The Bachelor's Guide
To Life

The Bachelor's Guide To Life

✦

Answers To Common and Not-So-Common Questions Every Single Guy Often Asks

Jason R. Rich

iUniverse, Inc.

New York Lincoln Shanghai

The Bachelor's Guide To Life
Answers To Common and Not-So-Common Questions Every Single Guy Often Asks

iUniverse books may be ordered through booksellers or by contacting:

iUniverse
2021 Pine Lake Road, Suite 100
Lincoln, NE 68512
www.iuniverse.com
1-800-Authors (1-800-288-4677)

ISBN-13: 978-0-595-35593-8 (pbk)
ISBN-13: 978-0-595-80077-3 (ebk)
ISBN-10: 0-595-35593-5 (pbk)
ISBN-10: 0-595-80077-7 (ebk)

Printed in the United States of America

Contents

Introduction

Are you a bachelor? Are you living alone for the first time? Perhaps you've recently gotten divorced and are re-learning how to take responsibility for yourself now that you're once again on your own. Are you confused about how to accomplish everyday tasks, like how to properly do your laundry, take care of yourself, meet women, plan an awesome vacation, find a high-paying job or choose a place to live? Well, *The Bachelor's Guide To Life* is chock full of information and strategies for improving your life, pursuing success, surrounding yourself with cool stuff, setting goals and achieving true happiness.

While most guys won't be bachelors forever, this book will help you get the most out of those pre- or post-marriage years when you're on your own, independent and experiencing life as a single guy.

Who Should Read This Book?

If you're a bachelor (someone who is unmarried and living alone or with roommates), then you'll find this book to be an excellent resource and guidebook to help you successfully get through the trials and tribulations of everyday life. This book will appeal to:

- College students leaving home for the first time to attend school.

- Guys moving into their own home or apartment, who will be totally independent for the first time in their lives.

- Men who are recently divorced and must readjust to "bachelorhood" while re-discovering how to take care of themselves and be independent.

- Gay guys.

- Wanna be "Metrosexuals."

- Single guys looking to improve their lives, find happiness and achieve success.

What *The Bachelor's Guide To Life* Offers

As the title suggests, each chapter of this book focuses on a different aspect of a single guy's life and provides advice from well-known experts in their field. Plus, the book offers details about hundreds of products and services you can begin using to improve your overall quality of life. This book is all about solutions for making virtually every aspect of your life easier, less stressful, more fun and happier. It's also about arming yourself with an arsenal of information that will help you make intelligent decisions as you pursue your goals and enjoy everything life has to offer.

Much of what you'll read in this book isn't taught in school. While some of what's covered deals with important issues, such as your health, money, career and education, there are plenty of less serious (but equally important) topics covered, like dating, traveling "bachelor style," how to entertain yourself and have fun, plus how to dress like a fashion icon. This book assumes you already know at least something about topics like sports, beer and partying, so these topics aren't covered in too much detail.

The goal of this book is to help you take a look at where your life is right now, figure out what, if anything, you'd like to improve, then effectively make changes by helping you to obtain the information you need and tap the resources that'll help you achieve success. More importantly, this book should help you take more control of your life and be able to do more of the things you truly enjoy.

As you read the many interviews included later in this book, you'll be learning from the successes and failures of others. These interviews offer the perspectives and advice of many experts, but the information is based on their personal opinions and sometimes promotes a product or service that they're affiliated with. While there's a lot to be learned from the experiences of others, what's important is that you read what these people have to say and then apply only what you believe directly relates to you and your situation.

For example, in Chapter 7, you'll learn about "speed dating" and how it offers an easy and fun way to meet women. In the interview with Tom Jaffee, the founder and CEO of 8minuetDating.com, he promotes his own company and uses it in examples relating to how you can successfully date women and make a positive first impression. While his company has been a pioneer in the speed dating trend, there are a handful of companies that offer similar services you could also utilize in order to meet women. The tips and dating strategies Tom offers, however, will work for virtually anyone involved in the dating scene, whether or not you actually participate in speed dating through 8minuteDating.

Likewise, in Chapter 5, you'll learn about Zirh men's skin care products and how to use them from the company's president, Brian Robinson. While the Zirh product line is top-notch, if you're interested in taking better care of your skin and looking younger and healthier, for example, there are also dozens of other product lines on the market. Zirh is featured in this book to demonstrate how the different types of products can best be used by a guy to achieve various types of results. From this section, you'll discover how to use these products, but you're then free to choose a specific product line that's best suited for you, based on your personal preferences.

While this book features information about hundreds of products and services (all of which real-life bachelors, like you, successfully use in their own lives), keep in mind there are almost always similar products and services from other companies available. Thus, instead of considering what you read in this book to be product endorsements, consider the featured products and services to be a sampling of what's available. Be open to shop around for similar products and services that may better suite your individual needs and/or budget.

Allow *The Bachelor's Guide To Life* to be your personal guidebook as you begin dealing with the positive and negative aspects of living on your own and being totally responsible for yourself. In many cases, being a bachelor means not having mommy around to cook and clean for you, or having a wife (or live-in girlfriend) to do your shopping, laundry or help you make important decisions. The actions you take and the decision you make are all up to you and will impact your life, your well-being and your future. As a bachelor living on your own, you'll be taking on an entirely new set of responsibilities and must learn to rely on yourself (and those you trust) to help you make intelligent decisions.

As you read this book, make full use of the resources that are discussed, whether it's a piece of advice from an expert, a link to a website that will allow you to obtain more information about a topic, or a strategy for somehow improving one aspect of your life.

Once you've read the book from cover to cover, you can then refer back to it as you encounter various events in your life, whether it's moving into a new home or apartment (Chapter 2); finding and landing a new job or earning a promotion (Chapter 3); managing your money (Chapter 4); discovering how to improve your appearance (Chapter 5); learning how to dress more fashionably and appropriately based on your lifestyle and budget (Chapter 6); dating and meeting women (Chapter 7); finding new ways to enjoy life and entertain yourself (Chapter 8); traveling "bachelor style" (Chapter 9); or fixing problems in your life and dealing with bad habits and/or addictions that cause you trouble (Chapter 10).

Everyone's life is different. Each of us has different values, goals, lifestyles and personalities. Thus, while this book was designed to offer general guidance and advice, it's up to you to determine what information you personally need and can benefit from, then gather whatever additional information you may require in order to make educated decisions based upon your personal situation. No book or resource can offer you *all* of the information you need to experience life. If you haven't discovered it yet, life is complicated. It's filled with challenges. How you approach these challenges, however, and what you learn from them will play a tremendous role in your overall success and well being. Any information you can obtain along the way, whether it's from this book or any other source, can and will help you make the right decisions for yourself.

Being a bachelor is about being independent, potentially self-sufficient and on your own to explore life and experience all that it has to offer. The first step, however, is to decide on a general direction in which you'd like your life to go. Develop a game plan for yourself, set goals and determine a plan for achieving those goals. This is what's covered within Chapter 1.

As you read this book and begin experiencing your bachelorhood, if you want to share some of the knowledge you've acquired firsthand or share something you think might help others, feel free to email your thoughts, ideas, comments and strategies to me, the author, at jr7777@aol.com. I also invite you to visit my website at *www.JasonRich.com* to learn more about me and some of my other books.

Whether you're totally clueless about life or you're looking for a bit of advice on how to improve your current situation, *The Bachelor's Guide To Life* is an excellent starting point for obtaining the information you need in one easy-to-read resource.

Oh, and when you're ready to end your bachelorhood, get engaged and ultimately tie the knot, be sure to read my book *Will You Marry Me? Popping The Question with Romance and Style* (New Page Books) for some exciting and innovative ideas about how to propose marriage to your girlfriend. You'll find a preview of what this book offers within Chapter 11.

—Jason R. Rich
www.JasonRich.com

1

You're On Your Own: Now What?

In case you haven't figured it out yet, life is full of ups and downs, trails and tribulations, celebrations and setbacks, as well as a lot of mundane activities. In addition to the ongoing challenges involved in earning a living, paying your bills and/or achieving good grades in school (if you're still a student), one of your primary responsibilities is to create a life and lifestyle for yourself that'll make you happy. In other words, once you decide what you want out of life and discover how to achieve your goals, it's up to you to make things happen for yourself.

Sure, you can look to religion and pray for success. You can also sit around waiting for it to fall into your lap or for others to make things happen for you. However, while other people are just sitting around waiting for their dreams to come true, you can start making things happen for yourself by taking a pro-active role in creating your own destiny.

Nobody has all of the answers you'll need to become successful at whatever it is you set out to do. What you can do, starting immediately, however, is create a positive path for yourself. With proper planning and hard work, this path will eventually lead you exactly where you want to go in terms of your personal, professional, spiritual (religious) and financial life. One of the tricks you'll need to master is to discover how to think for yourself and make educated decisions that are in your best interest. You also need to begin taking responsibility for yourself and your actions. You're a big boy now, so start acting like it. Don't worry! There will still be plenty of time for fun, entertainment and excitement in your life!

Your life can evolve into whatever you want to it be. Your personal, professional, spiritual and financial goals can all be achieved, over time, if you're willing to dedicate yourself to making positive things happen and invest the time and effort that's necessary. Unfortunately, there are no shortcuts!

Setting Life Goals

Before you can begin working hard to dedicate your life toward achieving true happiness and success, define for yourself what exactly these terms mean to you. "Happiness" and "success' are extremely subjective words when applied to your personal, professional, spiritual and financial life. Thus, it's up to you and you alone to figure out what you want and need to be happy and successful, then figure out exactly what it'll take for you to make positive things happen.

The trick to achieving any long-term goal is to take a well-thought out and organized approach to making it a reality. In this case, a long-term goal is one that will take you one or more years to achieve.

Here are some basic steps to follow as you create a long-term goal and then set out to achieve it. These steps can be applied to virtually any type of personal, professional, spiritual or financial goal you set for yourself:

Goal Setting Steps

1. Define the goal. What is it you want to achieve over time?

2. Understand your motivation for setting this goal. Know exactly *why* you want to achieve it.

3. Determine exactly what the benefits of achieving the goal will be to you (and those close to you).

4. Figure out approximately how long it will take you to achieve your goal. Set a realistic timeline for achieving it.

5. Based on your current situation, figure out all of the things you need to make happen or achieve in order to realize your ultimate goal. In other words, divide your long-term goal into a series of smaller, more achievable goals. As you accomplish each of these smaller goals, you'll be taking a step closer to achieving your ultimate goal. For each smaller objective, set a timeline or deadline for yourself and understand exactly what needs to be achieved.

6. In writing, create a detailed timeline and diary for your goals and what you're doing to achieve them. This can be done on a pad of paper, using scheduling software or a personal digital assistant. Keep careful track of deadlines, tasks that need to be accomplished and your ongoing progress. At any

given time, you should be able to look at your timeline and know how close you are to achieving each of your smaller objectives as well as your long-term goals.

7. On a weekly, monthly, semi-annual or yearly basis (depending on the goal), evaluate your progress thus far. Analyze your success. Also, make the necessary modifications to your game plan for achieving the objective, especially if you're not achieving the progress you had hoped for.

8. As you achieve your goals, develop others. This is a never-ending process that will help you achieve ongoing happiness and success in whatever you set out to accomplish.

Take a few minutes to consider what your life is like right now. Ask yourself these questions:

- In the next year, two years, five years and ten years, for example, what would you like to accomplish?
- How would you like your life to change?
- What are the things that would make you truly happy that are currently missing from your life?
- What would it take to add those missing things to your life in a beneficial way?

Apply these questions to every aspect of your life and begin creating a list of long-term goals. You'll probably find that some of your goals are inter-related. For example, in five years, you might want to be driving a flashy sports car. To achieve this, however, you need to begin earning more money, land a better job and begin saving more of the money you earn.

To land the better job, you may need to improve your education or obtain more training, for example. As you define each goal, follow the steps listed earlier and create a series of short-term objective that need to be accomplished (and deadlines that need to be met) in order to achieve each goal you set for yourself. Use the divide and conquer strategy. Pick a goal, divide it into a series of smaller, more achievable objectives, then complete each of those objectives, one at a time, until the initial goal is achieved. As you do this, be realistic.

While you want to set challenges for yourself, it's important to choose goals that are achievable and beneficial to you and those close to you. Nobody's life is perfect. After some self-analysis, focus on areas of your life that need improvement, then design goals that'll help you make the needed improvements. One of the biggest challenges you'll probably face after setting your goals it adapting a well-organized approach to making them a reality. For this to work, you'll need to properly manage your time and focus most on what's important by learning how to identify and properly deal with priorities.

You'll also need to keep yourself motivated about achieving your goals. To do this, set up a reward system for yourself. Once you achieve various milestones relating to your goal, do something to reward yourself for making progress. Everyone is motivated by different things, so figure out what drives you and what will keep you striving toward the success you'd like to achieve.

The Secrets of Effective Time Management

Are you always running late for appointments? Do the items on your daily to-do list never seem to get done fast enough? If there is never enough time in your day to meet your personal and professional obligations, you could be lacking important time management skills.

Learning time management skills won't add more hours to the day, but it will allow you to use all of your time more productively, reduce the stress in your life, allow you to better focus on what's important, and ultimately get more done faster.

Time management is easy to learn and requires just one basic tool—a daily planner, personal digital assistant (PDA) or specialized scheduling software for your computer. Paper-based daily planners or schedulers are available from office supply stores or directly from companies like Franklin Covey (800-360-8118/ *www.FranklinCovey.com*) or Day Timer (800-854-0346/*www.daytimer.com*). They come in a variety of sizes, designed to fit on a desk or within a jacket pocket or purse, plus they're available in many different daily, weekly and monthly formats.

A personal digital assistant (PDA) is a hand-held electronic device that can be used to store thousands of contact names and addresses, appointments, notes and other pieces of information. PDAs range in price based on their capabilities and are available from companies including PalmOne (*www.palmone.com*), starting at around $100.00.

The more advanced PDAs, such as the Palm Treo 650, are fully expandable, plus offer the ability to surf the Internet wirelessly, providing you with a vast amount of information virtually anytime, anywhere, at the touch of a few buttons. PDAs are available from office supply superstores and consumer electronics stores, such as Best Buy or Circuit City.

From a time management perspective, PDAs can be used to manage scheduling and organize to-do lists, plus store other important information that needs to be available to you within seconds. Thus, the right PDA can easily become an indispensable tool for helping to manage your time, responsibilities and your overall life.

A variety of different software programs for desktop computers, such as Microsoft Outlook (*www.microsoft.com*) or ACT! (*www.act.com*), can also be used to handle scheduling and help you better manage your valuable time.

It's important to choose a time management tool you're comfortable with, whether it's a traditional, paper-based planner, a high-tech PDA device or specialized computer software. The tool(s) you choose for yourself should easily fit within your lifestyle. If you're always on the go, you'll want a planner or PDA that's totally portable and can be carried with you. If most of your time is spent working from a desk, a desktop planner or software package for your desktop computer may be best suited to meet your needs.

Once you obtain a time management tool, spend several days carefully analyzing how you spend every minute of your day. Determine what takes up the majority of your time, but diminishes your productivity. Perhaps you experience countless interruptions from co-workers, participate in too many long distance calls, you don't have well-defined priorities, your work area is messy and disorganized, you have too much to do and become overwhelmed, or you're constantly forced to participate in unscheduled meetings at work.

As you examine how you spend your day, pinpoint the biggest time wasters that are keeping your from getting your most important work done. According to the DayTimer's *4-Dimensional Time Management* program, an audio cassette, video or CD-Rom-based course that teaches time management skills, to successfully manage your time, you must learn how to:

- **Focus**—Determine what's really important and what duties you're responsible to perform in a timely manner. Learn to differentiate between what's important and what's not in terms of how you spend your time.

- **Plan**—Discover how to properly prioritize your work and the items on your to-do list. Set goals based on your objectives, and figure out, in advance, how much time each task will take.

- **Act**—Based on your planning, take an organized approach to completing each of the high-priority tasks and items on your to-do list. Focus on the less important items and tasks later.

Every evening (after work) or first thing in the morning, take about 15 minutes to create a daily to-do list for yourself. After listing all of the things that need to get done that day, determine approximately how long each task will take. Now, set your priorities. On your to-do list, place an '1' next to the items or tasks that will produce the most valuable results. These are the items that *must* get done, no matter what.

Next, go back to the top of your list and place a '2' next to important tasks that *need* to get done, but aren't as critical or time sensitive as your '1' items. Finally, place a '3' next to items or tasks that *should* get done, but that aren't too important. During a day or week, a task's priority may change.

Take major projects, goals and objectives and divide them into smaller, more manageable tasks. You'll need to incorporate your to-do list into your daily planner, allowing you to schedule your time. Make sure you attempt to complete your high-priority items and tasks early in the day, giving those items your full attention.

Make sure you list all of your pre-scheduled appointments in your daily schedule, allowing ample time to get to and from the appointments, and if necessary, prepare for them in advance.

Once you commit to using a time management tool, first spend time learning how to customize and use it properly. Then, focus on remaining disciplined and using it continuously until it becomes second nature. Initially, you may have to spend up to 30 minutes per day planning your time and creating your to-do lists, but ultimately, you'll probably begin saving up to several hours per day.

Learning to better manage your time can have a positive impact on all aspects of your life. It can help boost your productivity, which will ultimately make you more valuable to an employer and put you in a better position to eventually receive a raise or promotion. With the time you free up for yourself by eliminating some or all of the things you do each day that waste valuable time, you'll be able to do more things that you enjoy more often, such as spending more time with people who are important to you. You'll also be able to find more time to just kick back and chill.

Finding "personal time" in your schedule is critical. This is time you spend each day or each week doing things that you personally enjoy, whether it's participating in a hobby, hanging out with friends or family, visiting a spa for a massage, attending professional sporting events (or watching sports on TV), working out, doing home improvement projects or dating. Determine how you like to spend your free time and then allocate time in your schedule for these activities. Chapter 8 focuses on ways to entertain yourself and spend your free time.

Taking On Adult Responsibilities

If you're about to embark on life as a single bachelor, living alone or with roommates, you're about to experience a whole new set of "adult" responsibilities, like having to pay your bills on time, doing your own laundry, earning an income and managing all aspects of your personal, professional, spiritual and financial life. While this may sound a bit daunting at first, have no fear, these are responsibilities you can handle.

The trick to managing your new found responsibilities is to face them head-on. In other words, don't pretend they don't exist or ignore important responsibilities, like paying your bills on time. Whenever you have questions, seek out the answers by asking for help from people you know and trust. You can also obtain the information you need by conducting your own research, on the Internet, for example.

When faced with new responsibilities:

- Determine what the new responsibility actually entails. Ask yourself questions like: What's expected? How much of a time commitment will it require? What will it cost?

- Use your personal planner or PDA to allocate the time in your schedule to complete your responsibilities, even if they're not "fun" or how you'd prefer to spend your time. Being a responsible person means successfully juggling your responsibilities with things you'd rather be doing.

As an example, suppose you need to start doing your own laundry. You're living alone now (or you're away at school) and your mom isn't around to keep your clothes clean. Set a plan for yourself to do your laundry on a weekly basis. This will probably mean spending about one hour per week doing two or three loads of laundry. Don't forget you'll need to clean your bedding (sheets, pillow cases and blankets) at least twice per month. Knowing this is now an ongoing obligation, determine how you can best utilize the time while you're waiting for the laundry's wash and dry cycles to finish. Can you use this as time to relax, to do your homework, catch up on reading or make personal phone calls? If you do your laundry on a regular basis, you'll always have clean clothes to wear and the piles of dirty clothes will never get too high.

Certain tasks you may need to accomplish in the not so distant future might include finding a place to live and signing a lease, buying or leasing a car, obtaining insurance, finding and landing a job and managing your money. Many of these responsibilities involve signing legal contracts. It's important that you fully understand whatever document(s) you're required to sign, before actually signing them.

Each chapter of this book focuses on a different aspect of your life. In the next chapter, for example, you'll discover some of what you need to know when looking for your own place to live.

2

Home Is Where Your Stuff Is: Finding A Place To Live and Setting Up The Ultimate Bachelor Pad

There's nothing that defines a bachelor more than his very own bachelor pad. You know, the house, apartment or condo where you keep your stuff and call home. A guy's bachelor pad is his kingdom. It's where he's the ruler supreme. Your mother isn't around to tell you to pick up your dirty clothes, and there's probably no live in female to add flowery trinkets or a feminine touch to the decor. There's also nobody (other than yourself or your roommate) to stock the refrigerator, clean up after you or hog the TV's remote control.

In addition to being a place to store your stuff and sleep, your bachelor pad should be a place where you can kick back and relax, chill with friends, entertain girlfriends and escape from the pressures of everyday life. Ideally you want a place that's clean, comfortable and functional, based on your everyday living habits.

No matter how much money you have or what you do for a living, your bachelor pad can and should be transformed into a clean, well organized and comfortable place. If you have plenty of money, you might hire an interior decorator and shop for furniture at someplace like Ethan Allan, plus treat yourself to the luxury of fine French bed linens from someplace like Yves Delorme, then equip your kitchen with top-of-the-line appliances that a gourmet chef would envy. You might also hire a maid to come by once or twice per week to clean up after you, do your laundry and keep your home spotless.

The fact is, however, most of us don't have the kind of money it takes to indulge in every possible luxury at home. Thus, if you want to live in a clean, comfortable and functional environment, you need to find the best furniture deals at places like Ikea, make full use of your George Foreman Grill (an absolute must in any bachelor's kitchen) and clean up after yourself. Your vision, creativity, personal taste and ability to take-on and complete do-it-yourself projects will determine how comfortable you ultimately are living in your bachelor pad. Even if you're living on a tight budget, you can still create an awesome living space for yourself.

Finding The Perfect Bachelor Pad

If you're moving into your own place, there's a lot to consider. For example, you need to determine:

- Where you want to live.
- What type of neighbors you'd like to have.
- What type of place you can afford.
- Whether you want to purchase, rent or lease your house/apartment.
- If you'll live alone or with one or more roommates.
- What amenities you need or want your home to be equipped with, such as its own parking spot, laundry facilities, air conditioning, a fireplace, hardwood floors (or carpeting), dishwasher, walk-in closets, additional storage space, etc.
- If the place you're planning to move into will mesh with your personal lifestyle and living habits.

When it comes to finding a place to live, location is everything. In addition to finding a clean and safe area, for convenience, you'll probably want to live near things like a supermarket, bank, video store, post office, pharmacy, dry cleaners and restaurants, for example. Ideally, you also want to be somewhat close to where you work (to avoid a long commute) and perhaps live near your close friends or relatives. As you decide where you'll live, location should be a major consideration.

Buying a home or condo carries with it a tremendous level of responsibility and a hefty financial commitment. This is why young bachelors often choose to rent or lease an apartment or house. In this situation, *renting* an apartment refers to a short-term commitment, where you pay month-to-month and can move out, typically with 30-days notice to the landlord, with no additional financial or legal obligations. A *lease* refers to a longer-term commitment, where you're obligated to stay in your apartment, typically for a period of 12 months (one year).

It's important to understand that when you sign a lease with a landlord, it is a legally binding agreement. You're obligated to pay rent on a monthly basis for the privilege of occupying the apartment. Once you sign the lease, you are bound to all of the terms within in, which is why it's extremely important to read your lease carefully and understand it, so you know exactly what the landlord expects.

In addition to paying your monthly rent (the amount should be clearly listed within the lease), you'll probably be required to provide the landlord with a security deposit upon moving in, and possibly pre-pay your last month's rent. Thus, when you initially move in, you'll be required to pay your first month's rent, deposit *and* last month's rent. This, however, will vary based on the landlord's requirements and the local laws where you live.

Your security deposit, which is typically equal to or less than one month's rent, will be held by the landlord and later used to pay for any repairs for damage you cause to the apartment. Thus, prior to moving in, it's important that you and the landlord agree in writing about the current condition of the apartment and list any damage that already exists. If you fail to mark down even minor damage on your "damages check-in sheet" (provided by the landlord when you move in), the landlord will assume that you caused the damage(s) and will charge you accordingly when you move out.

As you read your lease, make sure it clearly lists its duration and the amount of the monthly rent. The lease's start and end date should also be listed. You also need to know if upon the expiration of the lease if it will automatically renew, if you'll become a month-to-month tenant, or if the lease will need to be renegotiated should you choose to stay in the apartment. The lease should list other fees you're responsible for. Some landlords, for example, charge an extra fee if you pay your rent late or bounce a rent check. The penalties for breaking the lease should also be spelled out.

The lease you're required to sign prior to moving into an apartment will describe your responsibilities and the rules of the apartment building or complex. It will describe all of the community restrictions on things like parking, pets, alterations to the apartment, security, use of facilities, recycling, and trash collection. Make sure you're willing to adhere to all of the rules prior to signing the lease. If you'd like to make a change to the lease, discuss it with the landlord. If both parties agree, you can easily add a written addendum to the end of the document, which you and the landlord should then sign and date. Always keep a copy of your signed lease in a safe place, with your other important papers.

Finding The Perfect Apartment

Finding the perfect apartment isn't always easy. In fact, you may have to invest significant time reading ads, visiting properties and negotiating with landlords before you find a place that meets your particular needs. The local newspaper, the Internet, real estate agents (rental agencies that specialize in apartment rentals) and referrals from friends are all excellent ways of finding an apartment.

A website, called CraigsList (*www.craigslist.org*), is an excellent (and free) resource for finding a place to live, finding roommates and for buying/selling used furniture and appliances. CraigsList also offers online help wanted ads and a variety of other services that are easy-to-use, free and perfect for bachelors.

Other websites useful for finding apartments to rent include:

- *www.ApartmentGuide.com*

- *www.ApartmentLinks.net*

- *www.Apartments.com*

- *www.ApartmentZone.com*

- *www.ForRent.com*

- *www.Rent.com*

- *www.Rentals.com*

- *www.Roommates.co*m

- Yahoo! Real Estate (*http://realestate.yahoo.com/re/renting/*)

Once you think you found the perfect apartment, prior to signing the lease and moving in, make sure it will live up to your needs and expectations. Think about things like who your neighbors will be, the location of the apartment, whether or not there are a lot of noisy dogs and/or kids living in the immediate area, and what utilities are included with the apartment. If you'll be paying for all of your own utilities (heat, air conditioning, gas, electricity, garbage removal, cable TV, water, high-speed Internet access, etc.), these fees will add up quickly and need to be calculated into your monthly budget in addition to your monthly rent.

Other things to consider when evaluating a potential apartment include:

- The amount of closet and storage space the apartment offers.

- Whether or not there are laundry facilities in the apartment, shared laundry facilities, or if there's a nearby Laundromat.

- The number of electric outlets in each room and the age of the electrical wiring.

- Whether or not the landlord lives on the premises and will be available if you need assistance. If the landlord lives nearby, will he/she become too intrusive and often "drop by" expectedly?

- Whether or not the apartment offers enough space for all of your furniture and belongings.

- The parking situation for yourself and your guests. In addition to determining whether adequate parking is available, you need to determine how safe the parking is.

- Does the apartment have a problem with insects or rodents?

If you're not prepared to sign a 12-month lease, one option is to become a tenant-at-will and have a month-to-month rental agreement. Not all landlords offer this option. As the tenant, by not signing a long-term lease, you typically give up certain legal rights. For example, tenants with a month-to-month rental agreement can be evicted by the landlord at anytime, for any reason whatsoever, with 30-days notice. As the tenant, you can also vacate the apartment with 30-days notice to the landlord. If you've signed a 12-month lease, you can't be evicted unless you specifically violate the terms of the lease, but you're obligated to stay in the apartment for the full 12-month period (or for the term of the lease you sign.)

Prior to signing a lease, do your research, ask questions, learn about the community you'll be living in and understand exactly what you're signing. It's always an excellent strategy to have any legal document you're required to sign (including a lease) reviewed by an attorney.

Either right before or right after you move in, you'll need to contact the various utility companies to have service started in your apartment. Your landlord should be able to help you get in touch with the necessary companies relating to your utilities, which will most likely include:

- Phone (local and long distance service)

- Gas

- Electric

- Garbage Removal/Recycling
- Cable TV
- Internet Service

You'll typically need to allow several days to get these various services and utilities turned on within your new apartment. A deposit and/or one-time set-up/installation fee may also be required by the various utility companies.

If you have a roommate, you'll need to decide whose name each account will be set up under. The person's whose name is on the account is legally responsible for that bill. While you'll probably be splitting the utility bills with your roommate, the utility companies will typically only allow for one name to be put on the account.

Not paying your utility bills on-time or moving out of the apartment without paying the balance due to each utility company will have most likely have a negative impact on your credit rating. It'll also be harder for you to reestablish service later on when you move again into another place.

Get Insurance: Protect Your Home and Stuff

If you own the home you live in, chances are you already have home owner's insurance to cover your house and property against a multitude of disasters. Renters can also purchase insurance, called "Renter's Insurance," that will protect your belongings against natural disasters, theft, fire, vandalism and other disasters. The annual cost of this insurance is relatively low, and should be obtained since the insurance your landlord has will not cover your belongings, clothing, furniture, appliances, computers or other personal property.

For information about Renter's Insurance or to obtain a policy, contact an insurance broker. Well-known insurance companies, like Allstate, Liberty Mutual and State Farm Insurance, for example, offer Renter's Insurance policies. For a listing of brokers in your area, check the Yellow Pages or point your web browser to: *www.monstermoving.com/Mortgage_and_Finance/Department/Insurance_center*.

When obtaining this type of insurance, make sure the policy is active starting on or before the day you plan to move. This way, your property will be protected should something happen during the move itself. Renter's Insurance is even more important if you'll be living with a roommate and someone else will be using your furniture, appliances and belongings.

As with any type of insurance, the cost will depend on a number of factors, including where you live, the amount of coverage you need and the deductible you choose. According to the State Farm Insurance website (*www.statefarm.com*), to determine how much coverage you need, it's important to first determine how much your stuff is worth. "A great way to determine how much coverage you need is to take a complete inventory of your possessions. To do this, list each item, when you acquired it and the purchase price or current value. Next, total up the amounts of these items to give yourself a rough idea of what your property is worth. Once this is done, put your inventory list in a safe place, away from your home (such as in a bank safe deposit box). Consider adding photos of your belongings and apartment to your inventory. Photos can help if you someday have a claim."

Finding Roommates & Dealing with Them

Depending on your financial situation, you may discover it's not possible for you to rent a studio or one-bedroom apartment on your own. In fact, it might be more economically feasible for you to rent a two-bedroom apartment and split the rent with one or more roommates.

A roommate can be a friend or relative who agrees to split the rent with you, or it could be a total stranger you find through an ad. *Roommates.com* and *Craigslist.org* are two websites dedicated to helping people find the best possible match for a roommate.

It's important to understand, living with a roommate and sharing the financial responsibilities of the apartment, for example, requires a certain amount of trust, tolerance and flexibility on both of your parts. When choosing a roommate, you ideally want to find someone who is employed and who can pay their portion of the rent and utilities on-time. The person should be honest, trustworthy, responsible and have a similar lifestyle to your own. For example, if you're a non-smoker, chances are you'll want a roommate who also doesn't smoke.

Some of the questions you need answers to when looking for a compatible roommate include:

- Are you willing to live with a male or female as a roommate?
- Does the roommate have pets?
- Do you have a similar school or work schedule and overall lifestyle?
- Does the potential roommate have a criminal history?

- Does the potential roommate share similar religious, political and ethical beliefs as you? Is this important to you?

- Does the sexual orientation of the roommate matter?

- Is the person employed and capable of paying their portion of the rent and utilities on-time?

- Is the roommate clean and organized?

- Should the roommate be in a certain age range?

- Will the roommate often have overnight guests, such as a boyfriend or girlfriend?

- Will the roommate respect your privacy and property?

- Would you prefer a smoker or non-smoker?

Decide what's important to you when it comes to selecting a roommate. When interviewing perspective roommates, ask plenty of questions. It's often helpful to take notes and snap a Polaroid or digital photo of each potential roommate as you meet him/her. This will help you keep each person straight in your head as you meet lots of prospects. As you talk to each potential roommate, confirm that they know exactly what the rent, deposit and move-in date is and obtain multiple references from them.

Unfortunately, it's common for roommates to disappear in the middle of the night, for example, and break their lease. Make sure you have the name, address, phone number and details about the potential roommate's employer, closest relatives and friends. It's also a good idea to have the potential roommate co-sign the lease with you, so they're equally responsible to the landlord if there are any problems. Keep in mind, your landlord will most likely need to approve the roommate(s) you select.

Prior to your new roommate actually moving in, establish ground rules in terms of acceptable behavior within the apartment. Set a schedule, if necessary, for cleaning common areas, like the bathroom, living room and kitchen. If you'll be sharing items like a TV, computer, telephone, phone answering machine or stereo that you own, set rules for when and how these items can be used. Also, set rules about overnight guests and make it clear that your roommate is responsible for cleaning up after him or herself.

Even if you have a two bedroom apartment, chances are, the living space will be somewhat cramped. Thus, it's important that you and your roommate have a mutual respect for one another to insure a happy living situation.

The Bachelor's Guide To Moving

As soon as you decide a move or relocation is in your future, you'll quickly discover you're about to embark on a tremendous task that will take several weeks to properly plan and execute.

When it comes to choosing the best possible place to live and determining if you can afford to live in that city or town, there are many resources available to help with your research. *MonsterMoving.com* offers a special area that focuses specifically on issues of interest to people in the process of moving or relocating.

Monstermoving.com and *Moving.com* are two online-based resources designed to help people planning their move. Many real estate agents, moving supply companies and moving companies offer similar resources.

Once you know where you're going to move and when, it's time to figure out how you'll transport your belongings from your old home to your new home. As with every other aspect of the whole moving process, here too you have many options. Some of the most common moving options include:

Full Service Movers

These services handle just about every aspect of your physical move. This includes packing your furniture and belongings, supplying all packing materials (boxes, etc.), loading/unloading the truck, and driving your belongings from one location to the other. Many factors will contribute to determining the cost of using a full service mover, such as: the number of laborers (movers) required for the job, the size of the truck, the time of year, the distance of the move and the amount of furniture/belongings you'll be moving.

If you'll be hiring a Full Service Mover, be sure to shop around for the best price. Ideally, you want to hire a mover that's experienced, insured, has a top-notch reputation and that comes highly recommended by close friends or family members. Before actually hiring a mover, consider contacting the Better Business Bureau (*www.bbb.org*) or Chamber of Commerce in your area to insure the company you're about to hire is reputable.

A Full Service Mover should be registered and/or licensed by the state's Department of Transportation. One way to determine if the moving company you're about to hire is legitimate is to contact the Department of Transportation in your state.

Prior to the actual move, the people hired to do the packing and loading/unloading will review every item and check it for pre-existing damage. Make sure you are present for this inspection and that you agree with the assessment prior to the item(s) being packed and moved. Be on the lookout for items that are: bent, burned, broken, chipped, dented, gouged, rusted, covered in mildew, scratched, warn, torn, soiled, faded or loose.

When you initially make contact with a Full Service Mover in order to obtain a quote or estimate, you'll be asked a series of questions. The company will want to know where you're moving from and where you're moving to. The exact number of miles between locations will need to be calculated. You'll also need to describe how much stuff will need to be packed up and moved. You may be asked how many furnished rooms are in your current home, how much furniture is in each room, and how cluttered with stuff the various rooms are. From this information, the moving company will attempt to calculate the weight of your belongings and how many people will be required to pack everything up, load the truck and execute the move.

A Full Service Mover will provide you with a free quote or estimate that falls into one of three categories. Make sure everything you agree to is put in writing and is signed and dated by all parties. The type of quote you receive will be classified as one of the following:

- Binding—The mover provides you with a guaranteed price, within a small percentage of deviation. This price is based on a complete list of items to be moved and the type of service performed. To obtain this type of quote, a representative from the moving company will have to do an in-person inspection of your home and belongings.

- Non-binding or hourly rate—Instead of providing an estimate relating directly to the cost of your move, in this situation, you'll be provided with little more than a detailed price list regarding what the moving company charges for each of its services. The rates should, however, be based on the movers' previous experience with jobs similar to yours. Until the move is actually complete, you won't be able to calculate a exact cost of the move.

- Not to exceed—When a mover gives you a price, the actual final price for the move cannot exceed the estimate figure. From the mover's standpoint, the quote is binding. If the move comes in under the estimated amount, you'll be responsible to pay that lesser price.

If you obtain multiple estimates, and the price ranges vary greatly, make sure you ask plenty of questions to determine why one company is quoting a price that's so much higher or lower than the competition.

Hiring a Full Service Mover to handle your packing will save you a lot of time and effort, however, there are still certain things you'll want to pack yourself, such as your valuables (jewelry, memorabilia, family heirlooms, firearms, photo albums, items used in conjunction with your hobbies, medications and anything else that's valuable or can't easily be replaced). You'll also want to transport these items yourself, in your own vehicle, as opposed to placing them on a moving truck.

The American Moving and Storage Association (*www.moving.org*) offers a free, seventeen page guide called *Consumer Handbook: A Practical Guide To Interstate Moving* which explains what people should be aware of when hiring a mover.

Pick Up & Delivery Service/Self-Service Movers

If you can't afford a Full Service Mover, yet you don't want to deal with all of the responsibility of a Do-It-Yourself Move, consider hiring a Pick Up & Delivery Service (PUD) or Self-Service Moving Company. After evaluating your needs, this type of service will determine exactly what size moving truck you need and deliver it to your current home, typically at least two days prior to the actual move. It's then your responsibility to pack up your belongings and load the trailer.

Once the truck is fully loaded, it's picked up by a professional driver and driven to your destination. You don't have to drive the truck, but you are responsible for your own packing, unpacking and manual labor. The price you pay for this service is based primarily on the amount of space you fill in the truck (weight) and the distance of your move.

The Do-It-Yourself Move

When you hire a Full Service Mover, for example, you'll be given one estimate or quote for the entire move. Meanwhile, taking a do-it-yourself approach will mean having to price out and pay for each aspect of the moving process separately. You can, however, save a fortune. The following are some of the individual costs you'll need to consider:

- Dolly Rental
- Fuel Charges (for the truck and/or your vehicle)
- Furniture Pads
- Hourly Laborers
- Insurance
- Packing Materials (Boxes, Tape, Bubble Wrap, etc.)

- The Value of Your Time
- Tolls
- Truck Mileage Charges
- Truck Rental Charge
- Truck Rental Deposit
- Warehouse/Storage Fees

There are several pros and cons to managing and handling your own move. While you'll save considerable money, you'll need to make a significantly larger investment of your time, plus have to put forth a tremendous physical effort to carry, load and unload boxes and furniture. By handling your own move, you have total control over scheduling, but you're also taking sole responsibility for all of your belongings. If you pack something incorrectly and it breaks, it's your own fault.

If you check the Yellow Pages or visit any truck rental location, you'll find a wide selection of vehicles you can rent in order to make your do-it-yourself move possible. The size of the vehicle (truck, van or trailer) you choose should be based upon how much stuff you need to transport, how many trips between the two locations you plan to make, and cost.

Typically, when you rent a truck or trailer, you'll pay a flat daily fee for the vehicle itself, plus mileage and insurance. You'll also be responsible for gas, tolls and other related expenses.

According to U-Haul (800-468-4285/*www.uhaul.com*), moving the contents of an apartment or condo will require a smaller-size vehicle, such as a 10-foot truck, offering up to 368 cubit feet of storage space (5' x 10' x 8'). Other options include renting a van or sport utility vehicle or a trailer that can be towed behind your existing vehicle.

U-Haul, for example, also rents four different size trailers that can be towed behind most cars, vans, trucks or sport utility vehicles equipped with a temporary or permanent trailer hitch (also offered by U-Haul). To move the contents of three rooms, U-Haul recommends using a 6' x 12' trailer (offering 396 cubic feet of storage space). A smaller, 5' x 8' trailer (208 cubic feet of storage space) is suitable for moving two rooms worth of contents, while for smaller jobs, either a 4' x 8' trailer or 4' x 6' trailer may be suitable. For larger moves, U-Haul offers trucks with up to 1,538 cubic-feet of storage space.

When renting any type of truck, van or trailer, make sure your belongings can be locked up safely and that the storage area of the vehicle offers adequate space for everything you'll be transporting. As you pack the vehicle, remember you'll be dealing with boxes, odd shaped furniture, and items wrapped in pads. To get these items in and out of the truck, make sure you rent or acquire some type of dolly.

After you've taken inventory of what you need moved and have calculated approximately how many boxes (in addition to pieces of furniture) need to be transported, contact several truck/van rental companies to inquire about the cost of renting a vehicle. You need to be able to answer the following questions in order to obtain an accurate price quote:

- How much stuff needs to be moved
- How long will you need the vehicle for
- The date(s) the vehicle is needed
- The distance (in miles) that will be traveled
- The vehicle (trailer) size needed
- Will you be renting the vehicle for a one-way move and dropping it off at a different location?

In addition to national companies, such as U-Haul, Ryder Truck Rental (800-GO-RYDER/*www.yellowtruck.com*) and Hertz (888-999-5500/*www.hertztrucks.com*) that rent moving trucks and vans for do-it-yourself movers, you should also check the Yellow Pages to find other local truck rental companies.

Don't cut corners when packing your personal belongings. Make sure that each item is packed in the right size box and surrounded by ample packing materials to avoid damage. When you purchase your moving supplies, be sure to stock up on plenty of different size boxes.

The following are additional supplies you'll probably want on-hand to make your packing easier:

- Box Labels (including "Fragile" labels)
- Bubble Wrap
- Cardboard Boxes (Available from moving companies, truck rental companies, office supply superstores, supermarkets, etc.)
- Dish Dividers & Boxes
- Markers
- Packing Paper (It's best to avoid using newspapers)

- Packing Tape (two inches wide)
- Plastic Mattress Covers
- Stretch Wrap
- Styrofoam Peanuts
- Tape Gun/Dispenser

Announcing Your Move

Before your actual move (about 30-days prior to moving day), once you know exactly when and where you'll be moving to, you'll want to start notifying people about your move. First, contact the United States Post Office and complete a Change of Address Form. You can do this in-person at any Post Office or via the Internet by pointing your Web browser to *https://moversguide.usps.com*. Until people know about your move, the Post Office will either hold your mail for you, or forward it to your new address.

In addition to the post office, it's critical that you inform the Internal Revenue Service of your new address. To do this, call (800) 829-3676 or visit the IRS' Website at *www.irs.ustreas.gov* to obtain an official Change of Address form.

You might want to send out Change of Address cards to any or all of the following people/organizations on this list:

- Accountant
- Airline Frequent Flier Programs
- Bank(s)
- Cable TV Provider
- Clubs
- Credit Card Companies
- Current Landlord
- Dentist
- Department of Motor Vehicles
- Department of Social Security
- Doctor
- Dry Cleaners

- Electric Company
- Employer
- Financial Advisor
- Friends
- Gardener/Landscaper
- Gas Company (other Utility Providers)
- Girlfriend(s)
- Gym
- Insurance Companies
- Internet Service Provider
- Library
- Local & Long Distance Phone Companies
- Mortgage Company
- Newspaper/Magazines Subscriptions
- Optician
- Parole Officer
- Police
- Professional Acquaintances
- Relatives (including your in-laws)
- Religious Organizations
- School(s)/College(s)
- Stockbroker (Financial companies that manage your investments, retirement account, etc.)
- Union
- Veterinarian
- Voter Registration Office

Furnishing Your Bachelor Pad

Most guys hate the prospect of "decorating" their living space, yet creating an environment that's clean, functional and that showcases your personality and taste can be easy and inexpensive.

There are several benefits to having a well-organized, clean and function living environment. First and foremost, it provides a comfortable place for you to hang out and relax. Secondly, it gives you a place to entertain. A nicely decorated apartment, for example, will certainly impress any dates you invite over.

If you have money, you can visit a furniture store, like Ethan Allan, and have their staff of professional interior decorators furnish your home in a stylish and tasteful way using high-end furniture from their company. For most people, however, it's up to you to create your own living space, decorate it as you see fit and within a budget you can afford.

As you get started decorating your bachelor pad, The Sheffield School of Interior Design recommends focusing on each room separately. Your goal should be to design every room so it's functional, expresses a mood and exhibits a sense of harmony.

To accomplish these goals, ask yourself the following seven questions:

1. What will each room be used for?

2. How often will you actually be using each room?

3. How much lighting does each room get naturally and how bright do you actually want it to be?

4. What colors or color schemes do you personally like? How can you incorporate those colors into each room?

5. Knowing the primary functions of each room, what furniture is required?

6. Once you've selected your furniture, how can you arrange it so it looks good and provides the function you're looking for?

7. What trinkets, accessories, plants or artwork, for example, can you add to each room to personalize your living space?

As you decorate and design your bachelor pad, what's important is that it meets the needs of your personal lifestyle. Where you live should be functional, comfortable and clean. If you're on an extremely tight budget and can't afford brand new designer furniture, here are a few options.

Of course, as you save money down the road, you can always upgrade your furniture and improve the overall décor. Once you know exactly what furniture items you're looking for, here are some suggestions and resources for finding furniture bargains:

- Ask friends and relatives for furniture that they have in storage and that they're not currently using.

- Visit thrift stores.

- Visit garage sales, tag sales and flea markets.

- Go online, to a website such as *Craigslist.org*, and browse the online classified ads. You can find some incredible deals on used furniture and appliances. Just make sure you take a look at the items before purchasing them (and feel free to negotiate the price with the seller.) The great thing about services like *Craigslist.org* is that you can find items being sold in your immediate area. This is also a great resource for selling items you no longer want or need.

- Consider utilizing "assemble it yourself" furniture sold at places like Target, Wal-Mart or Ikea (*www.ikea.com*). Before purchasing items like desks, bookcases, tables, etc., make sure you look carefully at the fully built display model in the store. Make sure the quality is good and the size of the item works. Target, for example, offers a line called Furio Home, which features well-made, contemporary, assemble-it-yourself furniture.

- Look for sales at furniture stores. Many offer large discounts on discontinued items, returned items or slightly damaged (but still fully functional) items.

Can't afford a couch or don't have the space for one? There are a wide range of inexpensive alternatives. Consider purchasing a traditional love seat, reclining chair, a futon or a LoveSac (the 21st century version of bean bag chairs from the 1960s and 70s). LoveSacs (866-305-LOVE/*www.lovesac.com*) offers an overstuffed, extremely comfortable seating solution for apartments or homes. Instead of being filled with beans, they containing pieces of soft foam. A wide range of covers (in many different colors) are available to match any decor. The six-foot SuperSac, for example, can seat two or three adults, while the LotOLoveSac is ideal for one person.

For additional furnishing and decorating ideas, point your web browser to these free resources:

- SoYouWanna.com—*www.soyouwanna.com*

- The Renter's Mall—*www.therentersmall.com*

The Bachelor's Bedroom

People require sleep. So, unless you spend several nights per week at your girlfriend's place, chances are, you'll be spending at least six to ten hours per night at home, sleeping in your bed. Because so much time is spent wrapped up in your sheets, under your covers, hopefully comfortably in dreamland, it's important to invest in bedding that's well-made, comfortable and that looks good in your bedroom.

As a guy, you may find it difficult to find sheets, blankets and a duvet cover, for example, that come in a masculine pattern and color scheme. After all, you probably don't want your bachelor pad to feature a flowery or feminine design.

When putting together your bedroom and choosing your bed linens, focus on functionality, comfort, quality and looks. The most important piece of furniture in your bedroom is your bed. Start by choosing a bed size—twin, full/queen or king. Next, find a mattress and a bed frame that works for you. Most bachelors opt for a queen-size bed, because it offers plenty of room for one person, yet comfortably accommodates two people. The prices of mattresses vary greatly, so shop around and look for sales. Ideally, you want to purchase the highest quality mattress you can afford. Be sure that you don't get caught up in a sales pitch from a pushy mattress salesperson when choosing the best bed for yourself.

If money and/or space is a concern, or if you need an additional bed for occasional guests, check out the line of airbeds from Aero Products International (888-462-4468/*www.thinkaero.com*). The raised Aerobed, for example, comes in twin, queen and king sizes. Using the included (and built-in) electric pump, the bed/mattress inflates in under two-minutes to be the size and height of a regular bed. You can also adjust the firmness of the air mattress and use standard sheets, pillows and blankets. What's more, the Aerobeds are extremely comfortable and affordable, starting at about $100.00. When they're not being used, they can be deflated and stored in their own storage bag (which is about the size of a filled backpack.) This type of bed is ideal for someone living in a very tight space, such as a studio apartment, because when not in use, the bed can be deflated.

While you can certainly purchase a used bed frame and perhaps even a box spring, for health and sanitary reasons, it's always best to purchase a new mattress. Once your mattress, box spring and bed get delivered, choose a location in your bedroom that's conducive to getting a good night's sleep. Pay attention to windows and how light will shine through them in the morning. Also consider drafts, the location of air vents, where light switches are located and where you'll put items like a television, alarm clock and lamps, which you'll want to access from your bed.

Once your bed is in place, it's time to add the bed linens (your sheets, blankets, pillows, etc.). Most guys will find the bedding from Calvin Klein Home (available from major department stores, like Macy's, and bedding specialty stores, like Linen's & Things or Bed, Bath and Beyond) to be affordable. Calvin Klein Home also offers designs that will nicely complement any guy's bedroom décor, because it offers a handful of complete bedding sets with perfectly coordinated colors, textures and patterns, making it easy for a guy to put together a comfortable and great looking bedroom. You'll quickly discover that the color and pattern on your sheets, bedspread or duvet cover will help set the overall tone and look of the bedroom. Calvin Klein Home's The Khaki Collection, for example, is an ideal bedding solution for any bachelor's bedroom.

For the ultimate in luxury, Yves Delorme (800-322-3911/*www. yvesdelorme.com*) offers fine French bed linens, including: fitted sheets, flat sheets, pillow cases and shams, duvet covers, blankets and a wide range of matching accessories in several masculine designs. The company's popular Rabanne pattern offers a modern and masculine aesthetic, combining an abstract pattern with darker colors and an ultra-soft and extremely comfortable feel.

Ideally, when shopping for bedding, choose sheets created from 100-percent cotton, with the highest thread-count you can afford. Avoid sheets with a thread count under 200. This will provide you with comfort, luxury and years worth of use if the items are cared for and laundered properly. While you want your bedroom to look stylish, when it comes to bedding, comfort and quality are equally important.

"Calvin Klein Home offers a selection bed and bath products, as well as down-filled bed products, like comforters and pillows. What sets us apart from other companies are the designs we offer. We offer a very different esthetic. Our goal is to create bedding products that come out of the package and feel like you've been using them for years. We don't want our brand new sheets, for example, to be stiff, smell like chemicals or be uncomfortable," explained Barbara Deichman, Senior Vice President, Calvin Klein Home.

For a guy who has never bought his own bedding, Deichman explained that no matter what size mattress and bed you have, when it comes to sheets and bedding, you'll typically need at least:

- One fitted sheet (a 'bottom sheet' to cover your mattress)
- One flat sheet (also referred to as a 'top sheet')
- Two pillow cases
- A bedspread or duvet cover (to cover a down comforter, for example)
- Blankets
- Decorative pillow shams and extra pillows (optional)
- One bed skirt to cover your bed's box spring (optional)

"I recommend a down comforter, because it's extremely warm, but not heavy. It can be used throughout the year and covered with a duvet cover that matches the rest of your bedding and bedroom decor," said Deichman. "Pay attention to what the sheets are made from and what the thread count of the sheets is. As a general rule, the higher the thread count, the better the quality. How the sheets are finished and dyed by the manufacturer will also impact quality. I always recommend going with 100-percent cotton sheets. Check out the samples on display at the store, because a lot has to do with personal preference in terms of how a sheet looks and feels."

All bedding comes with proper care instructions from the manufacturer—follow them! "Make sure you don't overstuff the washer or dryer with your sheets and bedding. This creates wrinkles and keeps the linens from getting fully cleaned. Also, in the washer, don't mix light and dark colored fabrics," said Deichman. "When it comes to decorating your bedroom, I recommend starting with the bedding to set the color scheme and overall look, then decorate around the bedding, since it's the bed that's the largest thing in the room."

The price of bed linens varies dramatically, starting from under $10.00 for a basic, no-frills bed sheet. Mid-priced bedding, from companies like Calvin Klein Home, will average around $60.00 per sheet. For top-of-the-line bedding, from a company like Yves Delorme, a single, fitted Queen-size sheet could cost upwards of $120.00 or more.

No matter what type of sheets, pillows and blankets you purchase, be sure to shop around for the best deals. Department stores and bedding specialty stores (like Linens & Things or Bed, Bath and Beyond) often hold sales or offer discount coupons.

Home Gadgets Every Bachelor Needs At Home

In addition to everyday furniture items and your clothing, there are a handful of items, tools and accessories that should be staples in any bachelor pad, including:

- Air filter/purifier. Especially if you have allergies, an air filter or purifier in your bedroom will make the air you breath cleaner, because it will reduce or eliminate mold spores, airborne viruses and bacteria.

- First Aid Kit, fire extinguishers, smoke alarms, flashlight(s) and extra batteries. Be ready for the unexpected and have a supply of first aid and emergency supplies readily available.

- Home Entertainment System—The primary components you'll want might include: a television, VCR, DVD player, TiVo, video game system, stereo (AM/FM receiver) and a surround-sound speaker system.

- Phone and Answering Machine

- Tool kit—Whether you're a do-it-yourself project person or simply need to occasionally do your own minor repairs, having a basic set of tools on-hand is important. One excellent toolset is available from Hammacher Schlemmer (800-321-1484/*www.hammacher.com*). The Handyman's Chrome Vanadium Tool Set ($199.00) is a 107-piece set housed in a sturdy and well-organized case.

If you have the space and the budget, other must-have items for a bachelor pad include a pool table, a classic arcade-style video game (such as Pac-Man) and/or a hot tub. A home exercise machine is also an excellent investment.

Keeping Your Bachelor Pad Clean

The secret to having a comfortable and nice home, no matter where you live, is to keep in clean and sanitary. This means creating a cleaning schedule for yourself and sticking to it to insure that all of the rooms in your home, particularly your kitchen and bathroom, are regularly cleaned. You can do the cleaning and laundry on your own, or hire a maid to do the cleaning for you, depending on your budget.

If you're looking to hire a maid (to take your mother's place when it comes to cleaning), find someone who is reputable, responsible and who will to a thorough job. Obtaining a referral is always a good way to go, however, you can also hire a maid through a well-established service, such as Merry Maids.

Merry Maids (1-800-637-7962/*www.merrymaids.com*) is the largest home cleaning company in the world, with more than 900 franchises in the United States and Canada. The company cleans more than 300,000 homes, apartments and condominiums each month in North America and employs more than 8,000 home cleaning professionals.

According to the company, "Merry Maids provides customized cleaning services that are available weekly, every other week, monthly or one-time. Each home is custom priced in the presence of the homeowner to ensure our cleaning will meet your needs and budget. Service cost varies depending on location, size of home, condition of home and frequency of cleaning scheduled."

Service every other week for a 3-bedroom, 2-bath, 2,000-square-foot home, generally ranges from about $75 to $120 per visit. One-time and first cleanings typically start at $120 to $200 depending on the size, condition and location of the home.

In addition to regular cleaning, dusting and vacuuming every room, no matter who is doing the cleaning, here's a rundown of what cleaning a bachelor pad entails:

- Dust all window sills, ledges, ceiling fans, furniture, lamps and mini-blinds, as well as picture frames, knickknacks and hardwood floors. Cobwebs should be removed. Vacuum carpets and wash other types of floors (linoleum or tile, for example).

- Within the kitchen, clean all appliances, counters, cabinets, table and chairs. Clean, scrub and sanitize the sink. Countertops and backsplashes also need to be regularly cleaned and sanitized.

- Within the bathroom, focus on cleaning, sanitizing and deodorizing everything. Clean, scrub and sanitize the shower and bathtub, vanities, sinks and mirrors. Also, clean and sanitize the toilet. Polish all chrome, then wash the floors and tile walls.

In addition to an assortment of cleaning supplies, soaps, detergents, mops and dusting tools, a vacuum cleaner is an absolute must. Starting at about $100.00, you can purchase a good-quality, bag-less vacuum cleaner with built-in HEPA filter from stores like Target, Best Buy or Wal-Mart.

Look for a vacuum that's easy to use, light weight and powerful. Most come with an assortment of accessories to make cleaning easier. A built-in HEPA filter will help control dust and germs, while choosing a bag-less vacuum will eliminate the need to find and purchase replacement bags for your vacuum. Popular vacuum cleaner manufacturers include: Hoover, Eureka, Bissell, Oreck and Dirt

Devil. For quick cleanup of linoleum, hardwood or tile floors, for example, the Swiffer WetJet (*www.homemadesimple.com/swiffer/index_flash.shtml*) is an excellent and inexpensive product.

Bissell (*www.Bissell.com*) offers a line-up of products designed to make cleaning your home faster and easier. The CatchAll Bare Floor Cleaner ($50.00), for example, is ideal for sweeping and cleaning linoleum, tile or hardwood floors. It's a battery-powered, bag-less unit that's light weight. Using the Bissell Steam Mop ($80.00), you can clean and sanitize bare floors using steam as opposed to harsh and smelly chemicals. Both products are available from retailers such a Sears, Kohl's, Target, Wal-Mart and JC Penny.

For additional cleaning tips, point your web browser to:

- All About Home—*www.allabouthome.com/tips/cleaning/home.html*

- PageWise Home Cleaning Advice—*www.essortment.com/in/Home. Cleaning/*

Being a happy, prosperous and healthy bachelor involves a lot more than just finding and decorating an awesome living space for yourself. Being a bachelor is an all-encompassing lifestyle. The next chapter focuses on finding your dream job and pursuing a career (as opposed to a dead-end job).

3

You Need An Income: Landing Your Dream Job and Planning Your Career

When was the last time you went shopping, ate at a restaurant or called a company on the telephone and you were treated poorly by someone who appeared to hate their job? Unfortunately, this is an all too common occurrence. Many people graduate from school, feel anxious to land a job, and wind up accepting a dead-end position, doing something they have little or no interest in. These people, who are in no way challenged by their work, quickly find themselves getting burnt out and hating their career decision. This negatively impacts every other aspect of their lives.

Whether you're about to graduate from school and enter into the job market for the first time, or you currently find yourself stuck in a job that's leading nowhere, you can begin taking control of your own professional life and ultimately pursue a career path that's exciting, challenging and rewarding. The secret that all successful people share is that they have a true passion for their work and a dedication to it. Before you begin a search that will lead to a job you'll enjoy and prosper in, define whom you are as a person, what your strengths and weaknesses are, and where your true interests lie.

Your Professional Interests

Once you define the type of job you believe you would most enjoy, the next step is to be creative and discover job opportunities that will require you to incorporate your strengths and somehow involve your interests.

To help you define yourself and figure out what type of career you want to pursue, on a sheet of paper, write down all of your marketable skills and special abilities, as well as your interests, hobbies and the work-related activities that you really enjoy doing. Think about what the ideal work atmosphere would be for you, and what specific things you liked and disliked about your previous work experiences. After you have compiled lists of your skills, likes, dislikes, and interests, think about where potential job opportunities might exist.

Finally, start researching industries and individual companies that hire people with your skills, education and interests. To do this:

- Access the internet and do research about companies and industries.

- Attend job fairs.

- Contact the career counselor at your school.

- Network with friends and relatives to seek out advice and job referrals.

- Pick up the phone and call the human resources (HR) department of companies you're interested in.

- Read the 'help wanted' section of the newspaper.

- Visit a library to do research about companies and industries.

Remember, the majority of job openings aren't advertised, so it'll require you to do some serious work, networking and research to find them. Be persistent and be willing to put in the time necessary to find and land a job that you're ultimately going to enjoy and prosper in.

If you're about to graduate from school, yet you have no clue about where your career interests lie, you're not alone, so don't despair. Instead, spend time carefully and honestly analyzing yourself as a person and do some serious soul searching to help you determine what you're interested in. Don't allow anyone, such as a parent, friend or professor, to push you into a career that doesn't interest you. Your future lies in your ability to make decisions for yourself and in finding a career path that you're excited to follow.

Who Are You Anyway?

When you look in the mirror, what do you see? Who are you? What do you think about yourself? What do other people think about you? Before you can set off on a quest to find a job and start marketing yourself to potential employers, develop a good understanding of yourself. Understand exactly who you are and what your strengths and weaknesses are, before you can start marketing yourself to others.

No matter who you are, there are careers or professions that you can be highly successful in, based on your personality, education, your unique set of interests, and your personal skills. Finding a job that you're very good at isn't good enough. Ideally, your job should also allow you to exploit most, if not all of your personal strengths. Your work should involve performing tasks you enjoy. (Sure, every job will have things about it you don't like, but the trick I to make sure the positives outweigh the negatives by a significant margin.) As you start your job search, be looking for a job you'll love, and don't settle for less.

Even the smartest, most ambitious people, who are well rounded and appear to be the perfect candidate for just about any job they apply for, have weaknesses. These people, however, have learned to capitalize on and exploit their strengths, while being able to work around or compensate for their weaknesses. When analyzing a job offer, it's also important to know what you really want out your work experience.

Defining Yourself

Here are some questions to help you define your skills, goals, accomplishments, likes and dislikes. When you're creating your resume, writing cover letters, and analyzing job offers, refer back to the answers you provide to these questions.

1. What is your personal life like now?

    _____

    _____

    _____

2. What would you most like to change about your life?

    _____

    _____

    _____

3. What are three things you can start doing today to help you make the necessary changes in your life happen?

    1. _____

    2. _____

3. _____

4. How would you describe your current financial status?

_____

_____

_____

5. Assuming you'd like to improve your financial situation, what three things can you do to bring about improvements over the next one to five years?

   1. _____

   2. _____

   3. _____

6. What would you say are the three very best things about your life?

   1. _____

   2. _____

   3. _____

7. What are the three worst things about your life overall that you'd like to fix or improve upon over time?

   1. _____

   2. _____

   3. _____

8. What are the three qualities about yourself that you are most proud of?

   1. _____

   2. _____

   3. _____

9. What are some of the qualities about yourself that you know people don't like, or you think need improvement?

   1. _____

2. _____

3. _____

4. _____

5. _____

10. What can you do, starting today, to change the negative qualities that you listed in Question #9 into positive ones?

    1. _____

    2. _____

    3. _____

11. What three skills could you improve upon to make you more qualified for the type of job you hope to land?

    1. _____

    2. _____

    3. _____

12. If you were to pursue an advanced degree or continue your education, what subject(s) or degree(s) would you pursue and why?

    _____

    _____

    _____

13. What course of action can you take, starting immediately, to help you improve your skill set?

    _____

    _____

    _____

14. If you could spend more of your free time doing something (pursuing an interest, activity or hobby), what is it you'd like to be doing?

    _____

_____

_____

15. What are your long-term career, personal and family goals?

    Career Goals:

    _____

    _____

    Personal Goals:

    _____

    _____

    Family Goals:

    _____

    _____

16. List five accomplishments from any aspect of your life that you are the most proud of.

    1. _____

    2. _____

    3. _____

    4. _____

    5. _____

17. What were your strongest subjects in school? Which subjects were your favorites? Why?

    _____

    _____

    _____

18. What are your interests (hobbies) and what type of work-related activities do you enjoy?

    _____

_____

_____

19. What would you say are your biggest weaknesses?

_____

_____

_____

20. Describe what would be the ideal atmosphere for you to work in? (Do you like working with people or working alone? Do you perform better in a structured job or one that allows you to take initiative and make decisions? Do you enjoy traveling on business or spending time driving in your car to and from meetings? In what work environment are you the most productive? Do you want a smoke-free work environment? Is working in an office building with windows that open important to you? Do you prefer a corporate atmosphere or a more laid-back work environment?)

_____

_____

_____

21. What were the five things you hated about your last job?

    1. _____

    2. _____

    3. _____

    4. _____

    5. _____

22. What work-related tasks are you really good at?

    1. _____

    2. _____

    3. _____

    4. _____

5. _____

23. What are the five qualities that you hope to find in your new job?

    1. _____

    2. _____

    3. _____

    4. _____

    5. _____

24. What kind of co-workers would you like to have?

    _____

    _____

    _____

25. How do you define personal and professional success? What would it take for you to consider yourself personally and professionally successful?

    My definition of personal success is:

    _____

    _____

    _____

    My definition of professional success is:

    _____

    _____

    _____

Your Skills Are What Makes You Marketable

When applying for virtually any type of job, at some point in the process you'll be provided with a description of the position. This will be a listing of the core skills and requirements needed by you, the applicant, according to what the employer perceives its expectations and needs to be. Often, specific education, work experience or skills will be listed for the job opening.

As the job seeker, position and market your personal skill set so it's in line with exactly what the employer is looking for. While simply meeting the job's requirements in terms of your skill set is a requirement, to enhance your marketability as an applicant and perhaps enhance your earning potential, you'll want to carefully market yourself to a potential employer by showcasing all of your related skills.

Your personal and professional skill set can be any knowledge or ability that makes you a more desirable and productive person on the job. Depending on the industry you work in or the type of position you're looking to fill, your skill set goes beyond the core education you received in school. It includes the skills that ultimately allow you to meet the responsibilities of your job, whether it's working the computerized cash register at a retail store or managing a sales team of 50 people.

Being fluent in multiple languages, for example, can be an asset that will set you apart from other applicants when applying for a wide range of positions. Other sought after skills among employers include: sales, public speaking, management, leadership, typing, computer knowledge (literacy), bookkeeping, filing, telemarketing, performing online research, and/or organizational abilities.

Once you know what type of job you're applying for and have a general idea of what the employer is looking for, your cover letter, resume and employment application provide excellent initial opportunities to quickly showcase your personal and professional skill set.

The 'help wanted' ad or job description provided by the potential employer will offer valuable clues regarding the specific skills you should possess and which ones are of particular importance to an employer. Determine exactly what the employer is looking for before you devise a plan on how to best promote your skill set.

Simply stating you have a skill that's required for a job isn't enough. Within your resume, for example, you'll want to clearly spell out every skill you have that's directly relevant to the job you're applying for, then be able to provide specific examples of how you've already used each skill in a previous work situation. In other words, proof that you posses each skill is essential.

As you list each skill and describe how you've used it on the job, provide specific quantitative and qualitative details that convey the positive results of your abilities. You can later provide written documentation or support materials during a job interview.

Use your resume and employment application to list all of your relevant skills and to briefly describe how you've used them. Within your cover letter, emphasize one or two of your most marketable skills or job qualifications so they stand out, without blatantly repeating information within your resume.

Every marketable skill you posses has a value to an employer. Thus, having more skills than what's specifically spelled out by the employer will make you more desirable. It's your responsibility to demonstrate exactly how your particular combination of skills will make you a valuable asset to a potential employer.

The wording used to describe your skills within your cover letter, resume and employment application is important, since at this point in the job search process, you most likely won't have in-person contact with the employer.

By carefully describing your skills so that they're customized to the job you're applying for, you're more apt to get invited for an interview, at which time you'll be given the opportunity to discuss your skill set in-person. This is your opportunity to go into much greater detail about the skills you posses, describe how you've used them in the past, and explain exactly how they could be used in the future to meet the requirements of the job you're applying for.

An Internship Can Jumpstart Your Career

Most colleges do an excellent job educating students, but it's impossible to teach something that virtually all employers look for—real world experience. If you're a college student, one of the best ways to jumpstart your career while still in school is to participate in an internship program and work in the industry you hope to break into upon graduation.

Virtually all colleges offer structured internship programs, allowing students to work during their vacations or after classes (on a part-time basis), earn college credits and gain valuable real world experience. Many companies, in all industries, offer paid or unpaid internship opportunities. Even if a company you want to work for doesn't offer a structured internship program, if you have direct contact with an executive within the company, it's still possible to work as an intern.

Even if participating in an internship program isn't a requirement for landing a job within the field you hope to break into, having real world experience certainly makes you a stronger and more marketable job candidate upon graduation. In addition, working as an intern provides you with incredible networking opportunities.

Often, if you're able to demonstrate your abilities as an intern, you could easily parlay that into a full-time job upon graduating. Most employers prefer to hire people who have already proven themselves to be competent and who know their company.

Before looking for an internship program to participate in, determine what your goals are. Possible goals might be to get your foot in the door at a specific company, to learn about a specific industry, to obtain real world work experience doing something that interests you, to master skills that can only be learned on-the-job (as opposed to in a classroom), to earn college credit and/or to earn a paycheck.

Once you land an internship, consider it an audition for ultimately obtaining a full-time job. Always act professionally, ask questions, follow directions, display plenty of enthusiasm, volunteer to take on additional responsibilities, meet deadlines, and work closely with your boss/supervisor. Upon graduating, make sure to highlight your internship work on your resume.

Are You Earning What You're Worth?

Are you like most people, working too hard, for too many hours per week, yet not getting paid what you believe you deserve? Due to ever increasing competition, employers often push employees to work longer hours and take on more responsibilities, yet are offering less pay. Since salaries and compensation packages are typically kept confidential within a company, it can be difficult to determine if you're getting paid what you truly deserve based on your experience, skills, education and overall value to the company you work for.

Whether you're looking for a new job, hoping to earn a raise, or you're convinced you're not getting paid what you're worth in your current job, there are things you can do to discover your own true earning potential.

Many things contribute to someone's salary and overall compensation package. Work experience, education, skills, the size of the company, the industry, the geographic location of the employer, demand, the number of hours you work, and your ability to negotiate the best possible salary/compensation package all help to determine what you get paid.

Once you know exactly what type of job you're looking to fill (or you currently fill), by performing research you can determine what salary range someone holding a similar job title and responsibilities earns within your industry and/or geographic area. Using this information, you can then determine if you're currently earning less than what you're worth and take the necessary steps to either pursue a higher paying job or a raise.

No matter what industry you work in, its possible to pinpoint average salaries paid by employers for specific jobs. One of the best resources for gathering current and accurate salary information (available online or in printed form) is *The*

Occupational Outlook Handbook (*www.bls.gov/oco*) published by The Bureau of Labor Statistics. For each of the thousands of occupations covered, this directory describes the nature of the work, working conditions, employment opportunities, the job outlook (over the next decade), the earning potential/salary range, as well as information about related occupations.

On the Web, there are many research firms and other sources of salary information, however, when using these sources for research, its important to determine where the information is derived from, whether or not it's current, and if the data applies to your industry, occupation and geographic area. One of the best, most accurate and timely resources for salary information can be found at *www.salary.com*.

JobSmart (*www.jobstar.org/tools/salary/sal-prof.cfm*) is a free service that publishes profession-specific salary surveys online for over 60 professions, ranging from accounting to warehousing.

Through research, it's relatively easy to determine if you're getting paid less than what you're worth in today's marketplace. Knowing exactly what you're worth will help you participate successfully in a salary negotiation with your current or future employer.

During the salary negotiation process, always let the employer make a first offer. Once an offer is made, never accept it on the spot. Tell the employer you need at least several hours or a full day to consider the offer. If you know an employer is doing well financially and is desperate to fill the position you're qualified to fill, you'll have the advantage in a salary negotiation.

Never use your personal financial situation as a reason for requesting more money. Comments like "I need more money to afford my mortgage, rent or car payments," don't concern the employer. Instead, focus on the value you are offering to the company and be prepared to offer qualitative and quantitative information to back up your statements. By proving to an employer you're worth the salary you're seeking, your chances of receiving it increase dramatically.

Don't settle for earning less than what you know you deserve based on your research. Keep in mind, however, there's a big difference between earning what you're *actually* worth in today's marketplace and what you *think* you're worth.

Completing Job Applications

Most employers require applicants to complete a job application prior to an interview. An application is a questionnaire that takes a few minutes to complete, but is a useful tool for helping employers evaluate you as an applicant.

Job seekers often complete their applications by hand. The completed application demonstrates how well you can communicate on paper, how legible your handwriting is, shows whether or not you can spell and use proper punctuation, summarizes the information within your resume, and provides the employer with a list of your references. Thus, what you write on an application, in addition to how you write it, will impact an employer's decision about hiring you.

For each question within the application, think carefully about how you can answer it concisely and accurately. Neatly print all of your answers using a blue or black ball point pen. Avoid writing in script, crossing out mistakes, or using more space than what's provided. Don't use any words you don't know how to spell correctly. Employers will be looking for answers that are written in complete sentences, using proper English.

Most applications will ask you to fill in the position you're applying for and list what salary you're looking to earn. For the position, use the exact wording that was listed in the 'help wanted' ad or the job opening listing that you responded to. As for desired salary, instead of providing an actual figure, write "negotiable." Encourage the employer to make the first offer regarding salary.

When you fill in your educational background, keep in mind that employers will most likely contact the educational institution(s) you claim to have attended, so be sure that you have actually earned any degrees or diplomas you list.

Many applications will request that you write a paragraph listing any skills, research work, areas of interest, or special training you have. Refer back to your resume and make sure the information you provide is consistent.

Providing references is another key component to virtually all job applications. Prior to listing anyone's name and contact information, check with the people you want to list, then obtain permission to use them as references. Be sure to tell the person you'll be using as a reference exactly what position you're applying for, so they'll be prepared if one of your potential employers contacts them.

Never include an immediate family member as a reference. Employers don't consider relatives to be credible references. Previous employers and co-workers, prominent business people in the community who know you, former professors, and leaders of charity groups that you've done volunteer work for all make excellent references.

At the end of every application, you'll be asked to sign a statement that the information you provided is accurate to the best of your knowledge. Later, if an employer discovers you've provided false information, you could be fired.

By following all directions on the application, writing neatly, providing accurate and well thought out answers using complete sentences, and highlighting your skills and accomplishments in the space provided, you'll be one step closer to landing whatever job you apply for.

Creating A Cover Letter Is Easy!

If you understand the anatomy of a typical business letter and know what you are trying to convey within your cover letters, creating this document is relatively easy. Whether you are creating a cover letter that will be printed out, then hand-delivered, mailed or faxed (as opposed to emailed with an electronic resume), the content and format of the cover letter is the same. The only difference between the two is that an electronic cover letter will be placed in the main body of an email message, typically with your resume as an attached file.

As a general rule, never submit your resume to a potential employer unless it is accompanied by a personalized cover letter. This is a companion document to your resume. It's your initial introduction to a potential employer. It should get the recipient interested and even excited to read your resume. Your cover letters and resume should summarize your accomplishments, education and skills, using plain English. These documents should incorporate perfect spelling and grammar, and be written in a formal business style.

Just as your resume should be just one, 8.5-inch by 11-inch page in length, your cover letter should also be kept to less than one page in length. The shorter the better, since most people do not have time to read long letters.

Your Resume and Cover Letter Should Work Together

When creating a cover letter to accompany your resume, create these documents with synergy in mind when it comes to appearance and content. If you are creating a printed resume and cover letter (as opposed to an electronic resume for use with the Internet), always use the same paper, fonts and typestyles when creating both documents.

Virtually all employers put great value on an applicant with strong written and verbal communication skills. After all, a resume is typically a series of bulleted lists and short sentences, but a cover letter represents an actual writing sample.

Unless you impress an employer with your cover letter first, many HR professionals will not bother to read your resume. Thus, there is a chance your cover letter will be your *only* opportunity to convince a potential employer you are a viable job candidate. Both the wording and the overall appearance of your cover letter should nicely compliment your resume.

Your cover letter should not duplicate too much information that is already in your resume. Use your cover letter to:

- Introduce yourself
- State exactly what job you are applying for
- Seize the attention of the reader
- Peak the reader's interest
- Convey information about yourself that is not in your resume
- Briefly demonstrate your skills/accomplishments
- Convince the reader to check out your resume
- Ask the reader for an action to be taken

Your cover letter and resume will most likely arrive on a potential employer's desk along with many other pieces of mail, and possibly dozens of other resumes from people applying for the same position as you.

If you want your cover letter and resume to stand out, it needs to look extremely professional. Put considerable thought and attention into the appearance of these documents. First impressions, in this case, are extremely important. The first impression your cover letter and resume make will be based on their appearance.

While the reader of your cover letter will, of course, be looking at the letter's content and meaning, your writing style, spelling, punctuation and the format of your document will also be evaluated. What you say in your cover letter is important, but you should also think carefully about how you want to say it, and make sure that your overall presentation is professional and visually appealing. Each cover letter should be custom written for the job you are applying for, and be personalized using the name and title of the recipient.

Easy Steps For Creating Your Cover Letters

Before sending your cover letter and resume to anyone, call the recipient's office and ask for his/her full name and title. Obtaining the correct spelling of the recipient's name along with the company's name is important.

It is also critical to confirm the recipient's gender, so you can address the envelope and cover letter to Mr., Ms., Mrs., (insert last name). Refrain from making assumptions.

For your cover letter to have the desired impact, you must obtain and include the following information. So, before you actually sit down to write a cover letter, make sure you know:

- The Recipient's Full Name
- The Recipient's Job Title
- The Company Name
- Mailing Address
- Phone Number
- The Exact Position You're Applying For
- The Recipient's Fax Number (Optional)
- The Recipient's Email Address (Optional)

At the top of your letter, be sure to list *your* full name, address and phone number. If you have personalized stationary that matches your resume paper, use it. Your contact information should be followed by the recipient's address and the date (using a standard business letter format).

Next comes the salutation, the opening paragraph, your marketing message, one or two support paragraphs, your formal request for an interview, and finally some type of closure.

Just like in a verbal conversation (where you begin by saying "hello"), your cover letters should start off with a salutation, such as:

- Dear (insert recipient's first name),
- Dear Mr./Mrs./Ms./Dr. (insert recipient's last name):
- Dear Sir or Madam:
- To whom this may concern: (This is the worst salutation you can use for a cover letter. It is impersonal and demonstrates that you did not take the time necessary to determine to whom the letter should be sent.)

The opening paragraph of your letter should be short and simple. Answer the questions: "Who are you?" and "Why are you writing this letter?" Keep this part of your cover letter no longer than two or three sentences. Be sure to mention specifically what job opening you are applying for, especially if you are responding to an ad.

Following the opening paragraph, use the next paragraph or two within the body of your cover letter to quickly set yourself apart from the competition and position youself as the best applicant for the job you are apply for.

Addressing the employer's needs is the primary goal of this portion of the cover letter. Through research (and from the wording of the Help Wanted ad or job description you are responding to), you should have a basic understanding of what the employer's needs are, and then be able to use a few examples of how you can fill those needs.

Use the next paragraph to answer this question: *What is it about the employer that peaked your interest?* This is your opportunity to kiss up, compliment the employer, and demonstrate you have done some research about their organization and industry. Prove you have a strong knowledge regarding what the company is all about.

The next section of your cover letter should contain a request for the reader to take action and invite you in for an interview. Remember, the person you are writing to is probably very busy, so take it upon yourself to follow up with a telephone call. Do not simply send out your resume, then sit by the telephone and wait for a response.

Your cover letter should conclude with a formal closure and your signature. Be sure to thank the reader for their interest, time and/or consideration.

Formatting Your Cover Letter

Traditional business correspondence can follow several basic formats, any of which are acceptable for a cover letter. All correspondence should be typed or created on a computer, not hand-written. Sending your cover letter as the body of an email message is appropriate when submitting a resume via email to a potential employer.

Sample Cover Letter Layout

Your Name
Your Address
Your Phone Number
Your Fax Number (Optional)
Your Email Address (Optional)

Date

Recipient's Full Name
Recipient's Title
Company Name
Address
City, State, Zip Code

Dear (Mr./Mrs./Mrs./Dr.) (Insert Recipient's Last Name):

Opening Paragraph

Support Paragraph #1

Support Paragraph #2

Request For Action Paragraph

Closing Paragraph

Sincerely,

(Your Signature)

(Your Full Name Typed)

Your Resume Must Summarize Who You Are

For many job applicants, one of the most challenging tasks you will embark upon during your job search process is creating a resume. After all, it will most likely be the information on one single-sided, 8.5-inch by 11-inch sheet of paper that will determine whether or not an employer has any interest in inviting you to come in for an interview. On one sheet of paper, you must concisely summarize, using examples, all of the reasons why a potential employer should hire you.

Every potential employer that evaluates your resume will have the following questions they'll want instant answers to as they read your resume:

- Who are you?
- What position are you applying for?
- What are your skills and qualifications?

- What work experience do you have that directly relates to the job you are applying for?

- Are you worth the salary the job pays? What will be your worth to the employer if you get hired?

- What will you bring to the company that other applicants can't or won't?

- Will hiring you benefit the company in the short-term and long-term?

- If you get hired, will you be able to help the employer solve the problems or challenges it is currently facing?

- What sets you apart from all of the other applicants?

When a potential employer reads your resume, it needs to shout out, "Hire Me!" not "File Me!" Creating a powerful resume is a challenging process that takes time, planning, thought and the willingness to make revisions until you have created what you believe to be the perfect document.

What A Resume Is…And What It Isn't

Your resume is a tool that will help make a positive first impression on a potential employer. Even if you create the perfect resume, it doesn't guarantee you will receive a job offer. The goal of a resume is to peak a potential employer's interest in you enough so that you get invited in for a job interview.

There are several commonly accepted styles and formats for a resume. It is critical to adhere to one of these accepted formats as you create your own resume. The format and style you choose should best showcase who you are as an applicant.

This section describes the popular resume styles and formats, plus includes questions to help you choose the best resume style to utilize as you create your own resume.

Resume Type: Chronological Resume

Resume Description

This popular resume format describes your work history and education in *reverse chronological order*. It is best used by job seekers who already have real-world work experience, no gaps in their employment history, and multiple on-the-job accomplishments to showcase. It's the most commonly used and widely accepted resume format.

The primary purpose of this resume format is to show you have been steadily employed. It can demonstrate upward or lateral mobility in your career path as you have moved from job-to-job. Assuming you have the work experience to properly utilize this resume format, you will be able to demonstrate career direction. The job you are applying for now should be the "next step" upwards from your most recent work experience.

Sample Resume: Chronological Format

Your Full Name
Street Address, City, State, Zip
Phone Number/Cellular Number
Email Address

Objective: A one or two sentence summary of your accomplishments and your career objective. This should be specifically targeted to the job you are applying for.

Work Experience

200#–Present   Your Job Title   Employer, Employer's City, State
A one sentence description of your responsibilities.

- Using three to five bullet points, include short, concisely written accomplishments (listed one at a time). Use specific facts and figures to support your statements.

- List a second accomplishment.

- List a third accomplishment.

- List a fourth accomplishment. Since this is your most recent job, include more information about it. For subsequent jobs, list fewer bulleted points. Be sure to list any awards or recognition you received, plus highlight specific skills you used to succeed in each job.

19##–200#   Your Job Title   Employer, Employer's City, State
A one sentence description of your responsibilities with the company.

- Using two to four bullet points, include short, concisely written accomplishments (listed one at a time). Use specific facts and figures to support your statements.

- List a second accomplishment.

19##–19##   Your Job Title   Employer, Employer's City, State
A one sentence description of your responsibilities with the company.

- Using two to four bullet points, include short, concisely written accomplishments (listed one at a time). Use specific facts and figures to support your statements.

- List a second accomplishment.

Education

> School Name (City, State)
> Highest Degree Earned, Graduation Date
> Major, GPA

(List each school separately, and include all degrees, honors, credentials and licenses earned.)

Resume Type: Functional Resume

Resume Description

This resume format organizes your past work experiences into functional categories. You will incorporate the same basic information as you would when creating a resume using the Chronological format. Instead of focusing on employment dates, however, the information listed in your resume will focus on your past job responsibilities and job titles. Using this resume format, your skills are highlighted while your previous employers, employment dates, and job titles are given less prominence.

The Functional resume format is best used by applicants who want potential employers to discover what they can do (and are capable of) as opposed to when and where they have been employed. When using this resume format to showcase your skills and capabilities, you will be answering the question, "*What specifically can you do for the employer?*"

Sample Resume: Functional Format

Your Full Name
Street Address, City, State, Zip
Phone, Fax, Email

Objective/Job Title You are Pursuing

In one or two sentences, explain your specific career goal(s) or convey to the reader what job title you are looking to fill and why you are qualified.

Experience

List Your Most Marketable Skill (It must relate directly to the job you are pursuing)

- List your most impressive achievement using that skill, followed by the name of the employer and the employer's city and state.

- List a second achievement you have accomplished using that skill thus far in your professional career.

- List a third achievement. Since this is your most marketable skill—the biggest reason why you should be hired, use up to five bullet points.

List Your Second Most Marketable Skill

- Include up to three bullets describing how you have used this skill thus far in your career. Each bullet should include one example and list the name of the employer, plus the employer's city and state.

- List another example of how you have used this skill successfully.

List Your Third Most Marketable Skill

- Include up to three bullets describing how you have used this skill thus far in your career. Each bullet should include one example and list the name of the employer, plus the employer's city and state.

- List another example of how you have used this skill successfully.

Provide Another Reason Why You are Qualified For The Job You are Applying For

- List up to three or four achievements, areas of proficiency, specific skills, etc. (using separate bullets) that the employer will find impressive.

Employment History

200#–Present   Job Title   Employer's Name, Employer's City, State
19##–19##   Job Title   Employer's Name, Employer's City, State
(List each employer)

Education

Include a listing of degrees earned, the educational institution(s), graduation dates, etc.

Resume Type: Combination/Targeted Resume

Resume Description:

If you pinpoint a specific job opportunity, within a specific company that you choose to apply for and you want to create a customized resume specifically for that potential employer, you might consider using this resume format. All of the information included within this type of resume is used to support the statement, *"I am the perfect applicant for this job, because…"*

Use this resume format if you already know the exact requirements and skills the job you are applying for will require. When using this resume format, focus on why you are qualified to meet the job's requirements, based on the skills you already have.

Using a Targeted Resume format allows you to combine elements of the Chronological format and Functional format. When listing your employment history (in reverse chronological order), the focus will be on showcasing your most marketable skills. The dates of employment, however, can be tucked away at the end of each employment listing, so it takes the emphasis away from any gaps in your employment history.

This resume format can be utilized by someone who knows exactly what job they want and who understands the exact job requirements of the position. Thus, your resume can be custom tailored specifically to what you know the employer is looking for. This type of resume also works well for someone with the skills needed to fill a specific job, but who does not have related work experience.

Using the Combination/Target resume format, the following is an example of what one of the listings might look like under the 'Employment' section of your resume:

Job Title Held, Top Skill Used   Employer Name, Employer's City, State

   Short description of your most marketable skill (one sentence)

   • Work-related accomplishment that involved using this skill successfully

   • A second work-related accomplishment that involved using this skill

   Short description of another marketable skill of interest to a potential employer

   • Work-related accomplishment that involved using this skill successfully

   • A second work-related accomplishment that involved using this skill

(Employment Dates) 19##–2000

Resume Type: Electronic Resume

Resume Description:

An electronic resume is one that will be sent to a potential employer via email, posted on a career-related website, such as The Monster Board (*www. monster.com*), or included within an online resume database. Some employers that accept electronic resumes have a specific pre-defined resume form on their website that must be completed online in order to be accepted. This also holds true for the majority of career-related websites.

When creating an electronic resume, be sure you adhere exactly to the formatting specifications provided by the employer or career-related website. Instead of following the same format as a traditional printed resume, you will want to use *keywords* as opposed to action words to describe your employment history, skills and education.

Anyone taking advantage of cyberspace to apply for jobs online must have an electronic resume. This includes people using any of the career-related websites or who plan to apply for a job directly through a company's website. Electronic resumes are also ideal for sending via email. The majority of medium and large size companies accept electronic resume submissions.

Using an electronic resume, you can:

- Find and apply for jobs online using popular career-related websites, such as The Monster Board (*www.monster.com*), HotJobs (*http:// hotjobs.yahoo.com*) or CareerBuilder (*www.careerbuilder.com*).

- Apply for and submit your resume directly to employers by visiting the company's website or sending your resume directly via email.

- Add your resume to one of many resume databases that are used as an applicant search tool by potential employers, headhunters and employment agencies.

The biggest difference between a printed resume and an electronic one is that the electronic (or digital) resume is created on a computer and is kept in a digital format. As a result, it can be emailed to an employer, posted on a website, added to an online database and later easily imported into applicant tracking software used by potential employers.

While you will not have to deal with issues like choosing resume paper, picking the perfect font or ink color, or formatting your resume to look perfect on the printed page, there are other issues you will need to contend with when creating an electronic resume.

Keep in mind, there are no standard guidelines to follow when creating an electronic resume, since employers use different computer systems and software. Thus, it is important you adhere to the individual requirements of each employer in terms of formatting, saving and sending your resume electronically.

When completing an online-based resume form, be sure you fill in all fields with the appropriate information only. Be mindful of limitations for each field. For example, a field that allows for a job description to be entered, may have space for a maximum of only 50 words, so the description you enter needs to provide all of the relevant information (using keywords), but also be written concisely. Since an electronic resume is as important as a traditional one, consider printing out the online form first and then spending time thinking about how you will fill in each field (or answer each question).

Don't attempt to be clever and try adding information that wasn't requested in a specific field in order to provide more information about yourself to an employer. For example, if you are only given space to enter one phone number, but you want to provide a home and cell phone number, don't use the fields for your address to enter the second phone number.

The majority of online resume templates you will come across on the various career-related websites and sites hosted by individual employers follow the same basic format as a traditional Chronological resume, however, you will be prompted to enter each piece of information in separate fields, and you will most likely be limited to the number of fields you can fill in order to convey your information.

When sending a resume via email, the message should begin as a cover letter (and contain the same information as a cover letter). You can then either attach the resume file to the email message or paste the resume text within the message. Be sure to include your email address and well as your regular mailing address and phone number(s) within all email correspondence. Never assume an employer will receive your message and simply hit 'respond' using their email software to contact you.

When creating an electronic resume, follow these formatting guidelines:

- Avoid using bullets or other symbols. Instead of a bullet, use an asterisk ('*') or a dash ('-'). Instead of using the percentage sign ('%') for example, spell out the word 'percent.' (Within your resume, write '15 percent', not '15%').

- Use the spell check feature of the software used to create your electronic resume and then proofread the document carefully. Just as applicant tracking software is designed to pick out keywords from your resume that showcase you as a qualified applicant, these same software packaged used by employers can also instantly count the number of typos and spelling errors in your document and report that to an employer as well.

- Avoid using multiple columns, tables or charts within your document.

- Within the text, avoid abbreviations—spell everything out. For example, use the word 'Director', not 'Dir.' or 'Vice President' as opposed to 'VP'. In terms of degrees, however, it is acceptable to use term like 'MBA', 'BA', 'Ph.D.' etc.

Remember, keywords are the backbone of any good electronic resume. If you don't incorporate keywords, your resume will not be properly processed by the employer's computer system. Choosing the right keywords to incorporate into your resume is a skill onto itself that takes some creativity and plenty of thought.

For example, each job title, job description, skill, degree, license, or other piece of information you list within your resume should be descriptive, self-explanatory and be among the 'keywords' the potential employer's applicant tracking software is on the lookout for as it evaluates your resume. One excellent resource that can help you select the best keywords to use within your electronic resume is the *Occupational Outlook Handbook* (published by the U.S. Department of Labor).

Resume Type: Keyword-Based Resume

Resume Description

Use this type of resume if you know or suspect the employer utilizes applicant tracking software. This means a computer scans and analyzes your resume and picks out pre-defined keywords and phrases. A person does not initially read your resume.

Applicant tracking software is a computer application that allows an employer to create a list of keywords for each job opening it has available. These keywords are used to describe the job's requirements, the necessary skills and the educational background for the ideal applicant. Once this list of keywords is created by the employer, the software allows employers to take traditionally printed resumes and/or electronic resumes and automatically scan or import them into a database without ever actually getting read or evaluated by a human.

Once an applicant's resume is entered into the database, the software deciphers it word by word and compares each word to the listing of keywords created by the employer. Out of all the resumes an employer receives, only those applicants that have resumes with a pre-defined number of keyword matches will be flagged as potentially qualified applicants for a job opening. After the software has selected the top candidates, an HR professional reads only those applicants' resumes and/or invites those people in for interviews.

As a job seeker, if you will be applying for jobs at medium to large-size companies that use applicant tracking software, it is important to create a resume that will be compatible with applicant tracking software. Focus on using keywords within your resume that you believe will match up with the keywords the employer has already selected.

Someone creating a keyword-based resume can follow any of the formats of a traditional printed resume, however, the wording you will use when actually writing the résumé's content will be different. After the Heading section of your resume, some applicants choose to add a section called 'Keywords' which is simply a listing of nouns, phrases, industry terminology and buzzwords you know the computer will be searching for when it evaluates your resume.

Just because you are creating a printed resume you believe will be read by a computer, you should still follow the resume design tips used to create a traditional printed resumes. After all, there is always a chance a human might look at your resume and you want them to be impressed.

The biggest rule to follow when creating a scannable, keyword-based resume is to create the content by incorporating nouns and keywords into the text as opposed to action words (verbs).

10 Tips For Creating Your High-Impact Resume

These ten tips will help you create a resume that contains the information employers are looking for.

1. Start by writing out answers to the following questions: What are your skills and qualifications? What work experience do you have that directly relates to the job you're applying for? What can you offer to the employer? Specifically, how will hiring you benefit the employer? Can you help solve problems or challenges that the employer is facing? What sets you apart from other people applying for the same job? Answering these questions will help you determine what information to include in your resume.

2. The main sections of a resume are the: Heading, Job Objectives, Education, Accreditation and Licenses, Skills, Work and Employment Experience, Professional Affiliations, Military Service, References and Personal Information. Choose what information about yourself should be included under each of headings. The actual wording for each resume section can be modified. Also, only include the sections that apply to you.

3. In the Heading, include your full name, address, telephone number(s), fax number, pager number and email address. If you're trying to keep your job search a secret from your currently employer, don't list your work telephone or fax number. Also, make sure that there's an answering machine connected to the telephone number that's listed on your resume, so a potential employer can reach you anytime. Missing a message could result in a missed job opportunity.

4. When listing your education, don't include your grades, class rank or overall average unless this information is extremely impressive and will help to set you apart from other applicants. The first piece of information listed in the Education section of your resume should describe the highest degree you've earned or that you're in the process of earning.

5. To decide what work experience to include on your resume, start by listing all of your internships, after-school jobs, summer jobs, part-time jobs, full-time jobs, and your volunteer and charitable work. Be prepared to provide specific dates of employment, job titles, responsibilities, and accomplishments for each position. How you convey this information in your resume will ultimately be critical. Ultimately, you may have to refrain from including some of the less pertinent information in order to conserve space.

6. As you sit down to write your resume, use action words, which are usually verbs that make your accomplishments sound even better, without stretching the truth. What your resume says about you, and more importantly, how it's said, is what will make your resume a powerful job search tool.

7. Choose a resume format that best organizes your information for an employer. Using a 'chronological' format is the most popular. Your employment experience is listed in reverse chronological order, with your most recent job listed first.

8. Keep your resume short and to the point. Make sure all of the information is well organized and is stated as succinctly as possible. Remove words and phrases the are redundant.

9. Print your resume on good quality, white, off-white or cream-colored paper. Use 24 or 28-pound bond paper made of 100 percent cotton stock. Your finished resume should look neat and well-balanced on the page. It should be inviting to the reader and not look cluttered.

10. Before distributing your resume to potential employers, proof read it carefully. Even the smallest spelling or grammatically error will not be tolerated and could result in your missing out on a job opportunity.

Spending extra time on your resume is an excellent investment in your future. Pay careful attention to detail, and make sure that your resume promotes you in the best possible way. To assist in formatting and designing your resume, consider using specialized resume creation software. Since the design and formatting of a resume is so important, check out one of the many books available that explain and demonstrate the resume creation process.

Make A Positive Impression During Your Job Interviews

Assuming your resume does its job and captures the attention of an employer, you'll be invited to participate in an in-person job interview. This is your opportunity to sell yourself to a potential employer by demonstrating through your words, appearance, attitude and body language that you're the very best candidate to fill the job opening available.

Whether or not you receive a job offer after participating in one or more interviews has nothing to do with luck. The employer's decision will be based on your skills, experience, education and how well you present yourself and perform during the interview.

The following are strategies to help you properly prepare for an interview and make a positive first impression:

- Do research about the company you're interviewing with, the industry you'll be working in, and if possible, try to learn as much as possible about the individual who will be conducting the interview. Failure to prepare properly for each interview is a guaranteed way to stay unemployed.

- As part of your preparation, participate in mock interviews with a friend, relative or career counselor. Practice answering common interview questions out loud, and compile a list of at least five intelligent questions you can ask the employer during the interview.

- Be sure to get a good night's sleep before the interview. You want to look and feel rested and be totally awake and alert.

- Before your interview, take a shower, shampoo your hair, clean your fingernails, brush your teeth, shave, and apply antiperspirant and deodorant. Your appearance is the very first thing a potential employer is going notice when your arrive for an interview. Making a positive first impression is critical.

- Make sure your interview outfit is clean, wrinkle-free and fits you perfectly. Also, be sure your shoes are shined and coordinate well with your outfit.

- Make several extra copies of your resume, letters of recommendation, and your list of references and bring them to your interview. You'll also want to bring your daily planner, along with your research materials, a pad and a working pen. All of this paperwork will fit nicely in a briefcase or portfolio. On your pad, write down the company's name, interviewer's name, address, telephone number and directions to the location of the interview.

- The morning of your interview, read a local newspaper and watch a morning news program so you're aware of the day's news events and will be able to discuss them with the interviewer. Many interviewers like to start off an interview with general chit-chat. You want to appear knowledgeable about what's happening in the world around you.

- Arrive to your interview at least 15 minutes early and check in with the receptionist. While it's okay for an interviewer to keep you, the applicant, waiting if he or she is running late, it is never appropriate for the job seeker to show up for an interview even one minute late. Next to being unprepared for the interview, arriving late is the worst mistake you can make.

- If you're asked to sit in a waiting room until your interview begins, use the time to compose yourself, review your research notes and visualize yourself succeeding in the interview.

- From the moment you arrive at the interview location and step through the front door, be in interview mode. Act professionally and be polite to everyone, including secretaries and receptionists.

- As the interview gets underway, sit up straight. Listen carefully to the questions posed to you, take a moment or two to think about each answer, and then answer using complete sentences. Words like, "yeah", "nope", and "umm" should not be used as part of your professional vocabulary.

- Throughout the entire interview, in addition to what you say, you will be evaluated based on how you conduct yourself and use body language. Prior to your interview, spend the necessary amount of time learning to control your nervous habits. If you know what your nervous habits are, they'll be easier to control in stressful situations.

- During the later part of your interviews, make a point to come right out and ask for the job you're applying for. Explain exactly why you want the job, what you can offer to the company, and why you're the best candidate to fill the position.

- No matter what questions are asked during the interview, what the employer ultimately wants to know is if you're the best person for the job. Will you be an asset to the company if you're hired? Do you have the skills, knowledge and experience necessary to successfully achieve the job's requirements? Will you fit nicely into the corporate culture within the company? Are you a hard worker who is dedicated and honest? Using specific examples, it's your job to convey whatever information is necessary and tell your story during an interview situation.

Anticipating Job Interview Questions You'll Be Asked

As part of your job interview preparation, determine the types of questions the interviewer will ask. Spend time developing well-thought-out, complete and intelligent answers to these questions. Thinking about answers, or even writing out answers on paper will be helpful, but what will benefit you the most is actual practice answering interview questions out loud, and having someone you trust evaluate your responses honestly.

Most of the questions you'll be asked will be pretty obvious, however, be prepared for an interviewer to ask you a few questions that are unexpected. By doing this, the interviewer wants to see how you react and how well you think on your feet.

As you answer all of the interviewer's questions:

- Avoid talking down to an interviewer or making him or her feel less intelligent than you are.

- Be prepared to answer the same questions multiple times. Make sure your answers are consistent, and never reply, "You already asked me that."

- Don't be evasive, especially if you're asked about negative aspects of your employment history.

- Don't lie or stretch the truth.

- Never apologize for negative information regarding your past.

- Never imply that a question is "stupid."

- Use complete sentences and proper English

The following are common interview questions and suggestions on how you can best answer them:

1. What can you tell me about yourself? [*Stress your skills and accomplishments. Avoid talking about your family, hobbies, or topics not relevant to your ability to do the job.*]

2. Why have you chosen to pursue your current career path? [*Give specific reasons and examples.*]

3. In your personal or professional life, what has been your greatest failure? What did you learn from that experience? [*Be open and honest. Everyone has had some type of failure. Focus on what you learned from the experience and how it helped you to grow as a person.*]

4. Why did you leave your previous job? [*Try to put a positive spin on your answer, especially if your were fired for negative reasons. Company down sizing, a company going out of business, or some other reason that was out of your control is a perfectly acceptable answer. Remember, your answer will probably be verified.*]

5. What would you consider to be your biggest accomplishments at your last job? [*Talk about what made you a productive employee and valuable asset to your previous employer. Stress that teamwork was involved in achieving your success, and that you work well with others.*]

6. In college, I see you were a (insert subject) major. Why did you choose (insert subject) as your major? [*Explain your interest in the subject matter, where that interest comes from, and how it relates to your current career-related goals.*]

7. What are your long-term goals? [*Talk about how you have been following a career path, and where you think this pre-planned career path will take you in the future. Describe how you believe the job you're applying for is a logical step forward.*]

8. Why do you think you're the most qualified person to fill this job? [*Focus on the positive things that set you apart from the competition. What's unique about you, your skill set and past experiences? What work-related experience do you have that relates directly to this job?.*]

9. What have you heard about this company that was of interest to you? [*Focus on the company's reputation. Refer to positive publicity, media atten-*

tion or published information that caught your attention. This shows you've done your research.]

10. What else can you tell me about yourself that isn't listed in your resume? [*This is yet another opportunity for you to sell yourself to the employer. Take advantage of the opportunity.*]

Changing Careers

People in entry-level jobs all the way up to top-level executives sometimes feel the need to change careers, perhaps because their personal goals and interests change, or maybe after working within an industry, they realize that they've made bad career decisions. If you feel the need to change careers, for whatever reason, understand that this can be done successfully, but it'll be a bit more difficult than simply finding and landing a new job.

A career change refers to going from one occupation to another. You'll be taking on new responsibilities and challenges, because you'll be working in a totally different industry. For example, a career change could involve going from a managerial position at a retail store, to earning a law degree and becoming an attorney, obtaining a real estate license in order to sell houses, or earning a teaching license to become an educator.

The first step is to carefully analyze why you want to change careers. What is it about your current career that you don't like? How will your life improve if you change careers? Next, it's important to do some intense research to determine what type of career you'd ultimately want to have. This might require meeting with a career counselor to help you clearly define your interests and objectives. You should also take full advantage of your networking skills and speak with people currently working in the career you hope to break into.

Before pursuing any new career opportunities, compile a detailed list of all your work-related skills, education and accomplishments. Once you know what career you're interested in pursuing, compare your skill set and educational background to what the job requirements are for the new career. Your skill set, which might include being computer literate, having good public speaking abilities, and having strong managerial or organizational skills, could be transferable to a new career, even if the actual work experience you have acquired while using these skills isn't directly transferable.

Determine what knowledge and skills you're lacking, and decide how you'll go about acquiring the needed education and skills. Chances are, you'll have to obtain additional schooling or training, so consider the amount of time it'll take, the cost, and the overall commitment that will be necessary to obtain the needed education. Is returning to school full-time or part-time an option? Are there night or weekend classes you can take that will allow you to remain in your current job so you can continue to earn a paycheck?

By changing careers, you're actually starting again almost from scratch, as if you're first graduating from high school or college, because you have little or no related work experience. It's this work-related experience that employers are looking for, so while you might have proven skills that can be applied to a new career, your goal is to determine a way to position yourself as a qualified applicant, without stretching the truth.

Upon obtaining the necessary education and licenses (if applicable) that you'll need to land a job in the new career that interests you, choose a Functional resume format that allows you to showcase your skills and accomplishments, while at the same time, downplaying your past employment history. The goal of your resume and cover letter should be to communicate everything about your skills, experience and education that relate directly to the new career. Any well-written resume book can assist you in formatting your resume to achieve this objective.

Try to obtain related work experience, even if it means doing volunteer work or accepting an unpaid internship. Ideally, you want to show some work-related experience on your resume when you attempt to change careers. If you have the necessary education and skill set, however, you should be able to sell yourself to a potential employer and successfully change careers.

In terms of job interviews, be prepared to explain honestly why you're changing careers and how your skills fit nicely into the career you're now pursuing. Focus on what you can offer to the potential employer, and be prepared to answer the question, "Why doesn't your past work experience relate to the job you're applying for?"

Be sure to use whatever networking contacts you have to help you find and land a new job. Through a personal introduction to a company, you're more apt to get the attention of employers if you come highly recommended by someone who understands your accomplishments and skills. Also, take full advantage of the services offered by the career placement office at whatever educational institution you return to for the specialized or advanced education you need for the new career.

Finally, don't act too quickly. Before quitting your current job, make sure you have a formulated plan and a complete understanding of what you're getting into. Understand the financial risks involved. If possible, stay at your current job until you have the additional education you need and you've actually found a new job that offers a career change opportunity.

In the next chapter, you'll discover strategies for getting the most out of the money you earn. You'll learn how to control your spending and develop a realistic budget for yourself.

4

You're No Donald Trump: Living On A Budget

Who needs a budget anyway? The answer to this question is simple—everyone! Whether you're trying to live on a relatively low income or have multiple millions, developing and maintaining a budget for yourself will help to insure you maintain the highest quality of life possible, without squandering your money on unnecessary things, such as impulse purchases or paying excessive interest on loans.

Out of all the chapters in the book, this one deals with taking control of your financial situation here and now—starting today. By managing your money properly, you should be able to improve your overall quality of life.

Determine How and Where Your Money Is Being Spent

Have you virtually dedicated your life to working for a paycheck that barely covers your cost of living? Do you feel like the majority of your life is spent on the job? Does virtually every penny you earn get spent on necessities, with little or nothing left over after each pay period? Have you been relying on credit cards, for example, to help make ends meet? Do you find yourself getting deeper and deeper into debt, with no relief in sight? Have you been negatively impacted by the slow economy, forced to pay higher prices for what you need, while at the same time, you're earning less money?

This, unfortunately, is the financial situation faced by countless millions of people, from all walks of life. While there are no magical answers for quickly getting yourself out of debt or guaranteed ways of building wealth, once you fully understand the financial situation you're in, there are strategies you can easily implement to help you more easily meet your financial obligations and achieve your realistic financial goals.

When it comes to making your paycheck last and building wealth, you must first understand several basic realities. First, there are no easy solutions. Second, improving your current financial situation is going to take hard work, proper planning, plus a major commitment and effort on your part. So, unless you happen to win the lottery or receive a large inheritance from a long lost relative, if you want to receive the maximum benefits from the money you have, you'll need to plan and strategize.

Your Current Financial Situation

Developing a true understanding of your current financial situation is the first step to making your paycheck last and building greater wealth in the future. In this section, you're about to evaluate your current financial situation. This means developing an understanding about:

- How much money you have now, in savings and investments, for example.
- How much money you're presently earning (your income).
- What your current debts, expenses and liabilities are.

First, let's create an accurate "net worth statement." This is a detailed listing of what you own (your assets) and your debts (liabilities). Complete the following worksheet to the best of your ability. This worksheet will help you determine your current net worth. Once the worksheet is complete, to determine your net worth, subtract the total value of your liabilities from the total value of your assets.

Total Assets—Total Liabilities = Net Worth

If the total value of your assets are greater than your liabilities, you have a positive net worth (you're worth more than you owe). If the value of your assets is lower than your liabilities, you have a negative net worth. It's very common for people with a mortgage and various types of loans, for example, to have a negative net worth.

One of your long-term financial goals should be to ultimately achieve a positive net worth. As you begin taking steps to adjust your spending, save money, reduce your debt, and improve your overall financial situation, you'll want to recalculate your net worth every few months. This will help you track your progress.

Net Worth Statement Worksheet

Asset Description	Value ($)
Cash in Savings Account(s)	
Cash in Checking Account(s)	
Current Cash Value of Life Insurance	
Current Equity in Your Home, Condo or Apartment (If applicable)	
Value of Car(s)	
Value of Investment(s) (Mutual Funds, Stocks, Bonds, CDs, Commodities, etc.)	
Value of Personal Property	
Value of Retirement Account (IRA, Keogh, etc.)	
Other Assets	

Total: $_____

Liability Description	Value ($)
Bank Loan(s)	
Car Loan(s)	
Credit Card Balance(s)	
Mortgage Balance	
Personal Loan(s)	
Other Liabilities	

Total: $_____

Your Current Net Worth: $_____

Knowing your net worth is important. It allows you to look at the big picture in terms of your financial situation. For the short-term, what's more important to understand is how much money you're earning each month or pay period. Also, you need to determine exactly how you're spending the money you receive from each paycheck. To help you calculate this information, complete the following worksheets.

Monthly Income Worksheet

Directions: Complete this worksheet using income from a one month period. You can also take your annual net income (take home pay) and divide it by twelve to determine your average monthly income.

Income Type	Value ($)
Take Home Pay & Earned Income (Salary After Taxes)	
Interest, Capital Gains and Dividend Earnings from Investments	
Other Income	

Total: $_____

Monthly Expense Worksheet

Directions: For a one month period, calculate all of your fixed expenses, followed by your flexible expenses. A fixed expense is one that is the same every month, such as your rent, mortgage or car payment.

Fixed Expense Type Month: _____ Year: _____	Cost ($)
Auto Insurance	
Car Payment	
Disability Insurance	
Home Insurance (Renter's Insurance)	
Life Insurance	
Medical/Health Insurance	
Other Loan Payment(s)	
Rent/Mortgage	
Alimony/Child Support Payments	
Payment to Retirement Account(s)	
Investment to Stocks, Mutual Funds, etc.	

Total: $_____

Directions: Ideally, you'll want to track your spending carefully for between three and six months to ultimately determine how your money is being spent. For each month you track your flexible expenses, complete this worksheet.

Flexible Expense Type Month: _____ Year: _____	Cost ($)
Cable TV Bill	
Cellular Phone Bill	
Child Care/Babysitting	
Clothing	
Commuting Costs	
Credit Card Payments	
Dining out/Take Out Food Expenses	
Donations to Charities	
Dues for Clubs, Organizations and/or Religious Institutions	
Education	
Electric Bill	
Entertainment/Recreation Expenses	
Food & Groceries	
Fuel Bill	
Gas Bill	
Gas for Auto/Vehicle(s)	
Gifts	
Home Maintenance/Upkeep Costs	
Internet Connection Fees	
Laundry/Dry Cleaning	
Medical, Drugs (Prescriptions) and Dental Expenses	
Newspapers, Magazines and Books	
Parking for Your Vehicle(s)	
Personal Care & Grooming Products/Fees	
Pet Supplies and Expenses (Vet, Food, Grooming, Etc.)	
Taxes (Real Estate, etc.)	

Flexible Expense Type Month: _____ Year: _____	Cost ($)
Telephone Bill	
Trash Removal	
Vacations	
Vehicle Maintenance	
Water Bill	
Other Expense	
Other Expense	
Other Expense	

Total: $_____

By adding up all of your fixed and flexible expenses, you can determine how much money you need to earn per month to maintain your current lifestyle and quality of life. Now, take this figure (total expenses) and subtract it from your total monthly income. Do this basic calculation to determine your Net Available Cash Flow (also called your Discretionary Income):

Total Income—All Expenses (Fixed and Flexible) = Net Available Cash Flow

If each month you're earning more than you need to survive and maintain your current quality of life, you're starting off in good shape. This means you have discretionary income at your disposal because your Net Available Cash Flow is a positive number. Next, determine the best ways to improve your quality of life and properly invest or utilize this left-over money each month, while at the same time, determine ways to cut your spending to save additional money.

For a multitude of reasons, many people find themselves spending more each month than they earn. Thus, to cover expenses, they're forced to tap into their savings and/or use credit cards to make up the difference. In this situation, there is no discretionary income. This means you're living beyond your means and you need to take steps to avoid financial disaster, before it's too late. These steps might be as simple as cutting a few costs. Based on the severity of the situation, it might require a drastic change to your spending habits and lifestyle in order to get your financial situation under control.

Understanding Your Financial Woes

Now that you've calculated your net worth and net available cash flow, perhaps you've seen proof of something you've known for a while—financially, you're in trouble! Well, whatever you do, don't panic! Whatever the cause of your financial situation, you'll quickly need to discover ways to:

- Control your spending.
- Reduce your debt and make better use of your credit.
- Deal with unexpended financial disasters.
- Learn how to save money in your everyday life.
- Implement strategies for saving and investing.

After reviewing the financial worksheets you completed earlier in this chapter, answer the following questions:

1. What is the biggest financial obstacle you're currently facing?

    _____

    _____

    _____

2. What needs to change in order to improve your financial situation?

    _____

    _____

    _____

3. What are the primary causes for your financial problems? Check all that apply:

    __ Overspending

    __ Lack of understanding about my finances and how to manage them

    __ Carelessness

    __ Employment Problems (Being laid off, downsized, pay cut, etc.)

    __ Health-related problems

__ Unexpected emergencies

__ Not adhering to a budget or miscalculating financial needs

__ Poor investment decisions/strategies

__ Too much debt or poor use of credit

__ Living well beyond your means for too long

__ The country's bad economy

__ Not properly planning for major expenses (retirement, buying a home, purchasing a car, sending your children to college, etc.)

__ Other: _____

4.   What's currently keeping you from improving your financial situation?

_____

_____

_____

Once you've considered some of the reasons behind your current financial situation and perhaps given a few minutes worth of thought toward what it'll take to improve your situation, it's time to take stock in your own abilities and potential. While reducing your spending, increasing your savings, and implementing proper money management strategies will help make your current paycheck last, it's also highly worthwhile to develop strategies for earning more money in the months and years to come. So, as your cost of living increases, so will your ability to meet those financial challenges.

Take Control Of Your Spending

As you make your purchases, think about how they're being paid for. If you're using a credit card or financing your purchase, will you be paying off the balance immediately or will you be paying interest charges over a period of time? If you're financing your purchase, calculate in the amount of interest and additional fees you'll be paying and add them to the actual price of what you're buying.

When making a purchase, ask yourself these questions:

• Is the purchase absolutely necessary?

- Do you have the money to afford what you're buying?

- What options are available to save money when making this purchase? Can you use a coupons or take advantage of a sale or special promotion?

- Is there a similar product/service that would be less expensive?

- Have you done the necessary research to insure you're getting exactly what you need at the best possible price?

- What benefit(s) will you receive from the purchase?

The LowerMyBills.com (*www.lowermybills.com*) and BillSaver.com (*www.billsaver.com*) websites are two resources for quickly finding the best deals on a wide range of products and services, including: long distance telephone service, home refinancing, various types of insurance, credit cards, Internet services and debt consolidation services. When making any type of large purchase, use the Internet to see if online coupons are available. You'll be surprised to find you can save money on almost anything by utilizing online coupons.

Evaluating Your Expenses

First, let's evaluate your necessary expenses. Chances are, things like your mortgage (rent), car payments and insurance premiums are among your necessary expenses. While you can't eliminate these expenses from your budget, you might be able to reduce them. For example, you could potentially refinance your mortgage at a lower interest rate and save several hundred dollars per month. Or, if you're paying rent and drastic money saving measures need to be taken to cure your financial woes, you could move into a less expenses home or apartment or take on a roommate.

As for your car payments, you could potentially refinance your car or trade in your vehicle and purchase/lease one that will require lower monthly payments. Even insurance premiums could potentially be reduced if you shop around for the best rates and/or raise your deductibles. (Warning: Before raising your insurance deductibles, consider the financial consequences if you actually need to make a claim. For example, if you get into a car accident, can you afford to pay a $1,000 deductible to repair your car as opposed to a $250 or $500 deductible?)

Looking at your other expenses, carefully evaluate each of them and consider ways you might be able to reduce each of them (not necessary eliminate them.) For example, could you do a better job shopping for the best deal for your cell phone service and cut your monthly bill from $65 per month to $30 per month, simply by reducing the number of daytime or anytime minutes you have available to talk on your cellular plan?

On your regular phone bill, can you sign up for an all-inclusive plan that offers unlimited local and long distance service for a flat monthly fee? Companies like Verizon, AT&T and MCI offer this type of service. This all-inclusive type of plan allows you to talk as much as you want, but know in advance exactly how much your monthly telephone charges will be.

As you start evaluating your monthly expenses, depending on how much money you want or need to reduce from your overall budget, consider eliminating some or all of your least critical expenses, as opposed to just reducing them. Once again, consider your priorities and what's truly important to you and your quality of life.

Finally, take a look at all of your totally frivolous expenses each month. Your best option for these is simply to eliminate them from your budget and teach yourself discipline when it comes to making impulse buying decisions. Just because something you see is on sale, it doesn't mean you absolutely must purchase it, no matter how good the deal is. If you don't need the item, don't purchase it! When it comes to reducing your monthly expenses, your frivolous expenses should be the very first things to get cut or drastically reduced.

Making Your Money Work Harder for You

If you're like most people, chances are you have a pre-determined monthly income. Of course, if you earn commissions or work overtime, you'll earn more, however, you can pretty much assume your monthly income will be within a specific range. So, since drastically increasing the amount of money that comes in each month isn't an option (at least in the short-term), it's important to evaluate your overall budget and determine ways to make the money you have work harder for you.

There are countless things you can do to better utilize the money you now have available. Every month, if you save just $100 by doing very simply things, that money you save will add up quickly ($1,200 per year!)

Here are just a few ideas on how to make your money work harder for you:

- If you use credit cards, apply for cards with the lowest possible fees and interest rates, then transfer your outstanding balances from higher interest rate cards.

- Immediately work toward reducing your credit card balances so you're not paying so much interest per month. Likewise, consider refinancing your home and/or car to reduce the amount of interest you're paying.

- When choosing a bank, select one that pays the highest interest rates for money in savings accounts, plus has the lowest fees to maintain a checking account. In some situations, you'll find that a Credit Union offers the best rates. Shop around for the best deals.

- If you have a significant amount of money sitting in a low interest earning savings account, consider putting those discretionary funds into some type of investment, such as mutual funds. While you may incur some additional financial risk, the financial rewards could be worthwhile. Be sure to consult with a financial advisor and do your research before making any type of financial investment, plus be sure to diversify your investments. (Don't invest in a single stock or mutual fund, for example.)

- Find ways to reduce your utility expenses. For example, throughout your home, use more energy efficient (and/or lower wattage) light bulbs and turn down the air conditioning or heat during the day when you're at work. When purchasing major appliances, pay attention to their energy efficiency rating and look for the Energy Star label (*www.energystar.gov*). Energy Star is a government-backed program helping businesses and individuals protect the environment by promoting better energy efficiency. The Department of Energy Efficiency offers free information at *www.eere.energy.gov/consumerinfo/energy_savers*. This information is also available by calling (800) DOE-EREC.

Strategies for Sticking To Your Budget

Once you set a budget for yourself, it's important to stick with it. Sorry, those impulse shopping sprees need to stop. Hopefully, you've already begun to discover ways you can immediately reduce your monthly expenses. As you decide what expense cutting strategies you'll utilize, consider the following:

- Why are you implementing each expense cutting strategy? What's your specific goal or objective?

- What will the benefit be (short-term and long-term) of each strategy?

- What will the immediate impact be on you and your lifestyle?

- What do you anticipate the financial outcome will be after implementing each cost-cutting strategy?

As you implement each strategy, focus on your objectives and evaluate the results on an ongoing basis. After implementing cost cutting strategies and a budget, the biggest challenge will be sticking to it and allowing it to work for you. Choosing ways to save money or creating a budget is only the first step. Now, you must adjust your lifestyle and adhere to the cost cutting measures you've selected and make a conscious effort *not* to deviate from the budget you create.

Your personal motivation will be one of the key factors that will help you stick to the budget you create, plus adhere to the expense cutting and money saving strategies you implement. Your motivation should be driven by your long-term goals.

Don't allow yourself to justify reasons for straying from your budget. At the end of each month, each quarter and each year, evaluate your progress. This alone should help keep you motivated as you see yourself getting closer and closer to achieving your long-term financial goals. Develop an ongoing series of well-thought-out financial and budgeting strategies for achieving your financial goals. Implementing a random strategy here and there and not being consistent will keep you from achieving long-term success.

Balance Your Checkbook Monthly

There are two important reasons for a budget conscious person to balance (or reconcile) their checkbook on the regular basis. First, doing this allows you to keep careful track of how much money is available in your checking account. Second, it helps avoid costly errors. If, for example, you forget to take into account bank fees, or forget you made an ATM withdrawal, you could accidentally bounce a check due to insufficient funds. Not only can this be embarrassing, but it can be costly, since you'll be forced to pay additional fees, which for someone on a tight budget, should definitely be avoided.

As you take control of your personal budget and spending, start by balancing your checkbook, especially if you're watching every penny. To pay bills and cover living expenses, the average person writes at least 240 checks per year. In addition, a growing number of people are using their debit card or online banking to pay bills using funds from their checking account, without actually having to write a check.

When you write a check, the money is taken from your checking account. In addition, money gets removed from your account when you use a debit card, ATM (automatic teller machine), pay a bill using check-by-phone or automatic payment options and/or you pay related banking fees. Especially if you're on a tight budget, it's important to have ongoing knowledge of exactly how much money is available within your checking account in order to avoid accidentally bouncing checks and incurring additional fees from the bank.

Balancing (or reconciling) your checkbook requires a minimal time commitment and little mathematical skill. Furthermore, you can use a calculator, computer or PDA to make the process even easier. This process should be done every month when you receive your checking account statement from your bank. If you use online banking, it can be done on an ongoing basis, because you'll be able to see exactly when deposits and checks clear.

Follow these easy steps to balance your checkbook:

1. Keep an ongoing record of all transactions relating to your checking account as they happen. It's too easy to forget making a transaction if you don't write it down immediately. When recording a transaction, write down the date, type of transaction, the amount of money associated with the transaction, plus any additional notes. All of this information can be recorded in your checkbook register (provided with your checks) or recorded using your computer, with a program like Microsoft Money or Quicken.

    You'll want to keep track of:

    -   All transactions made using a bank teller
    -   ATM transactions
    -   Bank fees
    -   Checks that are written
    -   All deposits (direct deposits, ATM deposits, teller deposits)
    -   Online banking transactions
    -   Purchases made with your debit card
    -   Recurring automatic payments
    -   Transfers of money between your accounts

    Your checkbook register will probably look something like this:

Check Number	Date	Transaction Description	Payment/ Debit (-)	Code	Fee (-)	Deposit /Credit (+)	Total For Transac- tion

Note: In the 'Code' column of your check register, you can enter the type of transaction. Use this list to make it easier:

- D = Deposit
- DP = Debit Card Purchase
- ATM = Cash Withdrawal
- AP = Automatic Payment
- FT = Fund Transfer
- I = Interest Earned
- SC = Service Charge or Bank Fee
- TD = Tax Deductible

2. As soon as your monthly bank statement arrives, compare all of the transactions you recorded in your check register with the transactions listed on your statement. Each time you see a match, place a checkmark next to that entry in your check register and on the bank statement. Use a pencil, in case you need to correct an error.

3. In a perfect world, the balance on your statement should match the balance in your checkbook register for the date the statement was printed by the bank. In reality, however, this rarely happens. There will most likely be transactions listed in your check register, such as un-cleared checks, that aren't yet listed on your bank statement. Likewise, there may be banking fees on your statement that you forgot to list in your check register. To deal with this, subtract from your bank statement's total balance any checks, debit transactions, fees and service charges, for example, that are listed in your register but not listed on your bank

statement. Next, add to the bank statement's total balance, any deposits that are listed in your check register, but not included on your bank statement. This adjusted bank statement balance should now be identical to your checkbook register's balance.

4. Look for common errors. If, after making the necessary adjustments, the total listed on your bank statement does not match your check register (for the date the bank statement was issued), determine if any outstanding checks cleared, for example, perhaps from two or three months ago. Also, recheck all of your mathematical calculations and make sure you didn't transpose any numbers. Make sure you remembered to calculate in all of the various banking fees.

To make balancing your checkbook a bit easier, complete these two worksheets each month, then perform the following calculations:

Worksheet #1—Outstanding Checks

(List any checks you wrote that have <u>not yet been included</u> on your bank statement. Be sure to list any other debit card transactions and transactions involving money being taken out of your checking account that don't yet appear on the bank statement. Note: List banking fees separately.)

Check Number or Transaction Description	Amount

Total: $_____

Worksheet #2—Outstanding Deposits

(List any deposits or transactions involving money put into your checking account that <u>are not listed</u> on your bank statement.)

Deposit or Transaction Description	Amount

Total: $_____

Once these two worksheets are complete, perform this calculation:

	Ending Balance on Your Bank Statement	$_____
ADD (+)	Total Outstanding Deposits (Total From Above Worksheet #2)	$_____
SUBTRACT (-)	Total Outstanding Checks (Total from Above Worksheet #1)	$_____
SUBTRACT (-)	All Banking Fees	$_____
ADD (+)	Interest Earned (if applicable)	$_____

New Balance: $ _____

(Your New Balance should be equal to the balance listed in your check register.)

Who Can Afford To Save?

Ideally, it's an excellent strategy to have enough money in savings to support yourself financially for at least three months, assuming for some reason, you can't work and earn an income. In addition to saving for your retirement and other long-term expenses, putting money aside each month into a separate savings account will help you plan for an unexpected emergency or allow you to have the funds available if there is something you want to purchase that isn't calculated into your budget.

Depending on what your goals are, there are many ways to find money within your monthly budget that can be saved instead of spent. For example, on your nightstand, keep a jar for loose change. At the end of each month, deposit that jar of coins into a separate savings account. If you're like most people, you'll wind up collecting $25 to $100 (or more) in loose change every month.

The best way to start saving, however, is to automatically take a percentage (say 20 to 30 percent) of your discretionary income—the money from your paycheck that's left over after you pay *all* of your expenses—and put it immediately into savings each month. Use this formula:

Step 1) Take Home Income—All Expenses = Your Discretionary Income

Step 2) Your Discretionary Income x .20 (or .30) = Amount To Be Saved

Right now, you might not have any left over disposable income (discretionary income). Hence, you have no money to put into savings. Your first task is to implement your budget. This will allow you to systematically begin cutting expenses and reducing your debt. Once you begin incorporating these strategies, if done correctly, you should begin to see your discretionary income increase.

Using Personal Financial Software

Developing and maintaining a budget, tracking expenses and managing all of your personal or family finances becomes much easier when you use a popular software package, such as Microsoft Money (Microsoft Corporation/ *www.microsoft.com/money/*Price: $49.95 to $89.95, depending on version and ongoing rebate offers) or Quicken (Intuit/*www.quicken.com/*Price: $49.95 to $89.95, depending on version.)

If you use one of these programs on an ongoing basis, you'll spend much less time actually managing your finances, plus make fewer errors as a result of incorrect mathematical calculations. In addition, these programs are designed to integrate seamlessly with the online banking services offered by many banks and financial institutions, so data from your accounts can automatically be downloaded into the financial software.

Whether you're trying to organize your finances (gather all of your financial information in one place), balance your checkbook, track your spending, reduce your debt, pay your bills, manage investments or create and implement a budget, one of these programs is an ideal tool for helping to improve your financial situation.

Microsoft Money and Intuit's Quicken both use colorful graphics and easy-to-understand screens, they are easy to set up and use. Don't worry, there are no cumbersome manuals to read and understand. Everything you need to know is explained on the screen, using each program's help features and informational pop-up windows.

Whether you choose to utilize computer technology to manage your finances or opt to rely on pen, paper and a calculator, it's important to develop a thorough understanding of your personal financial situation, focus carefully on how you're spending your money, and then choose the appropriate strategies to help make your paycheck last based on your own personal situation and objectives.

Managing, Reducing and Ultimately Eliminating Debt

For financial institutions. like Citigroup, MBNA America, Bank One, Chase, Capital One, Providian, Bank of America, Household Bank and Fleet, issuing credit cards to consumers is a very profitable part of their business. In fact, in 2001, the global sales volume for Visa, MasterCard and American Express was $2.1 trillion, $986 billion and $298 billion respectively (as reported by CardWeb.com).

For the consumer who relies on credit cards and carries a significant balance, interest charges, annual fees, late fees, over limit fees and other charges from the credit card issuers can be significant. It's often these fees and charges that contribute to people getting themselves into debt and not being able to easily remedy the situation.

Unfortunately, the credit card companies make it easy to apply for and often obtain credit cards, especially if your credit rating is average or better. In a typically year, the credit card companies mail over five billion applications and offers to approximately 200 million people in America alone. Thus, the average American adult receives at least one credit card offer per week.

Using incentives, rewards, the knowledge that many people with financial problems will rely on their credit cards to pay their everyday living expenses in order to make ends meet, and by capitalizing on people's lack of understanding of how credit actually work, credit cards generate huge profits for financial institutions, while many consumers are getting themselves deeper and deeper into debt.

Sure, credit cards are convenient and in some situations beneficial to the consumer, but only if they're used correctly. Part of successfully utilizing credit cards involves taking steps to shop around for the best deals and offers.

Of course, credit cards aren't the only type of debt people accrue. Banks and financial institutions offer mortgages, second mortgages, home equity loans, personal lines of credit, and a wide range of other opportunities to borrow money and pay it off over time, with interest.

This section will help you better understand credit and how it can help you or hurt you, depending on how you use (or abuse) it. Developing a good credit rating is critical in today's society. Taking advantage of the credit you're given is perfectly acceptable, assuming you use it responsibly. If, like so many other people, you've already gotten yourself into some trouble by relying too much on your credit or by racking up extremely high balances on your credit cards, for example, it's important to immediately change your spending and credit use behavior.

Begin developing a plan to reduce and eventually eliminate the debt you've already acquired. Once you acquired massive credit card debt, for example, until those balances are paid off (or settled) the interest charges, late fees, over limit fees, etc. keep adding up, month-after-month, whether or not you continue to use your credit cards. It's in your best interest financially to reduce and eventually eliminate your high interest debt as quickly as possible.

Calculating Your Debt

In this section, begin by adding up all of your current debt in order to better evaluate the situation you're in right now and begin developing a plan to reduce and eventually eliminate this debt. Every month, your goal should be to pay off at least a small portion of your outstanding debt, without incurring new debt. Only by doing this will you break out of the cycle of racking up new debt and paying ongoing interest, month after month and year after year.

Credit Card Debt Worksheet

Take an inventory of all the credit cards you have right now. To complete the following worksheet, you may need to contact the various credit card issuers to obtain your APR and current balances. This information will also appear on your monthly statement. Be sure to list all of your different Visa, MasterCard, Discover, Diner's Club and American Express cards, plus your store credit cards and gas station credit cards. To insure you don't forget any cards, you might want to compare the list you compile here with what's listed on your credit report, obtained from Experian, Trans Union and/or Equifax. (See the section later in this chapter, called 'Understanding Your Credit,' to learn more about these credit reporting agencies and your credit report.)

Credit Card Name/ Account Number	Phone Number of Credit Card Company	Annual Fee(s) ($)	APR (%)	Other Fees/ Charges ($)	Credit Limit ($)	Monthly Payment ($)	Current Balance ($)

Total: $_____ $_____

Strategies for Reducing Your Debt

Your ability to lower your long-term debt will reply on several factors, including:

- Your current credit rating/credit score—People with the best credit are always given the lowest interest rates and best loan options.

- Your ability to make additional payments and/or payoff long-term debt (like your mortgage or car loan) early. Doing this will lower the balances of your loan and in the long-term save you significant money in interest payments, etc.

- Your willingness and ability to refinance the loan(s) at better rates and/or for shorter terms. With interest rates for mortgages constantly changing, you might be able to save hundreds of dollars per month, thousands over the term of the loan, if you refinance at a lower interest rate and/or for a shorter term. Whether you're looking to refinance a mortgage or a car loan, for example, contact at least three reputable financial institutions to see what interest rates and loan(s) you qualify for, then use a mortgage calculator, for example, to determine if you'll be able to save money. Make sure you take into account any fees, closing costs, points, etc. that may be involved in refinancing your long-term loan(s). The more time you invest in finding the best deals, the more money you'll ultimately save. Lowering your loan's interest rate just one-quarter of one percentage point, for example, can make a tremendous difference over a 15, 20 or 30 year period for a mortgage. Keep in mind, however, that if you've already damaged your credit rating, refinancing your mortgage or car loans will be significantly more difficult and you will not be able to obtain the most competitive rates. Companies that claim to offer credit to consumers, "regardless of their credit history", are usually either flat out scams or those lenders charge very high interest rates and fees.

There are several things you can do to immediately reduce and take control of your credit card debt, especially if your credit rating is at least average. Some of your options include:

- Find and apply for better deals on credit cards (in terms of lower APRs, annual fees, etc.) then transfer your existing balances from the high interest cards to the lower interest cards. The section of this chapter, called 'Find The Best Credit Card Deals,' will help you shop around for the best credit card offers. Once you transfer your balances, close the accounts with the high interest rates once those balances reach zero. The goal isn't to acquire more credit cards, but to reduce what you're paying in interest and fees on your existing debt.

- If your outstanding credit card debt is extremely high and spread over multiple cards (all of which are maxed out, or close to it), you might consider a consolidation loan. This is one loan (typically available at a much lower interest rate than your credit cards) that would allow you to pay off your multiple credit cards in full, then pay off just one loan over time. It's easily to obtain this type of loan if you already own a home and/or have average or above average credit.

- To reduce your credit card debt, on a monthly basis, pay more than the minimum required payment listed on your credit card statement. The minimum required payment covers the interest charges and fees related to the credit card. Only a very small portion (if any) of the minimum payment typically gets applied to the principle you actually owe. To reduce your debt, you need to be lowering your principle (the balance of what you owe) on an ongoing basis, not just pay the related interest charges and fees. Even paying $10 to $50 above the minimum payment each month will be beneficial to you in terms of reducing your debt and improving your long-term financial situation. To protect your credit rating, you always want to pay at least the minimum payment due on each credit card, for example. Don't just ignore incoming bills and monthly statements you can't afford to pay. When you're late on payments, the credit issuers will start making non-stop collection calls to your home, possibly your place of work, and also send countless collection letters until they're paid. They'll also report your delinquency to the credit bureaus, which will be reflected negatively on your credit report.

- If your credit card situation is out of control and you simply can't afford even to make the minimum monthly payments, consider negotiating a settlement (or payment plan) with each credit card company as soon as possible. When you settle with a credit card company, for example, your credit card account(s) will be closed and each settlement will be reported to the credit reporting agencies (Equifax, Experian and Trans Union) as a Settlement (as opposed to a 'Charge Off', for example). Each Settlement will damage your credit rating and stay on your credit report for up to seven years, but you'll often be able to settle for between 40% and 60% of what you actually owe and/or set up an installment plan for paying off the debt, while stopping interest and late fees from adding up. While a Settlement doesn't look good on your credit report, a Charge Off (where the balance is unpaid and written off by the credit issuer) is much worse for your credit rating. It's important that you take control of the situation and try to work with the credit card companies in good faith before your account goes into collection or gets charged off. Even after a charge off takes place, you could get sued for the full balance you owe, plus all fees, etc.

- To maintain your good credit, ideally you should carry a balance that's equal to no more than half of your credit limit on each card. You'll also want to pay more than the minimum amount due each month. Ideally, you should maintain a zero balance on your credit cards by using them, but then paying the bill, in full, when you receive your monthly statement. This allows you to enjoy the convenience of using a credit card, without incurring any interest charges.

Understanding Your Credit Rating/Credit Score

Your credit report is a document compiled by three different credit bureaus—Equifax, Experian and Trans Union. It contains detailed information about you, including your social security number, address, where you work and your bill payment history. This report also shows if you've been arrested and/or have filed for bankruptcy.

Companies that issue credit, such as credit card companies, mortgage companies and other businesses have access to your credit report and use this information to determine whether or not you are credit worthy. Companies that have already issued you credit or loans report monthly to the credit bureaus about whether or not you pay your bills on-time and as promised.

Negative information about your payment history, for example, can stay on your credit report for up to seven years. Information about bankruptcies can remain on your credit report for 10 years, while details about any criminal activity (such as arrests and convictions) can stay on your credit report indefinitely.

In addition to simply listing all of your creditors, the credit bureaus also calculate a credit score (also called FICO Score) that is part of your credit report. To calculate your credit score, information about your bill-paying history, the number and type of accounts you have, late payments, collection actions, outstanding debt, and the age of your accounts is all taken into account. Your credit score is a primary indicator, used to predict how creditworthy you are. Credit scores range between 300 to 850. The higher your score, the better your credit rating is.

Obtaining Your Credit Report & FICO Credit Score

Every six months, it's an excellent idea to review your credit report from all three credit bureaus. This will help you determine your credit worthiness, plus allow you to identify any errors on your credit reports. You can obtain your credit report online (within minutes) by purchasing a copy of it. You can, however, obtain a free copy of your credit report if you are denied credit as a result of information on one or more credit reports. By mailing a letter (containing your request along with your name, address, phone number, social security number and date of birth) to each credit bureau, you can also purchase a printed copy of your credit report for $9.00 per copy.

The addresses and phone numbers for the three credit bureaus are:

- Equifax, P.O. Box 740241, Atlanta, GA 30374-0241—(800) 685-1111—*www.equifax.com*

- Experian (TRW), P.O. Box 2002, Allen, TX 75013—(888) EXPE-RIAN—*www.experian.com*

- Trans Union, P.O. Box 1000, Chester, PA 19022—(900) 916-8800—*www.transunion.com*

For a monthly or annual fee (or a one-time fee per report), you can obtain copies of your credit report and credit score online and/or subscribe to monitoring services that will notify you as changes, updates or inquiries are made to your credit report. Many of these services also make it easier to correct errors on your reports. These services are offered online by all three credit bureaus. For about $30.00, you can also obtain a 3-in-1 credit report, which combines information from all three credit bureaus into one report. To save time, you should obtain your credit reports online (which takes minutes) as opposed to requesting the reports by mail, which can take upwards of 30-days.

If you're planning to purchase a home, buy a car (or other big ticket item using credit), or apply for any type of credit or loan, it's an excellent idea to review your credit report and develop and understanding of your credit score in order to determine whether or not you qualify for various types of loans or credit.

Improving Your Credit (FICO) Score

There are many things you can do to improve your credit score over time, such as:

- Pay your monthly bills (credit cards, mortgage, car loan, etc.) on-time, for at least six months in a row.

- Reduce the balances of your existing credit cards and loans.

- Consolidate your credit card balances.

- Pay off past due and uncollected debts, such as charge-offs or bills that have been forwarded to collection agencies.

- Establish (or re-establish) your credit by obtaining one or more secured credit cards and using them responsibly.

- Have a co-signer, who has good credit, apply for a credit card, car loan or mortgage with you.

- Correct any errors on your credit reports.

- Seek out assistance from a legitimate credit counseling or credit consolidation service. For example, the Consumer Credit Counseling Service (CCCS) is a non-profit organization offering free or low-cost financial counseling to help families solve their financial problems. CCCS can help you analyze your situation and work with you to develop solutions. There are more than 1,200 CCCS offices in the United States. For more information, call (800) 388-2227 or visit this website: *www.cccsatl.org.*

Credit Cards, Secured Credit Cards and Debit Cards

There are major differences between credit cards (Visa, MasterCard, etc.), Secured Credit Cards and Debit Cards. Here is a description of each and a brief explanation about how each works.

Credit Card—A credit card, such as a Visa or MasterCard, allows you to pay your balance through monthly installments and/or a revolving line of credit, with the pre-set spending limit set by the credit card issuer. Your monthly payment can range from a minimum amount, set by your bank, to your entire outstanding balance. As a general rule, if you pay the entire credit card bill at the end of the month, you will be charged no interest. When you maintain a balance, however, the interest you are charged will be at a predetermined Annual Percentage Rate (APR). The APR of every credit card is different. This rate determines how much you'll actually pay each year for the privilege of having credit and for maintaining a balance.

Secured Credit Card—This type of credit card is ideal for someone first trying to establish (or re-establish) credit. Virtually anyone who is over the age of 18 and has a valid Social Security number can qualify for a secured credit card. This type of card offers many of the privileges of a regular credit card, however, your credit limit is determined by the amount of money you keep in a separate savings account with the financial institution that issues the card. This savings accounts acts as insurance for the credit card issuer, in case you default on your payments. The minimum initial deposit is usually $200 (or more) and the fees associated with obtaining a secured credit card tend to be higher than the fees associated with a traditional credit card. There's often a required annual fee, one-time application fee, plus processing fees. On your actual credit report, however, there's no difference between a secured credit card and a regular credit card.

Debit Card—This type of card is linked directly to your checking, savings or mutual fund account. While for making purchases, debit cards are accepted wherever Visa or MasterCard are accepted, and the amount of your purchases is immediately deducted directly from your checking, savings or mutual fund account. In other words, a debit card works just like a paperless check. These cards also work as ATM cards for handling your regular bank transactions, such as making deposits or checking your balances. You're not actually using credit when utilizing a debit card to make purchase because the funds are instantly taken from your account. Even if you have plenty of money in your checking account, some financial institutions pre-set per-purchase spending amounts on debit cards. For example, without prior authorization, you may not be allowed to make a single purchase over $200.00, $500.00 or $1,000.00.

Find the Best Credit Card Deals

There are literally hundreds of financial institutions that offer credit cards to consumers. To ultimately make the most of your credit and save money in fees and interest, shop around for the best deals. The following are some of the things to consider when evaluating a credit card offer:

- **Perks and Rewards**—Depending on the offer, you may receive anything from cash back (rebates) on your purchases to frequent flier miles for your favorite airline, simply for using the credit card. Credit cards with special perks or rewards associated with them typically charge an annual fee. Other benefits associated with some credit cards include discounts on certain products/services, insurance and/or credit protection. As you'll see, what's offered varies greatly between card issuers.

- **Annual Fee**—This is a fee you pay once per year for the privilege of having that specific credit card. Some card issuers call this a membership or participation fee, and it can vary anywhere from $15 to $150 per year. To be competitive, many credit card issuers charge no annual fee. The fees typically run significantly higher for people with poor credit or those applying for a secured credit card.

- **Application Fee**—This is a one-time fee for filling out the application for the credit card and having that application processed. You may be charged this fee whether or not you are accepted and issued a credit card. There are many credit card issuers that charge no application fees. The application fee may be in addition to the card's annual fee. In some cases, you may also be charged a one-time or monthly 'processing fee.'

- **APR (%)**—This is the Annual Percentage Rate of interest you'll be charged. This represents how much credit will cost you on a yearly basis. This is a pre-determined percentage that the credit card company must disclose to you. In addition to the APR, make sure you pay attention to the Periodic Rate associated with the credit card. This is the rate the card issuer applies to your outstanding balance to calculate your finance charges for each billing period. Also, may attention to how the credit card issuer computes the balances for purchases.

- **Balance Transfer Opportunities**—When applying for a new credit card, some issuers will offer you an extra low APR for a pre-determined period, if you transfer balances from your other credit cards to this new account. This can be a way you can save money on interest payments, Make sure you read the fine print and understand the deal being offered before accepting it. After the pre-determined period, the APR on your outstanding balance could jump dramatically.

- **Billing Cycle**—This represents the length of time between each billing statement. A billing cycle is typically 30 days.

- **Credit Limit (or Credit Line)**—When you receive a new credit card, this is the maximum amount of credit the issuer is making available to you. The credit limit will depend on a number of factors, primarily your credit history (credit score). Periodically, the card issue will increase or decrease your credit line based on your payment history.

- **Customer Service**—Many credit card companies offer 24-hour customer service that's available seven-days-per-week via telephone or the Internet. Others offer limited hours when customer service is available. Ideally, you want to work with a card issuer that is available anytime to answer your questions and deal with issues that may arise.

- **Grace Period**—A "grace period" is the number of days the card issuer doesn't charge you interest on purchases. When applying for any credit card, be sure to read the fine print. Some credit card issuers give you a grace period only if your account is paid up and doesn't have a balance carried over from the previous month.

- **Introductory APR**—To encourage you to apply for its credit card (as opposed to the competition's), many credit card issuers offer special introductory deals for the first three months, six months or one year you use their card. This is a temporary, usually low, interest rate (expressed as a yearly rate). Remember, the introductory rate you're offered will typically expire after a pre-determined amount of time. After this introductory period, the APR you're responsible for will increase, sometimes significantly.

- **Late Fee**—If you're late on making your monthly payments, the card issuer has the right to impose various fees. In addition, if you're late on payments several times in a pre-defined period, your APR could automatically increase as well. In addition to charging late fees, the credit card issuer will report late payments to the credit bureaus, which will be reflected on your credit report.

- **Other Fees**—When reviewing any credit card application, read the fine print to determine if there are any other fees or hidden charges you'll be responsible for. An example of an additional fee is if you use the charge card to obtain a cash advance. There may also be a small monthly fee associated with the card, whether or not you use it.

- **Over Limit Fee**—If your credit limit is $1500, for example, and your balance goes to $1600 as a result of too many purchases or various fees being added to your balance, you will be charged an additional Over Limit Fee by most credit card companies.

Chances are, you receive a new credit card offer in the mail at least once or twice per week. In addition, you probably see ads on TV and see all kinds of offers when surfing the net. Make sure you apply for a credit card that offers you the best possible deal, based on your credit rating and needs. You can research various credit card offers by visiting these free Websites:

- Bank Rates—*www.bankrate.com*

- Card Locator—*www.cardlocator.com*

- Card Offers: The Credit Card Directory—*www.cardoffers.com*

- Credit Cards Plus—*www.credit-cards-plus.com*

- CreditLand—*www.credit-land.com*

- The Credit Card Catalog—*www.creditcardcatalog.com*

There's Much More To Learn

It takes much more than one chapter of a book to truly understand what you need to know about managing your personal finances and investing. For more detailed information, check out the book, *Making Your Paycheck Last* (The Career Press). You should also make a habit of reading financial publications, such as *The Wall Street Journal*, plus utilize the tools and information available to you on the Internet.

Unfortunately, aside from winning the lottery, there are no overnight ways to get rich quick. Thus, you'll need to plan and organize every aspect of your life to insure that you're spending your money wisely, saving and planning for the future.

5

Keeping It Clean:
Personal Grooming & Hygiene

As important as it is to maintain your physical fitness and overall health, proper personal grooming habits will make you look healthier, feel better about yourself and could easily help you look and feel younger. This chapter is all about personal grooming. It offers advice about: skin care, shaving, hair care and dental hygiene.

Keep in mind, the people interviewed in this chapter are all experts in their field, however, it's important to understand you always have a wide range of options in terms of the product(s) and service(s) you utilize to achieve various objectives and results. It's important to choose the products that work best for you, based upon your lifestyle, personal preferences and budget.

A Guy's Guide To Proper Skin Care

For decades, women have been encouraged to use dozens of different skin care and cosmetic products to make themselves look healthier, take better care of their skin, look younger, and be more beautiful. Meanwhile, a typical guy's skin care regime consisted of using a standard bar of soap and tap water. This, however, is changing. More and more guys are realizing that by spending just a few minutes each day to care for their skin, they too can look and feel better, younger and healthier. In fact, in recent years, over a dozen companies have developed skin care products specifically for guys.

Zirh Skin Nutrition (*www.zirh.com*) is a leading men's skin care company which offers a wide range of products for shaving, cleansing and skin treatment. Available since 1995, Zirh is the fastest growing prestige level men's skin care brand worldwide. The products are sold in over 500 department and specialty stores throughout America (and in 40 counties around the world.) Products can also be ordered from the company's website, where you'll find extensive information about the entire product line and how to best utilize each product in your own skin care regime. All Zirh products are made in America and do not use animal testing in their development.

The company's philosophy is simple. It develops products specifically for guys that are easy to use, fragrance free and that utilize the best ingredients available. For example, Zirh's skin care system involves three products (sold separately)—Clean, Correct and Protect—which are designed to exfoliate, clean, soften and moisturize your face and neck area.

Clean, as the name suggests, replaces a typical bar of soap and can be used to cleanse and exfoliate the skin on your face. It should be used twice per day. The next step involves using Correct, which is a cream-like multivitamin problem solver that replenishes the needed vitamins in your skin to improve skin texture. At the same time, this product moisturizes and softens your skin while fighting acne causing bacteria. Finally, the Protect product can be used on your face as the third step in your skin care regime.

Protect helps fight the negative effects of free radicals, sun damage and dryness. It's designed to moisturize your skin, slow down the aging process and improve your skin's texture and elasticity without leaving an oily film. It's also designed to help heal sores, bruises and abrasions on your face. As you've probably guessed, a moisturizer adds moisture back to the skin.

To handle special needs, like the area under your eyes, Zirh's Restore product can be used to make this sensitive area stronger, healthier and more resilient by healing collagen and locking in moisture. This product is also designed to reduce the visibility of fine lines, wrinkles, puffiness and dark circles (often caused by lack of sleep). When using an under-eye product, like Restore, place it in the refrigerator for several hours prior to use. By doing this, you'll create a cold compress-like experience when applying it to your under-eye area. This will feel extremely soothing.

If you're face or neck area has visible blemishes and minor irritations, the Fix product can be used to help heal the affected areas by reducing redness and dissolving impurities. This product can also be used to reduce the appearance of fine lines, brown spots and black heads. To care for the rest of your body's skin, Zirh offers several options, ranging from its popular Body Bar to its Body Scrub and Shower Gel.

Whether you decide to use Zirh or any other line of skin care products, the regime you adopt should involve three primary steps—cleaning, exfoliating and moisturizing. The process takes only minutes per day. Within a few weeks, you will see noticeable improvement in your skin's health and appearance, no matter how old you are.

According to Brian Robinson, president of Zirh, "When the company was formed, we saw a need for a masculine skin care line. Most guys look for simplicity and ease of use when it comes to caring for their skin. Anyone who is fashion conscience, affluent or in the 18-to-35 age group, for example, is a typical user of our products."

Unlike competing product lines, Zirh develops its products specifically for guys, while some competitors simply take products already being sold to women and add more male-oriented packaging. "Our research shows that guys do not like skin care products that contain fragrances, so our products are fragrance-free. If guys want to smell nice, they can wear cologne," added Robinson, who believes that more and more guys are using skin care products because they want to look and feel younger.

"Pollution and exposure to sun does damage to your skin. Using skin care products can help counteract that damage and offer added protection. If someone uses Zirh skin care products regularly, they can expect a nicer, healthier glow to their skin. Our products focus on exfoliating the skin, which means getting rid of the dead skin cells on the surface, allowing for healthier looking skin to show. Before using any skin care products, take a piece of clear tape and put it on your face for a few seconds, then remove it. You'll see dirt, oil and dead skin cells from your face sticking to the tape. If you do this test again after using Zirh's Clean, Correct and Protect products, you'll discover that the tape will be totally clean when you remove it. Removing dirt, oil and dead skin cells is what exfoliation is all about. Our products also helps control the skins pH levels, to better control problems resulting from dryness or oily skin," said Robinson.

One of the biggest misconceptions most guys have about using skin care products is that they're too complicated or by using these types of products, it'll somehow reducing their masculinity. "For someone who is first starting to use these types of products, I suggest that before they go out and spend a fortune on a complete skin care product line, which could include costly niche products, such as under eye creams, I suggest trying the basic products to clean, exfoliate and moisturize. Try a single product line for several weeks to determine what works best for you," explained Robinson. "The best way to get started using any skin care product line is to visit a department or specialty store, for example, and have someone demonstrate the products to you. Have the salesperson explain what each product does and how to properly use it."

To properly care for your face and neck area, it shouldn't take more than three to five minutes per day. It's important, however, to use the same products consistently and not mix and match products from different manufacturers or use the products sporadically if you want to achieve the best possible results. Unlike other skin care product lines, Zirh is designed for people with any skin type—normal, dry or oily. Thus, as the user, you don't need to understand your skin type to take good care of your skin.

Robinson explained, "Having the healthiest and best looking skin possible requires more than simply using a good skin care product line. It also involves leading a healthy lifestyle, drinking a lot of water, taking vitamins, maintaining a proper diet, and avoiding too much direct sunlight without proper protection."

The cost of skin care products varies dramatically. Traditional soap and water can cost under $1.00 per bar of soap, while premium skin care products, such as those from Zirh, can cost between $50.00 to $150.00 for a one to two month supply. Zirh's Clean (8.4 ounce), Correct (1.7 ounce) and Protect (3.4 ounce) products are priced at $14.50, $24.50 and $24.50, respectively. Discounts are offered when the products are purchased in packages. For example, the Zirh Starter Kit (containing Clean, Correct, Protect and Shave Gel) is priced at $59.00.

There are also lower-priced men's skin care product lines that will cost between $20.00 and $100.00 for a one to two month supply, but these more mass-market products typically don't use the best available ingredients or were not designed specially for men. Properly taking care of your skin, like anything else, requires a dedication and investment on your part.

Proper Shaving Technique

A typical guy will shave over 20,000 times during his lifetime. A good skin care regime should also include using good quality shaving products, such as pre-shave oil, shaving cream or gel, and aftershave to better protect your skin. Zirh also offers a complete men's shaving line for use with a standard razor, such as the Gillette Mach 3 Turbo (*www.mach3.com*).

As opposed to a traditional razor, you also have the option of using an electric razor for your daily shave. What you use is a matter of personal preference. Electric shavers, from companies like Braun, Remington and Panasonic, offer a wide range of functionality, such as the ability to shave in the shower (with a wet/dry razor). If you're switching between a traditional razor and an electric razor (or vice versa), keep in mind it'll probably take your face at least a few days to adjust, so expect some mild, but temporary irritation after each shave.

The best time to shave is during a hot shower or immediately after one. You typically want to apply hot water to your face prior to shaving in order to moisten your skin and open your pours. Instead of using hot water, however, you can apply a small amount of pre-shave oil, such as Zirh's Prepare product. Pre-shave oil is extremely popular throughout Europe and has been for decades. It creates a slippery surface on your skin (where you'll be shaving) and also helps to soften your beard.

Once your face has been pre-treated with hot water and/or a pre-shave oil, you'll want to apply a quality shaving cream or shave gel. The Zirh Shave Cream or Shave Gel, for example, contains about 85 percent aloe vera (other products contain only five or 10 percent aloe vera), which acts as a powerful moisturizer, plus creates a slicker surface for shaving to greatly reduce or totally eliminate razor drag, burns, nicks and cuts.

According to Robinson, "Many guys like our Shave Gel, because it's totally clear. You can see through it and it does not turn into foam. This is great for people with skin imperfections or goatees, for example, who want to see exactly where they're shaving. Our shave gel is designed for people with normal facial hair growth, while our shaving cream can be used by people with thicker beards."

Immediately after shaving, guys can control razor burn and heal cuts and nicks faster by applying an after-shave gel or lotion. Zirh's Post Shave Healer, for example, reduces redness, irritation and sting caused by the razor. "I recommend keeping the after shave gel in the refrigerator. Applying the cold gel on your face after shaving feels incredibly soothing," added Robinson.

If you're using a multi-step shaving regime, there's typically little need to apply a separate moisturizer. Allow the after shave to soak into your skin for 20 to 30 minutes prior to using other skin care products, like Clean, Correct and Protect, on your face. It's important to allow your skin time to heal after shaving before applying other products.

If you're using a traditional shaver with a disposable blade, such as the Gillette Mach 3 Turbo, change the blade regularly. Using a dull blade will cause more damage to your skin and increase the frequency of cuts and abrasions as a result of shaving. How often you change blades depends on your shaving habits and the thickness of your beard. According to Gillette, The Mach 3 Turbo, for example, features an "Advanced Indicator Lubricating Strip" that changes color from blue to white when you're no longer getting the optimal Mach 3 shaving experience. When the strip changes to white, you should swap the blade.

Instead of using the inexpensive shaver handle that comes with most disposable shavers, you can purchase fancier shaver handles and accessories from a company such as The Art of Shaving, which has locations in New York City, Dallas and Miami (212-986-2905/*www.artofshaving.com*). This company offers its own line of high-end shaving products, including pre-shave oil; shaving creams and gels; as well as after shaves, which are also available at upscale department stores nationwide. If you happen to be in the New York, Dallas or Miami area, The Art of Shaving retail locations feature a unique "Barber Spa", offering haircuts as well as a straight edge shave experience by a professional barber ($25 or $45) that utilizes the company's best shaving products. It's a relaxing and enjoyable experience that offers the ultimate in a close shave.

The Art of Shaving's Five Steps to Better Shaving

The Art of Shaving's website offers these tips for shaving using a traditional razor, such as the Gillette Mach 3 Turbo:

1. **Prepare**—This is done to soften the beard and protect the skin. It's important to shave after or during a hot shower, not before. Also, always use hot water while shaving, plus use a pre-shave oil to protect your skin and soften your beard.

2. **Lather Up**—For a close and comfortable shave, avoid using foams, gels or other shaving products that contain a numbing agent, such as benzocaine or menthol. These ingredients tend to close pores and stiffen the beard. When applying shaving cream, you might consider using an optional shaving brush (made of badger hair). This type of brush will soften and lift the beard from the face, and help generate a very good lather.

3. **Shave**—Use a good handle and proper technique. Always shave with the grain first—in the direction the hair grows. Shaving against the grain first can cause ingrown hairs and razor burn. For an even closer shave, re-lather and shave lightly across or against the grain. Use a razor handle that provides proper weight, balance and comfort for better control. The Art of Shaving's razors, for example, can be used with the Mach3 or Sensor blades by Gillette. Finally, avoid applying too much pressure on your razor. This is often the cause of razor burns and skin irritations. Always glide the razor gently over your face.

4. **Treat**—To rejuvenate and purify your skin, use an after-shave product. This type of product will also provide relief from razor burns, ingrown hairs, and skin irritations, while replenishing necessary nutrients lost during the shaving process.

5. **Moisturize**—To soothe and regenerate your skin, use a face moisturizer created specifically for men. Avoid a moisturizer that contains alcohol, which can irritate and dry out the skin. In the event of nicks or cuts, The Art of Shaving recommends using an antiseptic alum block to stop the bleeding.

Taking Care of Your Hair

Hairstyles change, but how you style and maintain your hair communicates a lot about you, especially in terms of making first impressions. Sure, you can drop into your local barber and get a $12.00 haircut, but for more personalized attention to your hair and its style, you'll want to visit a stylist—someone who can cut, style, highlight, color and/or treat your hair to create an improved look that's uniquely you.

World famous hairstylist José Eber (310-278-7646/*www.joseeberatelier.com*) works from his salon on Rodeo Drive in Beverly Hills, California, where he's considered the "stylist to the stars." As the most recognized name in hair styling, he also owns a chain of upscale salons located in cities throughout America. Based upon his over 40 years worth of experience as a stylist, Jose Eber explained, "A stylist looks at the overall person, the shape of their face, personality and their lifestyle, then creates a hairstyle for that person that works for them. These are things a hairstylist will focus on, which a tradition barber probably won't."

Eber believes someone's hairstyle contributes a lot to the first impression they make to the outside world. "When a guy meets a girl for the first time, for example, the first thing she'll look at is the guy's appearance. If a guy doesn't make a positive first impression with his appearance, he often loses the chance to showcase his personality, because its looks that people are attracted to first," said Eber. "The best way to find a hairstylist is through word-of-mouth. Look at the hairstyles of other guys and see what you like, then ask them who their stylist is. I also suggest that guys look at fashion and entertainment magazines for ideas about how they'd like to style their hair."

When choosing your hairstyle, pay attention to your lifestyle and how much time and effort you're willing to invest on a daily basis to maintain and style your hair. Next, choose a style that nicely compliments the shape of your face. "A hairstylist can style a guy's hair to highlight certain physical attributes and downplay others. Now, more than ever, it's become totally acceptable for guys to color or highlight their hair, especially if they're still young in spirit. Highlights, for example, can be used to give someone a younger, sportier look. It's important, however, that a guy go to the right place to have their hair styled, colored or highlighted. If it's done improperly, it could wind up looking foolish," added Eber.

If you choose to get your hair colored or highlighted, ask questions prior to having the work done. Ask what will be involved in the upkeep of the new hairstyle and how often the color or highlights will need to be redone. You also want to know if any damage will be done to your hair as a result of the process.

In terms of choosing a style, Eber stated, "Many types of cuts can be styled in several ways. This means, you can have a more traditional style while at work, then add some styling gel to your hair and make it look totally different for when you're going out to a club or on a date. As you leave your job, mess up your hair a bit to create a great look."

There are hundreds of different hair care products, shampoos, conditioners and styling products on the market. Eber recommends trying a handful of different products to find what works best for you. "Try products and ask others what they use," said Eber. "Don't rely on advertising to help you pick your hair care products. You really need to test each product for yourself. The goal is to make your hair look and feel good and to obtain a overall clean feeling. When choosing your products, beware of perfumes added to the products. Most guys don't like those flowery scents given off by many shampoos and conditioners, for example. It's far more important for a guy's hair to smell clean and fresh. That's what girls like when they're close to their guy."

With all of the different brands of hair care products, Eber said it's totally okay to mix and match brands. For example, you can use one brand of shampoo, another brand of conditioner, and the styling moose or gel from another company. "It's all about what works for you and your hair," he added.

No matter which products you use, Eber warns against over washing your hair. "This can cause the natural oils in your hair to disappear, which will result in dry, unhealthy hair over time. Also, avoid constantly wearing some type of hat or cap on your head day after day. Your hair needs to breath," he said. "In terms of blow drying your hair, this is totally safe, providing you use the included attachment that fits onto the hair dryer's nozzle that keeps the intense heat from burning your hair and scalp. Guys typically don't use this snap on nozzle, but it has a purpose. It's a protector."

Since hair is such an important part of any guy's overall look, if you're seeking a dramatic change to your look, seek out a skilled stylist (as opposed to a barber) who specializes in working with guys. "Don't ever be a slave to fashion," said Eber. "It's okay to be daring and to take chances, however. Of course, you'll want to look fashionable to a certain extent, but don't be a slave to the latest trends in hairstyles."

As many guys get older, their hairline recedes and they start loosing their hair. If you're faced with this situation, perhaps prematurely, there are things you can do to slow down or perhaps reverse the process. It's important, however, to seek out professional guidance early on, from your stylist and/or doctor, so you can begin taking advantage of the appropriate products and/or services. "I've seen guys have good experiences with products like Rogaine for slowing down hair loss. This won't cause hair to grow back necessarily. The good news is that shaved heads are extremely popular and sexy. Whatever you do, don't try to hide your baldness. You're not fooling anybody," said Eber.

When it comes to guys and their hair, you'll probably want a style that's easy to maintain and requires minimal upkeep, yet you'll want a style that makes you look the best you possibly can. Don't neglect this important aspect of your overall appearance.

Proper Dental Hygiene

If you want clean, healthy and ultra-white teeth and gums, not to mention fresh breath, there's no substitute for following a proper dental hygiene protocol. For example, it's recommended that you visit a dentist for a cleaning and check-up at least twice per year (every six months). Between dentist visits, however, it's up to you to maintain proper oral hygiene, which means brushing and flossing regularly.

Contrary to popular belief, visiting a dentist doesn't have to be painful or expensive. In fact, a typical cleaning and semi-annual exam should cost between $40.00 and $100.00. If you have dental insurance as a benefit through your job, however, your out of pocket cost will be significantly less. Plus, thanks to various advancements in dental care procedures, even the most complex dental procedures can be virtually pain free. By properly caring for your teeth, you'll easily be able to avoid dental problems and keep your teeth and gums healthy for many years to come.

When it comes to driving a car, you can travel around town in a Honda Civic, for example, and know you're within a reliable and practical automobile. That same trip around town, however, can be a lot more luxurious and fun if you're behind the wheel of a Porsche or Ferrari. Well, when it comes to toothbrushes, you have a wide range of options. There are those $3.00 toothbrushes that will keep your teeth clean, there are slightly more expensive battery powered tooth-brushes, and then there's the Sonicare toothbrushes from Philips Oral Healthcare (*www.sonicare.com*). Any of these toothbrush options, if used correctly, will help keep your teeth and gums clean and healthy.

Philips Oral Healthcare, however, guarantees that if you use the Sonicare, you'll have naturally whiter and cleaner teeth, plus healthier gums in 28 days. But, at a cost of between $119.00 and $139.00, it's truly the Porsche of tooth-brushes.

Jay McCulloch, senior director of marketing for Philips Oral Healthcare, explained, "Sonicare is truly the top-of-the-line of power toothbrushes. It offers the ultimate in home oral care, plus it makes it extremely easy to care for your teeth and gums. The bristles of the Sonicare move at very high speeds, so all you need to do is add tooth paste, put the brush head in your mouth, angle it at a 45-degree angle to your gum line, turn on the Sonicare and let it do the cleaning work for you. The Sonicare quickly removes plaque and stains. With its quad-pacer feature, the toothbrush divides your mouth into four areas and then beeps every 30 seconds. When you hear the beep, you simply move the brush to a different area of your mouth. You'll be done in two minutes."

The Sonicare is a high-tech toothbrush that makes regular, daily dental care easy and fast. The toothbrush works with your favorite toothpaste. Keep in mind, the Sonicare will help you brush your teeth properly, however, it's still recommended that you floss regularly.

When asked to describe the perfect home dental care procedures, McCulloch explained, "It all depends how fanatical you want to get about your dental hygiene. The more you do, the better off you are. First off, don't neglect your semi-annual dentist visits. In terms of your ongoing home dental care, brush your teeth at least twice per day for two minutes. You'll also want to floss your teeth after every brushing. It's a good idea to rinse your mouth with a mouthwash, like Scope or Listerine, after brushing. Many people also choose to use a pre-rinse, such as Plax, prior to brushing, in order to help remove more plaque. What I just described would be the ultimate in oral care, but not too many people do all of this as frequently as they should."

No matter what type of toothbrush you use, it's important to replace it every three to six months. You'll probably notice that the bristles will start bending and will get softer when it becomes time to replace it. If you use one of those inexpensive disposal toothbrushes, such as the Reach toothbrush from Johnson & Johnson, you might want to replace it monthly or every 60 days. After every use, however, always rinse off your toothbrush and shake off the excess water.

"Over time, the brush head will lose its effectiveness, which is why it needs to be replaced. For the Sonicare, we recommend replacing the brush head every six months to get the optimal performance," added McCulloch. "When brushing your teeth, be gentle. There's no need to use force or pressure by pressing the toothbrush against your teeth or gums."

Need a dentist? The best way to find one is through a personal referral. Ask a friend or family member for the name of their dentist, than schedule an appointment. You can also check the Yellow Pages, contact your dental insurance provider for a list of affiliated dentists, or call a dentist referral services (such as 1-800-Dentist). If your dentist believes you require extensive (and costly) dental work, seek out a second option before having major work done.

Similar to medical emergencies, you can't always predict when you'll develop a major tooth ache or experience some other dental emergency. Most dentists are always on-call and can be paged if a dental emergency arises. Of course, you may be charged extra for a 3:00am appointment booked on a last minute basis, but if it's truly an emergency, finding immediate dental care is usually as easy as calling your own dentist.

Developing A Whiter, Brighter Smile

Maintaining healthy teeth and gums is extremely important. More and more people, however, have also become obsessed with having whiter teeth and a brighter smile. In fact, seven out of 10 people don't like the color of their teeth and would like them to be whiter and brighter. To accomplish this, there are literally dozens of different treatments you can use to whiten your teeth, plus counteract the discoloring effects of drinking coffee, soda or tea; smoking and eating certain foods, such as blueberries.

There are special teeth whitening tooth pastes you can use daily when brushing your teeth, whitening gels you can apply to your teeth after brushing, teeth whitening strips that get placed over your teeth (Crest's Whitestrips have become extremely popular—Cost: Approximately $35.00 for a 14-day supply/*www.whitestrips.com*), and special procedures your dentist or oral hygienist can administer to make your teeth significantly whiter.

Depending on how much you want to spend, how quickly you'd like to see results and how white you want your teeth to be, you'll want to choose the teeth whitening procedure that makes the most sense for you. Most of the do-it-your-self teeth whitening procedures work over a period of 14 to 30 days and will whiten your teeth up to three or four shades. The results will last for about six months. Keep in mind, these whitening procedures only work on your natural teeth—not on caps, crowns, veneers, fillings or dentures. No matter which teeth whitening product or system you use, follow the directions carefully.

If you're willing to make a somewhat significant investment in your smile (to the tune of about $600.00), BriteSmile (800-BRITESMILE/*www.britesmile.com*) offers a teeth whitening procedure that takes about 60 minutes at one of its offices. The results will be immediate and significant. In fact, independent studies have shown that the BriteSmile procedure will whiten your teeth up to nine shades within the single visit and can last for three to four years.

BriteSmile operates more than 14 freestanding "spas" in major cities, like Beverly Hills, Boston, New York City, Atlanta, Denver, Chicago and Phoenix. The procedure is also available through a network of over 4,400 dentists who have been specifically trained to administer this totally safe, clinically proven and patented tooth whitening procedure that has thus far been used on over 500,000 people worldwide.

"I was amazed at how well the BriteSmile procedure worked in just one visit. Yes, during the one hour procedure it wasn't too comfortable sitting there in the chair with my mouth being held open, but there was no pain whatsoever," said Tristan Ferras Taylor, a 21-year-old patient who visited BriteSmile's Beverly Hills location for the procedure. "During the procedure, you sit in a private room and can watch television while the whitening it taking place. I had tried the Crest Whitestrips and other whitening systems in the past. They worked, but the results took several weeks to see and weren't anywhere near as dramatic as the BriteSmile treatment. The offices were clean and the people were incredibly friendly and knowledgeable. I am so much happier with my smile now."

Despite the relatively high cost, BriteSmile's teeth whitening procedure offers several compelling advantages over all of the other teeth whitening products on the market. The procedure itself is fast, safe and convenient, plus the dramatic results are instant and will last for up to three or four years.

Chris Edwards, vice president of marketing for BriteSmile, Inc., explained, "People notice your smile immediately. Having white teeth helps you make an even better first impression when meeting people. Most guys like instant gratification in whatever they do. BriteSmile offers instant gratification when it comes to professional teeth whitening in about one hour. In many cases, we can even accommodate same-day appointments."

Edwards explained that BriteSmile works using patented products and technology. The procedure utilizes a light activated process in conjunction with specially created teeth whitening gel. In terms of the cost, Edwards believes that as technology becomes more advanced and additional competition enters the marketplace, the cost of BriteSmile procedure will most likely drop at some point in the future. "In the meantime, we offer several different financing options to make the procedure affordable to the most people possible," he added. "We also offer a $75 to $100 discount for prepayment."

If the cost of BriteSmile is still beyond your financial means at the moment, consider using any of the popular over-the-counter teeth whitening toothpastes and kits. The results won't be as dramatic and will take longer to achieve, but the cost is significantly lower. In terms of other professional teeth whitening procedures done at a dentist's office, contact your dentist for recommendations.

No matter which teeth whitening procedure you use, it does not eliminate the need to visit a dentist twice per year for a professional cleaning and exam, or does it replace the necessity to brush and floss your teeth on a daily basis.

Putting It All Together

As you get more accustomed to taking better care of yourself, by developing your daily regime for taking care of your skin, hair, teeth, etc., you'll find your overall appearance will improve and you'll soon begin feeling better about yourself and more confident. Once you get into the habit of properly caring for yourself, you'll find the time investment will be relatively minimal. Keep in mind, however, you're cleanliness and personal hygiene is only one part of the overall picture. Your health, appearance and overall well-being will also be impacted by such things as how often you exercise, what you eat and what you wear.

6

Dress Like A Fashion Icon

You're a guy. You're single. Chances are, you want to show yourself off to the world as the hottest stud possible, especially if you're always on the prowl for new dates. Part of making a positive first impression involves always looking your best. This chapter is all about how you dress, your wardrobe and how to accessorize your outfits to complete your personalized look. You'll discover what's appropriate to wear at work, plus how to be fashionable and comfortable at play, and how to always look your absolute best.

Simply buying designer clothes isn't enough to make you look like a fashion icon. In fact, you can dress extremely well without relying on expensive designer labels. The clothing you wear needs to fit properly (to compliment and showcase your body) and be properly cared for. After all, you can spend hundreds of dollars for a pair of designer slacks, for example, but if you don't have them properly dry cleaned or ironed before you wear them, you'll look like a wrinkled mess. When expanding your wardrobe, it's important to purchase articles of clothing that:

- Look good on you

- Fit properly

- Will last a while (with proper care)

- Are easy to care for

- Coordinate well with articles of clothing you already own

Especially if you're on a budget, it's important to round out your wardrobe with staple clothing items that look good, are fashionable and that won't quickly go out of style. It's also an excellent strategy to choose new articles of clothing that can be mixed and matched with other items you already own in order to create several different and well coordinated outfits. Thus, to develop an awesome wardrobe requires planning, not necessarily a large budget.

Developing Your Perfect Wardrobe

If you're like most guys, you hate shopping for clothes and you probably rely on your girlfriend or even your mother to pick out new outfits for you. Well, if you consider yourself to be fashion inept, but you still want to look your best, one option is to hire a personal image consultant who will take you shopping, sort through your current wardrobe and develop a personalized and customized look for you. Most personal image consultants and stylists have been trained in fashion and are experts in helping their clients look their absolute best.

Currently based in New York City, Jenny Gering (212-352-1152/email: GoLight@Go-Lightly.com) is a fashion stylist to the stars. In addition to having worked on dozens of TV shows, commercials, music videos and movies, she's also helped some of Hollywood's elite dress fashionably.

To stay on top of the latest styles for guys, Gering suggests reading magazines, like *GQ* and *Details*, and using the fashion layouts for inspiration. The styles you see in high fashion magazines are typically expensive and difficult to achieve, but you can take bits and pieces of what you see from those magazines and adapt them into your own wardrobe with relative ease.

"I think there is some basic knowledge a guy needs when developing his personal wardrobe. The first step is to evaluate your lifestyle and determine your needs. No matter what, it's important to dress appropriately for who you are and what you're doing. Don't try to be anyone else. If you're 45-years-old and find yourself back in the single's world, don't dress like you're 20. Every guy needs to be totally comfortable with what they wear," she explained. "Be confident with who you are and develop your wardrobe around that."

To insure that you get the most out of your wardrobe investment, Gering recommends sticking to clothes made from natural fabrics. "Investing your money in five good quality garments, for example, is much better than buying 15 cheap articles of clothing. Always go for quality," she said. "Every guy's wardrobe should include a handful of staple items, such as a turtleneck sweater in a dark color. This can dress down a formal look or step up a pair of jeans. Polo shirts are also important staple items for any guy's wardrobe, as are long and short sleeve, cotton T-shirts. I also believe that a guy's wardrobe should include at least two good pairs of jeans. By that, I mean jeans that are clean and simple, on the darker side and that fit a little loosely. If you're not comfortable with basic Levis, for example, go with a brand like Diesel. Corduroy pants and khakis can also round out a casual wardrobe."

One of the great things about staple clothing items is that they can be mixed and matched to create many different outfits. Gering, however, warns that one pair of dress shoes, for example, can't be worn with every outfit you create. "Never wear dress shoes with jeans. A boot, for example, is more appropriate with jeans. Style is all about expressing yourself. Whether you're 20 or 50, what you wear helps communicate what you've learned so far in life, so never cut corners. What you wear helps to create that very important first impression," said Gering.

"In addition to basic casual wear, every guy needs a suit that's created from a season-less fabric so it can be worn year-around. "Stay away from suit jackets with more than three buttons. You can make a basic suit more interesting with the shirt and tie you select. It's critical that your suits fit perfectly and be wrinkle-free when you wear them," added Gering.

Guys needs to be more forward thinking when it comes to fashion. What you wear should always be appropriate for what your doing and what environment you'll be in, but there's always room to express your own personality. If you're looking to change your image for the better and update your wardrobe, this can typically be done well for as little as $500.00. Plus, you can always add to your wardrobe on an ongoing basis. Never try to rework your entire wardrobe during a single shopping spree.

The place to start when redefining or updating your wardrobe is your own closet. Go through every piece of clothing you own. Determine what you want to keep and what you can get rid of, then make a list of every additional item you'd like to add. Think in terms of mixing and matching articles of clothing to create full outfits.

Clothes Shopping On A Budget

1. Don't buy an article of clothing if you already have one just like it, in another color, for example.

2. Think carefully about if you'll ever actually wear the garment you're about to purchase, what you'll wear it with, when you'll wear it and whether or not it will truly compliment other pieces in your wardrobe. If you can only get one use out of a clothing item, you should probably avoid buying it.

3. Ask yourself: Will you look at the item in a month, six months or a year and wonder what you were thinking when you bought it? Is the item seasonal or trendy to the point it'll be totally out of style in a few months?

4. Give yourself guidelines in advance by determining what articles of clothing you actually need (or want) before leaving home to hit the mall, department stores or outlet stores.

5. Many people buy items that are on sale, even if they're not needed, simply because they think the price is right. Avoid this.

6. Focus on buying only quality items that look good on you and that fit well. Always choose quality over quantity. "You can't go wrong at places like The Gap, Banana Republic, Express Men, L.L. Bean, Abercrombie & Fitch, Old Navy and Brooks Brothers. Places like these tend to offer quality merchandise made from natural fabrics. The clothing also tends to come in colors that coordinate well with a wide range of things, making it easier to mix and match outfits. If the majority of your wardrobe is comprised of timeless and staple items, you can round it out by occasionally buying a trendy shirt, for example, from a store like Club Monaco," explained Gering. "Ralph Lauren always offers a classic style. The Ralph Lauren Blue Label, for example, is far more affordable than the Ralph Lauren Polo line."

7. If you're looking for designer labels, wait for sales at the end of each season or shop at designer outlet stores to save a fortune. If you're shopping at outlet stores, be prepared to hunt for the best deals.

Designer Fashions Aren't Always Best

Designer fashions tend to be cutting-edge, trendy and typically extremely expensive. To look like a fashion icon and dress well, it's not necessary to wear designer labels. "I believe it's much more important to develop your own sense of style and individuality when it comes to what you wear. It's totally acceptable to mix and match clothing labels. I recommend against ever dressing from head-to-toe in a single label's cloths, because it shows absolutely no personality, thought or originality," said Gering.

Choosing The Perfect Outfit For Any Occasion

Depending on what you're doing, what's appropriate to wear will vary greatly. Obviously, you'd wear a totally different type of outfit to a dance club than you would to an important business meeting.

The following are the most common outfit categories and examples of what's appropriate for each:

Casual Attire—This category covers a lot of territory. When dressing down, Gering recommends utilizing some of your older, more stylish clothes in less formal ways. For example, wearing an old Oxford shirt with the sleeves rolled up will go nicely with a pair of khaki or cargo shorts. You can round out the outfit with tennis shoes, a pair of loafers or even flip-flops. "You can look fashionable in casual attire by utilizing contrasts, such as a nice pair of shorts, jeans or khakis with an old Oxford shirt. That's casual, but a classier look than wearing an old pair of pants or shorts with an old T-shirt, for example," said Gering. "Conversely, you can wear an old, beat up (vintage) T-shirt with a nicer pair of jeans or pants to create a casual, but fashionable look. Instead of wearing all older clothes or all new cloths, I enjoy creating contrast in a guy's look." For basic casual attire, check out stores like The Gap, Abercrombie & Fitch, Old Navy, Express Men, Banana Republic or the men's department of any major department store.

Business Casual—"A lot of guys have a hard time defining what 'business casual' means, because it's different at every place of business. If your employer has what it calls a 'business casual' dress code, follow the guidelines provided. This usually includes a nice button down shirt tucked into a nice pair of khaki pants or formal slacks, for example. This might also mean wearing a Polo shirt with a sport jacket and a nice pair of jeans or casual slacks, but no tie," said Gering. Business casual can also mean wearing a more formal suit with a button down shirt, but no tie, or it could also mean skipping the sport jacket and tie all-together, but wearing dress slacks with a nice Oxford or button-down shirt. Whatever you wear, your outfit needs to be what Gering refers to as "crisp, clean and very neat."

When it comes to business casual attire, a bachelor's easiest options include wrinkle-free garments, such as Oxford button-down shirts and khaki pants. Wrinkle-free garments are the easiest to care for and require no ironing. They're ready to wear right out of the dryer. Docker's khaki pants (*www.dockers.com*), for example, are available in wrinkle-free and stain-resistant fabrics in colors designed to coordinate well with a wide range of outfits.

Formal Business Attire—"Men need to embrace the formal business suit. This can be a very powerful fashion weapon, especially if you're a younger guy trying to get the attention of women. A suit can be very sexy and help a guy communicate a put together image. It allows you to show you care about how you look. The suit needs to be perfectly tailored. Even the most formal business suit can be personalized with a stylish tie and a shirt that's not a traditional white or light blue," said Gering, who strongly recommends that a guy start his suit buying efforts at a store like Brooks Brothers or Barney's, which specialize in classic style suits for men. You can also visit the men's department at a major department store. When shopping for a suit, shop around and ask the salespeople a lot of questions. Determine what styles, fabrics and colors look best on you. Work with the salesperson to help you mix and match colored shirts and ties to compliment, enhance and personalize the look of the suits you purchase. The trick to wearing a suit is to make sure the suit itself goes nicely with the shirt, tie, belt and shoes you'll be wearing. You never want to look like you got dressed in the dark.

Need help learning how to tie your necktie, point your web browser to any of these websites for step-by-step illustrated directions:

- *www.mckinnonsc.vic.edu.au/school/ties/ties.htm*
- *http://fly.hiwaay.net/~jimes/necktie/tietie.html*
- *http://terhune.net/necktie*

Formal Attire (Black Tie)—Whether you're attending a gala charity event, wedding or some other black tie affair, every guy should eventually invest in a classic black tuxedo. Until the time when you're ready to add this type of suit to your wardrobe, you can always rent a tux that's suitable for whatever event(s) you'll be attending. Be sure to seek out the guidance of the salespeople at the tuxedo sales or rental stores to determine which styles are appropriate for the type of event you'll be attending. You also want to make sure you properly accessorize the tuxedo. This means knowing how to wear a cummerbund (the pleats always face north), use cufflinks and how to tie a bowtie.

Laundry 101: It's Not That Difficult!

It may seem like the nicer the clothing is that you own, that more care is requires when you launder or dry clean your outfits. The biggest thing to know about taking care of your clothing is to read the care label for each and every garment. For example, 'Dry Clean Only' means just that. Take the garment to a professional dry cleaners to be cleaned and pressed.

If you're on your own for the first time, this may be the first time in your life you have to do your own laundry. Well, don't worry. It's not as difficult as you might think. The first step is to go through your laundry, one garment at a time, and separate the colors from the whites. While you're doing this, empty out all of your pockets and separate any garments that requires special treatment or care when being cleaned.

There are several reasons to separate your whites and colors. First, when laundering whites, you'll typically use warm or hot water along with detergent. For colored laundry, you'll typically want to use cold or warm water to help keep the colors of your clothing vibrant.

Once you choose the laundry detergent you'll be using, read the directions carefully. Select a laundry detergent that's suitable for all types of clothes, such as Tide or Cheer. When you go to the store to purchase your detergent, you'll find you have many choices.

Now that your clothes have been sorted and you've selected your detergent, you're ready to use the washer. Place your cloths into the washer, without over stuffing them in. You're better off doing two or three loads than stuffing your cloths into one machine. This will help reduce wrinkles and allow your clothing to get cleaner.

You'll always want to follow the directions for using the washing machine. After your cloths are clean, you'll need to dry them. Make sure that all of your clothing can be placed in the dryer (and don't need to be line dried, for example). You may choose to add fabric softener, such as Bounce (Procter & Gamble, *www.thebouncehouse.com*), to the dryer to reduce static cling and to make your clothing softer and feel fresher. Remember, never stuff too many garments into the dryer.

Most clothing these days use colorfast dies. This means that when they're washed, the colors don't run. Over time, however, if not properly taken care of, the color of fabrics will fade. Likewise, most clothing made from cotton comes pre-shrunk. This means that it can be placed in the dryer and won't shrink. There are, however, many exceptions to these rules, so be sure to read the label on each garment carefully before washing it for the first time.

White fabrics (and colorfast fabrics) are best laundered in hot water. When mixed with pastels or colored laundry, whites, along with permanent press fabrics and 100-percent synthetic fiber fabrics, should be washed in warm water. To prevent fading, colored cloths should be washed in cold water. However, this will vary based on the fabric type and type of detergent you use, so read the garment labels and detergent directions carefully.

The following are the basic steps involved in successfully washing a load of laundry using a traditional washer and dryer with off-the-shelf detergent:

- Separate your clothing by color and fabric types, washing like items together.

- Empty all pockets!

- Turn down the cuffs of pants and shirts (turn jeans inside out to reduce fading).

- Close all zippers, snaps and hooks.

- Read the care labels on each garment and follow the directions.

- On the washing machine, set the load size.

- Select the cycle type on the washer.

- Choose the appropriate water temperature on the washer (hot, warm or cold).

- Determine the best laundry detergent for the job, then mix the appropriate amount into the washer when the directions on the determent say to do so. It's important to add detergent and fabric softeners at the right time in order to achieve the best cleaning results possible. In order to avoid staining when using liquid fabric softener in your washer, for example, the fabric softener should be diluted in water and not make direct contact with clothing as it's poured from its packaging.

- Deal with badly stained clothing separately. This may involve using a special detergent and/or allowing the stained garment to soak before putting it through a normal wash.

- When the washer cycle is complete, remove the garments promptly. Place each garment in the dryer (if applicable), keeping in mind that some types of garments need to be line dried and should not be exposed at all to the high temperature of a dryer.

- To minimize wrinkling, as soon as the dryer finishes, remove the garments immediately. You may then choose to iron or steam certain garments to completely eliminate wrinkles.

Choosing The Best Laundry Detergent(s)

When you walk up and down the laundry detergent isle of a supermarket, you're faced with literally dozens of options. In addition to many different brand names, such as Tide, Cheer or Wisk, detergents come in several forms, including:

- Capsules—This is an alternative to solid detergent tablets. No measuring is required.

- Liquid—These detergents are easy to measure and dissolve quickly. Liquids can often be used to pre-treat stains, but usually don't contain bleach.

- Powders—Usually more economic than liquids, powder-based detergent can be used in the dispenser drawer of your automatic washing machine.

- Tablets—While tablets offer the same cleaning power as liquid or powder-based detergents, no measuring is involved. Just drop in a single tablet into the washer (as described in the detergent's directions).

As you'll see when you shop for detergents, virtually all of the different brand names offer a complete line of detergent products. In addition to using detergent, you may also choose to add fabric softener into the washer (or dryer, depending on the product). As their name suggests, fabric softeners make clothing feel softer. They also help reduce wrinkles and static cling.

If you have a question about how to properly use a specific type of laundry detergent, don't guess! Call the manufacturer of the detergent and ask. Tide (800-879-8433/*www.tide.com*), Cheer (800-632-4337/*www.cheer.com*) and Wisk (800-ASK-WISK/*www.wisk.com*), for example, offer toll-free phone numbers and websites designed to answer laundry-related questions. Remember, your clothes are an investment. With proper care, most clothing will stay looking fresh and new for years.

Stain Removal Strategies

Stains are almost impossible to avoid if you live a normal lifestyle. Food, drinks, dirt, blood, grass, ink, motor oils, grease, wine, rust, chewing gum, perspiration, deodorants and antiperspirants are all common types of stains you'll have to contend with sooner or later. The good news is, if you approach each stain correctly, you should be able to make it disappear with relative ease.

Based on the type of stain and its severity, you may choose to have a garment professionally cleaned. You can also try pre-treating, presoaking, bleaching or pre-washing the garment, depending on the type of fabric and what caused the stain. Washing the stained garment in the appropriate water temperature and using the strongest possible detergent or stain remover will also help your battle against even the toughest of stains.

As soon as a stain is created, the manufacturers of Wisk recommend following these five steps:

1. Sponge stains promptly with cool water to prevent setting.

2. Always test your stain-removal agent on a hidden part of the garment first, to check for colorfastness and bleachability.

3. Before laundering, pre-treat stained articles with Wisk Liquid (or another detergent). Remember, washing and drying without any pre-treatment can set some stains.

4. Air-dry treated and washed items. Some residual stains are not visible when wet and heat from the dryer could set them, making them tougher or impossible to get rid of.

5. Follow all safety precautions on stain-removal product labels.

To deal with a wide range of stains, the laundry experts at Tide recommend the following:

- To remove a few small spots, apply undiluted liquid laundry detergent, such as Liquid Tide with Bleach Alternative, undiluted liquid dishwashing detergent, or suds from an Ivory soap bar, directly on the stained area. Launder immediately.

- For deep-set soils, old stains, extensive staining, or protein stains, like blood, grass, or "body soils," soak stained item(s) in a plastic bucket or laundry tub with the warmest water safe for the fabric and a good heavy-duty laundry detergent, like Tide, for a maximum of thirty minutes. Bleach-sensitive stains, like fruit juice or drink mixes, should be rinsed in cold water, and then washed with a non-chlorine bleach product. If stains remain, colorfast items may be laundered with a colorfast bleach, like Biz, and bleachable items may be laundered with chlorine bleach.

- For heavily soiled garments, like work or play clothes, run cloths through the pre-wash cycle with the recommended amount of detergent. When the wash cycle is complete, drain the pre-wash solution and launder in the hottest water recommended by the manufacturer.

OxiClean (800-781-7529/*www.greatcleaners.com*), from Orange Glo International, Inc., is a powerful oxygen based alkaline cleaner that attacks the toughest organic dirt including mildew, blood, pet messes, mold, wine, juice, baby formula and more. According to the manufacturer, "After removing your stains, OxiClean will break down into harmless oxygen and sodium carbonate. Oxi-Clean works over time, and some stains will require several treatments for best results. OxiClean has no odor so you clean without the harmful fumes. For the most effective stain removal, follow the mixing instructions provided with the product."

When used to do your laundry, Orange Glo International, Inc. recommends, "Adding one scoop of OxiClean to each load of laundry in addition to your regular detergent. OxiClean will boost your laundry detergent's cleaning power and is safe on most fabrics including jeans and colors. Do not use OxiClean on wool or silk. For extra tough laundry stains, fill the washing machine with hot water, laundry detergent and OxiClean (one to four scoops) and turn machine off. Allow the solution and the stained garment to soak at least 30-minutes (or even overnight). Run machine as usual after soaking."

Iron or Steam Your Clothes To Keep'em Wrinkle Free

Once the dryer cycle is done, be ready to remove your clothing immediately and start folding. This will dramatically reduce wrinkles. Of course, cotton garments will probably need to be ironed or steamed before they're wearable. In Europe, steamers have become more popular than irons to get rid of wrinkles. This concept is quickly catching on in America.

The Rowenta DG-980 Expert Steam Generator, for example is a cross between an iron and a steamer. It can be used as a steamer on hanging garments to remove wrinkles, or as a more traditional steam iron (on garments placed on an ironing table.) A professional steamer, like the Rowenta DG-980 ($300.00/ *www.rowentausa.com*), looks like a fancy iron, but generates twice as much steam as a traditional iron, which allows you to obtain better results much faster when ironing (a chore most people despise.)

Depending on your wardrobe, if a steamer is more useful to you than a traditional iron, the Rowenta Commercial Garment Steamer IS-7800 ($175.00) might be a better solution for removing wrinkles from virtually any type of fabric. Or course, a more traditional steam iron, priced between $30.00 and $100.00 (and available at places like Wal-Mart or Target, for example) can also be used to iron clothing and remove wrinkles. As a general rule, the more steam an iron generates, the faster your ironing will be and the better results you'll get.

For suits and dresses, for example, a steamer will allow you to freshen these garments between wearings, without having to send them to the dry cleaners each time their worn.

Easy Ironing Strategies

The Appliances.com website (*www.appliances.com*) offers the following tips on how to properly iron your clothing in order to greatly reduce or remove wrinkles:

- Set up the ironing board at the right height. You should be able to place your hand on the board without bending your arm or your back. Adjusting the ironing board to the correct height will reduce muscle fatigue.

- Be sure to correctly adjust the temperature of your iron prior to getting started. Begin by consulting labels for manufacturer's suggestions, especially when dry-ironing. For example, when ironing blended fabrics, use the setting for the lowest-temperature fabric in the blend. Most fabrics, however, can be done using the steam setting.

- Use proper motion and handling. Start ironing each garment in the middle and work your way outward. There's no need to press too hard, especially when using steam.

- Be sure to use extra care with certain types of fabrics. For example, all silks should be ironed on the reverse side. Cultivated silks should be ironed when evenly damp, but should not be sprayed because they may spot; raw silks should be ironed when dry. Velvet, acrylics, corduroy, embroidered pieces and synthetic leathers should also be pressed from the reverse side, with a clean towel or blanket on the ironing board. This will prevent these materials from ending up with an unwanted sheen.

- Whenever you're ironing clothes with different fabrics, save yourself time as well as a potential tragedy by sorting the garments and then starting with synthetics that call for cooler settings. By working your way up to things like high-temperature cottons, you'll avoid scorching and having to wait for your iron to cool down, which takes a lot longer than for it to heat up.

- When it comes to ironing using the heat of an iron, more is not always better. Be sure to use the right temperature for each of your garments. An overheated iron is the quickest way to make your clothes go from clean to crispy. Synthetics and silks react best to low or medium temperatures. Cottons and linens react best to the iron's highest temperatures. Wools respond best to medium to high (and the use of a press cloth to avoid shine.)

Start Collecting Quarters

Unless you live in an apartment, home or condo that has its own laundry facilities, chances are, you'll need to maintain an ongoing collection of quarters to feed into the washers and dryers at coin-op Laundromats or in your apartment building's shared laundry facilities.

Keep a jar on your dresser or in your closet where you can collect quarters. When you go to the bank, it's always a good idea to pick up a $10.00 roll of quarters to insure you'll have an ample supply to do your laundry. To save money, bring your own laundry detergent and fabric softener to the Laundromat. This is always cheaper than using the vending machines at the Laundromat. To save time at the Laundromat, consider dividing each laundry load into two dryer loads. This will cost a bit more, but your clothing will dry significantly faster.

A Guy's Guide To Buttons

Whether you have your shirts dry-cleaned or you launder and iron them yourself, buttons are apt to fall off and get lost. Most dress shirts, for example, come with extra buttons, however, when they need to be replaced, it typically requires some sewing on your part. Okay, don't panic. There's a solution for replacing buttons that doesn't require sewing. Best of all, it takes just seconds to replace a button on virtually any type of clothing. What you need is The Original Buttoneer. This little gadget costs under $15.00 and is available from many mass-market retail stores, like Walgreen's or Jo-Ann Fabrics, or it can be ordered by calling (800) 236-7996. Using plastic fasteners that are virtually invisible, buttons get attached to articles of clothing with ease. The Buttoneer is a must for any bachelor who dislikes sewing.

Accessorizing Your Outfit

How you accessorize any outfit allows you to showcase your personality, taste and sense of style. It's totally okay to wear jewelry, however, it can be a turn off if a guy wears too much jewelry. "Jewelry on a man is a tricky issue, because every guy pulls this off differently," said Gering. "If there's too much going on in terms of a guy's jewelry, such as earrings, bracelets, rings and chains, that can be a turn off for women, plus communicate the wrong image.

A nice, fashionable watch is always a great fashion accessory that can be used to compliment and enhance an outfit. Many sports watches for guys can do double duty as a stylish watch that coordinates well with a business suit. The jewelry and accessories you wear should showcase who you are, not be used in attempt to look trendy."

A wristwatch is a popular and functional fashion accessory for any guy. It's an accessory that's seen by others and helps to make a statement about who you are and your taste. According to BlueNile.com (a popular online jewelry store), it's important to choose a watch that matches your personal style and lifestyle. If you'll be investing a lot of money in a designer watch, choose a style that's considered traditional or timeless and not so trendy. This way, you can wear the watch virtually anytime and anywhere and have it compliment what you're wearing.

Always buy a watch from a respected brand. Based on your budget, there are countless brands to choose from. Whether it's an upscale brand, like Rolex or Tag Heuer, or a less pricy brand, like Swatch or Citizen, with proper care, a fine watch can last for many years.

Final Fashion Thoughts

Many guys simply don't care too much about their wardrobe or appearance, especially when not forced to wear business attire. One reason for this is the stereotypical thinking that if you look too clean cut or too fashionable, people might think you're gay. The best way to avoid this is to insure that what you're wearing is clothing you're totally comfortable in. Always try to look your best and express yourself and your personality with confidence.

Simply by investing a bit of time and money into your appearance, and updating your wardrobe, looking like a fashion icon is a relatively simple process, especially if you seek out the help of trained professionals, like a personal stylist or even the salespeople where you typically shop for clothes. If you believe your fashion sense leaves a lot to be desired and you're in desperate need of a wardrobe make-over, check the phone book or any Internet search engine for 'Personal Stylists', 'Fashion Consultants' or 'Image Consultants' in your area. These people tend to be paid by the hour for their services, so plan on spending at least several hundred dollars to hire someone to take a total hands-on approach to helping you revamp your wardrobe and overall look.

"If you're totally at a loss, but also living on a tight budget, I recommend looking at how celebrities and other people you look up to dress, then find ways to copy it," said Gering. It's almost always possible to recreate a designer look, without incorporating any designer labeled apparel. "If you're not 'Mr. Creative," copy someone else's fashion style and use that as a guideline," she added.

Of course, you can always copy what the display mannequins and models in the catalogs are wearing at your favorite stores, like Abercrombie & Fitch or Old Navy. You're better off, however, seeking the advice of a sales associate at the store you're shopping in and coming up with outfits that coordinate well and that showcase your individuality and style.

Buying Sunglasses Needn't Be A Clouded Decision

Whether you spend a lot of time outdoors, driving or simply want to look fashionable, sunglasses are an important accessory for protecting your eyes against the harmful UV rays and glare from the sun. If you choose the right pair, sunglasses can also be the perfect fashion accessory, whether you're dressed for the beach, participating in sports, driving or wearing a tuxedo to a black tie event.

All sunglasses have two primary components—the frames and the lenses. As you're about to discover, your options are plentiful when it comes to choosing the right pair of sunglasses. This is why many guys wind up having a small collection of sunglasses, with each pair suitable for different situations and for making a totally different fashion statement.

When it comes to buying sunglasses, you can pick up a basic, non-designer, inexpensive pair that may or may not offer the sun protection you need and want. You can also visit one of the over 1,700 Sunglass Hut International stores (*www.sunglasshut.com*) located across America and choose from hundreds of designer sunglasses, from companies like: Oakley, Revo, Ray-Ban, Versace and Gucci. Designer sunglasses offer some of the hottest styles and best eye protection available, but at a price starting at around $100.00 per pair (and going up considerably).

The prices for designer sunglasses tend to be higher, because better materials are used to construct the frames and the lenses, plus there's typically a premium added for high fashion designs and styles.

Choosing the best pair of sunglasses for you means finding a pair offering the right look, a perfect fit, and the best possible eye protection. It's also important to choose sunglasses designed for the activities you'll be participating in while wearing them. "If you'll be participating in outdoor sports, sunglasses with polycarbonate lenses, as opposed to glass, are the most impact resistant. A great all-purpose lens is one that's polarized, because this cuts glare," explained Paula Donnelly, Director of Product Development at Sunglass Hut International. "The sunglass frame size should be in proportion with your face size. This means that smaller frames are best for smaller faces, and larger frames work best on people with larger faces. The frame shape should contrast with, that is, be the opposite of, the shape of your face."

In addition to being manufactured out of different materials, sunglass lenses also come in a wide range of colors. Donnelly explained that grey lenses offer the least color distortion, so the colors you'll be looking at when wearing the sunglasses will look the most natural. A brown lens, however, offers more contrast and better visibility on a hazy day.

You can typically choose between plastic and metal frames. "Plastic frames have no nose pads. The frames simply rest on the wearer's nose bridge. Plastic frames come in many colors, allowing for bolder and more daring fashion statements. The metal frames, however, are thinner and offer nose pads that provide a better fit. Metal offers a more classic look. Titanium metal frames are great because they're extremely light weight, offer a thin profile and are corrosion resistant," added Donnelly.

With so many choices, Donnelly suggests matching your sunglass purchase with the types of activities you'll be doing when wearing the glasses. "People think of sunglasses as a fashion accessory, but forget that their true purpose is to protect your eyes from the sun. If you need sun protection, make sure the sunglasses offer the protection and glare reduction you need. Always wear sunglasses that offer '100 percent UV protection.' This is different from glasses that promote 'UV protection' or that claim to be 'UV protected.' Darker lenses that are polarized offer the best glare reduction," added Donnelly. "You want lenses that offer the best optics possible. Cheap sunglasses typically don't offer the best optics. If you wear an inexpensive pair of sunglasses, these could cause extra fatigue on your eyes and result in headaches."

Among the different designer brands of sunglasses, there are also major differences, not just in styles, but in the functionality of the lenses. Revo sunglasses, for example, offer a unique and complex light management system in the lenses. Revo lenses manage light, based on the situation the wearer is in. The lenses offer multiple layers of coatings to let in certain types and amounts of light, depending on the situation. The majority of the Revo lenses are also constructed from glass, as opposed to polycarbonate or plastic.

Choosing the right sunglass shape is also important, because you want the sunglasses to complement your overall look. "You want to create the image of having an oval face shape. If you already have an oval face shape, you can wear almost any shape sunglasses and they'll look great on you. If your face has a more rectangular shape, for example, glasses with more rounded edges will de-emphasize your jaw. For people with a round shape face, stay away from glasses that are circular in order to slim down the appearance of your face," said Donnelly, who suggested trying on a wide range of sunglass styles to see what looks best on you.

Just because a certain style of sunglasses is trendy right now, it doesn't necessarily mean that that specific style is suitable to your face or for what you'll be doing when you're wearing the sunglasses. Be sure to ask the sales associate for their input when choosing the best sunglasses for your needs. Make sure the glasses you purchase offer the lenses that are best suited for the environments where you'll be wearing them.

"It's important to remember that for most active people, one pair of sunglasses won't do everything for you that you need all the time. It's a good start to have one good quality pair of sunglasses, but you'll find that certain types of glasses are better for driving, spending time outdoors, participating in sports or for making a fashion statement. The sunglasses you wear when downhill skiing, for example, probably aren't suitable for wearing to a club as a fashion statement."

Okay, now that you've got your overcall look under control, you're ready to show yourself off to the world and enter the dating scene. Whether you already have a girlfriend and you're looking for some awesome date ideas, or you're a bachelor in every sense of the word, playing the field and exploring the dating scene, the next chapter will help you find the love, romance and companionship you desire.

7

Dating 101: Finding Your Dream Girl

Research shows that there are two things on a guy's mind more than anything else—girls and sex (but not necessarily in that order). This chapter is all about finding the perfect girlfriend and then planning dates that will be fun, memorable and romantic.

The decisions you make in regard to relationships are extremely personal. If you believe you're old enough to engage in sexual activities, for example, be mature enough to understand exactly what you're getting into. It's important to understand that many sexual acts involve some element of risk, especially if you're not in a monogamous relationship. Furthermore, for some, there are religious implications involved with how and when you practice any type of sexual activities.

To properly make decisions that are right for you, gather all of the information you need and get all of your questions answered accurately. Don't rely on friends, for example, to provide you with accurate information. Being uncomfortable or embarrassed to talk about topics relating to sex is not an excuse to avoid learning what you need to know.

Whether you're looking to meet potential dates and expand your proverbial little black book, or you already have a girlfriend and you're trying to come up with fun, romantic and relatively inexpensive date ideas, this chapter will be useful. It also offers ideas about gifts that are suitable for your girlfriend, whether you're celebrating a special occasion or holiday, or need to say you're sorry after a fight.

Building Up Your Little Black Book

Unless you're a chick magnet or hot muscle stud with an incredible personality and near perfect body, chances are, you're like most guys and face the ongoing challenge of meeting women, capturing their attention and scoring dates. If you don't currently have a girlfriend, but you're looking for someone to date, this section offers ideas about how and where to meet potential girlfriends.

Whether you're looking for a serious relationship or hoping to get more involved in the single scene and go on casual dates, you probably want to find prospects you'll get along with, find attractive and enjoy spending your time with. Step one is to figure out the type of woman you're attracted to.

Sure, every guy wants to date a Victoria Secret model or *Playboy* centerfold, but there's a lot more to finding the perfect girlfriend than simply dating a physically beautiful woman. Aside from her looks, think about all of the other qualities about a person that are important and attractive to you.

As you enter the dating scene, be on the look out for women with many of the qualities you deem important. In addition to finding someone you believe is physically attractive, consider some of these qualities and personality traits:

- Artistic/Creative
- Clean and Neat
- Family-Oriented
- Fashionable
- Goal-Oriented
- Good Sense of Humor
- Health Conscious and Physically Fit
- Independent
- Intelligent/Well-educated
- Outgoing and Friendly
- Professionally Successful
- Religious/Spiritual
- Sensual/Loving
- Someone with Similar Interests and Hobbies as You

Once you have a general idea of the type of person you're looking to date, consider where you're most apt to meet someone with those qualities and attributes. While the bar or club scene is a popular haven for singles, it's not always the best place to meet people you'd be compatible with.

The following are some ideas about where you might meet potential dates:

- **Bars/Night Clubs**—While many guys find hanging out at bars or night clubs to be fun, it's not typically the best place to meet your dream date. It requires a certain type of outgoing personality to approach a woman in a bar, for example, then strike up a conversation and ultimately obtain her phone number. If you consider yourself to be shy and not too outgoing, this probably isn't the best environment for meeting potential girlfriends.

- **Dating Services**—For a fee, a dating service can help you find other single people looking to be in a relationship. You'll find that most dating services cater to middle-age people, over the age of 25 or 30. If you decide to pursue this option, be sure to find a reputable service that will match you up with people your compatible with. Keep in mind, many dating services use high pressure sales tactics to sign up new clients. Be sure to find a dating service that makes you feel comfortable and that will generate results for you based on your personal situation.

- **Get Involved By Volunteering**—Charity work not only allows you to help others in need (and feel good about yourself), it also provides an excellent opportunity to meet people with similar interests in a casual environment. Whether you get involved with a Walk-A-Thon, volunteer your time at a local hospital or homeless shelter, or become a Big Brother, the time you invest in volunteering could become beneficial in many aspects of your life.

- **Health Clubs**—In addition to helping you stay healthy and physically fit, a growing number of health clubs are offering special services and events for singles. Once you join a health club, participate in the classes and special events. Also, be sure to strike up conversations with people on the treadmill next to you, for example.

- **Introductions by Friends & Relatives**—If you're looking to enter into a new relationship, seek out the help of friends and family who might know someone who would be a perfect match for you. Many people enjoy playing match maker, so put the word out that you're looking to meet single women.

- **On The Job**—While most people spend a considerable amount of their time each day working, depending on the type of work you do, it's typically not advisable to get involved in an office romance. Aside from the legal issues pertaining to sexual harassment, it can become awkward to work with someone after the romantic aspect of your relationship comes to an end. Instead of looking to date people from work, consider asking some of your coworkers if they know anyone outside of work (their own friends or family members) you might be compatible with.

- **Religious Groups, Professional Organizations or Clubs**—Anytime you can become actively involved with a group of like-minded people, with similar interests, you're more apt to meet women you're compatible with and would be interested in dating.

- **Single's Ad**—Using ads in the newspaper to find romance does work, but to generate the best results, you'll need to create an ad that truly stands out. Keep in mind, many women are hesitant to respond to a guy's ad, so in addition to placing your own ad, be sure to respond to ads placed by women that peak your interest.

- **Speed Dating**—This has become one of the latest trends in the dating scene, mainly because it works! In the next section, you'll learn more about 8minuteDating from the company's founder and president. No matter what type of person you're looking to date, speed dating provides a fun, casual and stress-free environment for meeting new people relatively quickly and effortlessly.

- **The Internet**—Participating in online chat rooms, posting ads and utilizing email are all powerful tools for finding romance in the 21st century. There are literally hundreds of online-based dating and match making services, so find one you're comfortable with and start surfing. America Online offers its own online match making service in addition to hundreds of chat rooms. There's also Match.com, which is an example of a popular online-based match up service well worth checking out. Plan on spending between $10.00 and $30.00 per month to access the popular online dating services, which typically allow you to browse ads with photos and respond instantly via email.

- **While Traveling**—As you plan your vacations or business travel, consider finding destinations, hotels and activities that cater to singles. Visiting a resort (such as Club Med) or vacationing on a cruise ship that caters to a singles crowd, for example, are two excellent ways of meeting people. Check out Chapter 9 for information about traveling "bachelor style."

Speed Dating: A Great Way To Meet People

Not every guy feels comfortable walking up to a woman in a bar and striking up a conversation. Whether you consider yourself to be on the shy side, have diffi-cultly meeting woman for whatever reason, or you're looking to improve your chances of meeting a potential girlfriend whom you're truly compatible with, one of the latest ways guys are meeting potential dates is through speed dating.

8-MinuteDating (*www.8minutedating.com*) is a pioneer in speed dating. The company's goal is to help the 82 million singles in America increase their chances of making connections. With events currently being held regularly in more than 80 cities across the U.S., in the first two years of the company's existence, more than 70,000 people have participated in 8minuteDating's events.

Tom Jaffee is the CEO and founder of *8minuteDating.com*. In this interview, he offers advice to guys on how to get the most out of speed dating, plus offers excellent strategies for dating in general. Whether you're relatively new to the whole dating scene or until now, you've simply not met the type of woman you'd consider entering into a serious relationship with, Jaffee offers some excellent strategies.

The typical client for 8minuteDating is a busy professional, who is attractive, smart and looking to meet people of the opposite sex (or of the same sex, if it's a gay event.) The organization's events provide a target rich environment that's very different from the traditional bar or club scene.

How did the idea for 8minuteDating.com come about?

Jaffe: "The concept came about as a result of my personal need as a single guy who was falling in and out of relationships for several years. I wasn't thrilled with what the single world had to offer, and I wanted a better way to meet women. There needed to be a better, faster, fun, safe and comfortable way for single peo-ple to meet each other. Until 8minuteDating and speed dating, the main way for single people to meet was at a bar. I found the bar scene to be one of the worst ways, however, to actually meet someone. What I wanted to do was provide a fun, party environment where it's really easy to meet new people and engage in fun and comfortable conversations with dating prospects. I believe a comfortable environment for people to meet is what's needed for two people to create that ini-tial spark."

How does someone get involved with 8minuteDating?

Jaffe: "The first step is to visit the 8minuteDating.com website to learn what events are taking place in your area. Simply choose a city and then select an event that's of interest. We have events for people in specific age ranges and that cater to specific groups of people, based on interest. We have special events for single professionals, Jewish singles, gay men, and golf enthusiasts, for example. Find the event that seems the most interesting to you, register for that event online, then simply show up and get ready to meet new people. The cost to attend one of our events is about $30.00."

Once someone shows up to an 8minuteDating party, what should they expect?

Jaffe: "You will be attending a social event. It's like a cocktail party where everyone is looking for the same thing. When you arrive, you'll check in and receive a three-digit number. People are asked *not* to reveal their last name or their contact information at anytime during the event. Instead, each person is given a special dating card on which they'll keep notes about the people they meet. Participants are also told not to ask anyone out on a date during the event.

"Once things get started, each participant will engage in at least eight, eight minute, one-on-one conversations with potential dates. During that those eight minutes, you to can get to know the other person and discuss whatever you want. After each conversation, if you're interested in meeting that person again, you can put a check-mark on your dating card in one of three categories. One category is for someone you'd like to see for a second date. Another category is for someone you'd like to develop a friendship with, and the third category is for potential business relationships.

"At the end of the event, if you wish to get in contact with someone you've met, and that person has also expressed and interest in meeting you based on your initial eight minute date, we'll provide you both with each other's contact information after the event. After everyone has participated in all of their eight-minute dates, there's an informal cocktail party at the end."

What are the benefits of 8minuteDating?

Jaffe: "First, everyone in the room is interested in meeting someone to date, so we provide a room full of prospects. When you meet a woman at one of our events, you know she's available and looking to date. We also provide a much friendlier atmosphere than the bar or club scene. We've discovered that 98 percent of the people who attend our events would come to another 8minuteDating event. About 90 percent of attendees meet someone who'd they'd like to see again. About 60 percent of attendees at each event wind up getting matched up and ultimately going on a second date. Unlike other types of blind dating experiences or online dating opportunities, for example, you already know there's a chemistry if you and someone else match up after your initial eight minute meeting."

What should a guy wear to an 8minuteDating event or any event where he'll be meeting women for the first time?

Jeffe: "You want to make yourself look as appealing as possible. First impressions really matter a lot! Take a look at where the event is being held and dress accordingly. Think about being stylish. Your clothes should look nice, fit properly, plus be cleaned and ironed. Spend some time styling your hair. Your overall package should look well put together, because that says a lot about who you are as a person."

When a guy meets a woman for the first time, whether it's during an 8-minute dating event or at a bar, for example, what types of things should they talk about?

Jeffe: "My advice is to keep things simple and friendly at first. You can discuss things like where you each grew up, your jobs, current events, hobbies or what movies you've each seen. The goal is to have a two-way conversation. Don't look at your initial meeting as an interview or a fact finding mission. Try to establish an engaging conversation and determine if you enjoy talking with that person. If there's a mutual interest and a connection, there will be plenty of time later to ask personal questions and find out the resume-type details about that person. It really doesn't matter what you talk about as long as you're both actively involved in what's being said. Remember, you're making a first impression, so avoid controversial or highly personal topics. Things like politics and religion are topics to avoid initially. As you engage the other person in conversation, try to discover things you have in common. The goal initially is to develop chemistry or that initial spark."

What tips do you have for developing a rapport with someone?

Jaffe: "Make eye contact, use the person's first name and create a positive way for your dates to remember you. Come up with something that fits your personality. Most important, make a good first impression and be yourself. Don't lie, because that could come back and haunt you later. Also, take a sincere interest in each person you meet. Pay attention to the things they say, and ask follow up questions. Show that you're interested in finding out about the person. People can tell when you're truly interested in them and what they're saying, and they appreciate that. It's important that both you and the other person are participating in the conversation. If you're spending the whole time talking about yourself, you're not off to a good start. Finally, always end your conversations on an up-beat and positive note."

What advice do you have for a guy who is very shy or who has trouble meeting women?

Jaffe: "What a guy needs to know is that they should always be themselves and on their best behavior when meeting women for the first time. At an 8minuteDating event, for example, there's no need for an opening line. Each event is orchestrated so each person meets several potential dates in a non-threatening and laid-back environment. All they need to do is be friendly, ask a few introductory questions and allow the conversation to flow. You don't need to worry about getting shot down or rejected, nor do you have to worry about getting the other person's phone number. There's no pressure."

What are some of the biggest mistakes you've seen guys make when it comes to dating and meeting women?

Jaffe: "The biggest mistake is that guys don't get themselves out there to meet people. Find ways you're comfortable meeting people and put some effort into it. When you start meeting women, it's important to make it clear early on that you have something positive going on in your life. Women want to know that you're going to be someone they'd like to spend their time with. Give them a sense that you're happy with yourself and don't have any serious issues or negative baggage. Somehow communicating that you're an unhappy person or involved in one or more bad situations isn't going to get you too far, nor will it impress the women. Step one is to pull yourself together. You want to show you're desirable to be with. Don't start thinking to yourself, 'Who would want to be with me? I'm such a loser!" If you believe that, other people will believe it too, because that's the image you'll convey."

After meeting a woman, what advice do you have for what to do on a first date?

Jaffe: "Set up a situation where there's an opportunity to end the date in a short amount of time, or extend it if it's going well. The date might be something as simple as meeting for a drink or a cup of coffee. It should be something that you both know will last for a finite period of time. If you two hit it off, you could then invite her to dinner or something. Have a plan in mind to extend the date if it's going well. If there's no spark, however, you can end the date after the coffee without things being awkward."

Planning A Date: 15 Cheap, Romantic and Fun Date Ideas

Once you find someone you're interested in dating, here are a handful of ideas for dates that are fun, potentially romantic and inexpensive. Keep in mind, you'll want to customize these date ideas to meet your own personality and the personality of your date.

To find events happening in your area or view a listing of clubs or events taking place in your city, point your web browser to *DigitalCity.com*, or check the "Calendar" section of your local newspaper.

Can't think of something fun to do with your upcoming date? Well, here are some ideas:

1. **An Evening At Home**—Enjoy a romantic evening at home together. Create the perfect ambiance with a fire in the fireplace, play some romantic music, enjoy a champagne toast and then prepare a romantic dinner for two. You could also rent a romantic movie or plan some other activity at home.

2. **Attend a Wine Tasting Event**—Many fine restaurants and vineyards, for example, host wine tastings. Spend a few hours tasting and learning about fine wines. These events can be romantic. Just don't plan on driving yourself home afterwards.

3. **Bake Something**—If you or your girlfriend have a fully equipped kitchen, plan on spending a few hours baking something from scratch,

such as a cake. You can also prepare a lavish multi-course meal, which you can later enjoy together.

4. **Go Bowling**—Bowling is a sport that virtually anyone can do. It provides for a fun, somewhat competitive and light-hearted way to spend time together. It's a great alternative to simply catching a movie, because there's more time to socialize and interact.

5. **Head to Starbucks for Coffee**—An excellent first date is to meet for coffee. It allows you and your date to sit down and chat in a relatively public setting. There's also no major time commitment. If there's no spark between the two of you, you can end the date after the coffee (within a half-hour), or you can invite your date to another activity after coffee if things are going well.

6. **Hike/Nature Walk/Rollerblade/Bike Ride**—If you and your date are active and enjoy the outdoors, spend a few hours hiking, bike riding or Rollerblading together. You could also visit a local park or beach and take a romantic walk.

7. **Karaoke/Piano Bar**—As an alternative to visiting a regular bar or night club with your date, you might enjoy visiting a Karaoke bar (and participating in the activities) or checking out the fun at a local piano bar and watching professionals perform.

8. **Lunch or Dinner**—As you're getting to know someone, consider inviting your date to a restaurant for lunch or dinner. This provides for a place to talk and get to know each other while enjoying a meal together. If you're also planning some other activity, such as a movie, participate in the activity first, then have your meal. This way, you'll have more to talk about when you sit down to eat.

9. **Movie/IMAX**—Perhaps one of the most generic (but fun) date ideas is to see a movie. While you can catch Hollywood's latest releases at your local theater, you might consider making the date a bit more exciting and unusual by seeing whatever movie is playing at the IMAX theater in your area. This provides a much more memorable date experience, plus most IMAX movies are under an hour in length. Looking for an IMAX theater in your area? Check out *www.IMAX.com* for a listing of theaters worldwide as well as information about the various IMAX films. Make sure you allow interactive time before and/or after the movie, since

movies do not provide a social or interactive environment that's conducive to spending quality time with your date and getting to know her.

10. **Museum/Art Gallery**—Visiting a museum or a special exhibit at a local art gallery can be a fun and cultural way to enjoy a date, if that's something you're both interested in.

11. **Nightclub/Dance Club**—If you and your date like to dance, why not take her to a local club and strut your stuff on the dance floor? Be sure, however, to find a club that plays the type of music you'll both enjoy and that offers a nice atmosphere.

12. **Picnic**—If you want to do something very romantic on your date, prepare a picnic lunch and take her to a park, beach or another rural location. Don't forget to bring a bottle of wine and a comfortable blanket you can cuddle on. Check out these websites to find picnic baskets that contain everything you need for a romantic date (minus the food, of course): *www.thetreasureshoppee.com*, *www.picnicplanet.com* or *http:// thepicnicstore.com*.

13. **Play a Board Game**—Depending on the type of people you and your date are and the board game you choose to play, you can enjoy fun and mildly competitive time together playing a game. Check out the selection of board games at your local toy store. If all else fails, you can always play cards. Strip poker anyone? Even if you're hooked on video games, chances are, your date isn't. So, focus on traditional board games you can both enjoy.

14. **Play Miniature Golf**—If the weather is nice, spending an evening playing a round of miniature golf can be a fun way to spend some time with someone and get to know them in a casual environment.

15. **Volunteer Together or Participate in a Charity Event**—You and your date can have fun, spend quality time together and help others in the process. Consider doing some volunteer work in your area. To find volunteer opportunities, visit any of these websites: *www. volunteermatch.org*, *www.volunteersolutions.org* or *www.redcross. org/services/volunteer*. You can also contact your favorite charity or a local hospital.

Five Celebration Ideas: Extravagant and Romantic Dates

As you get serious with your girlfriend, you'll probably want to plan some more romantic or extravagant dates, for example, to celebrate a holiday or special occasion, such as a birthday, anniversary, Valentine's Day or a promotion at work. Here are a few more extravagant date ideas you can use to help you make any special date even more memorable.

1. **Bed & Breakfast Get-Away**—Even if you don't have time to travel to a far off destination, you can still find a romantic bed & breakfast (as opposed to a hotel or motel) and spend a romantic night or weekend together. The InnKeeper.com (*www.theinnkeeper.com*) offers a national directory of B&Bs.

2. **Dinner at a Fancy Restaurant**—Instead of dining at your favorite restaurant or the place you and your girlfriend frequent often, find a five-star restaurant in your area and enjoy an elegant dinner together. If you're celebrating something special, be sure to notify the restaurant's manager when you make your reservation. A Japanese restaurant (where the food is cooked at your table) or a theme restaurant (such as The Rainforest Café, The Hard Rock Café or Planet Hollywood), make for fun dining experiences.

3. **Broadway Show, Live Performance, Sporting Event or Concert**—While you might not live in New York City, chances are there are professional theater companies in your area that present Broadway caliber shows. There are probably also concerts and other types of live cultural events taking place that could easily provide for an entertaining and romantic way to spend an evening with someone special. For a listing of events in your area, or to purchase tickets, contact Ticket Master (*www.ticketmaster.com*) or visit the box office at the venue where the event is being held.

4. **Theme Park/Amusement Park**—For those who are still young at heart, consider taking your date to a nearby theme park or amusement park, such as a Six Flags or Paramount Park theme park. It's a great way to spend a special day with someone. A County Fair, Renaissance Faire or carnival can also be fun places to visit.

5. **Take a Boat Ride**—If you live near water, consider taking a boat ride, chartering a boat or taking a whale watch cruise. A romantic dinner at sea can be extremely memorable and is a great way to celebrate a special occasion.

Gift Ideas For Your Girlfriend

Whether you're celebrating a special occasion, you want to present your girlfriend with a gift to demonstrate your love for her, or you're apologizing for somehow screwing up, here are some gift ideas to consider.

Remember, a gift should come from your heart. It can be something sentimental, that conveys a message or that's symbolic of your feelings. Try to make the gift as personalized and as special as possible. Demonstrate that you put thought and effort into your gift(s) and didn't just pick something up at the mall.

- **Chocolates/Candy**—Although many women are calorie conscious, most appreciate receiving a fine box of chocolates, from Godiva (800-9-GODIVA/*www.godiva.com*), for example. Fine chocolates aren't cheap (prices start at around $25.00), but they taste good and can be enjoyed as dessert after a romantic dinner.

- **Cook Dinner**—Instead of taking your girlfriend out to a restaurant, invest the time in actually cooking a multi-course meal at home for her. Be sure to create a romantic ambiance, with candlelight and music.

- **Flowers**—Virtually all women feel special when they receive a bouquet of fresh cut flowers. Keep in mind, the flowers you send can communicate a message. Red roses, for example, communicate a message of true love. Sending or presenting flowers can cost anywhere from $10.00 to $100.00 or more, depending on the arrangement. Visit any local florist or call 1-800-FLOWERS (*www.1800flowers.com*) to order flowers suitable for any occasion. Keep in mind, many florists can make same-day deliveries, if you happen to forget an important occasion.

- **Jewelry**—With all of the options available to you, including earrings, bracelets, necklaces, rings, etc., made from precious metals, such as Sterling silver, gold, platinum, stainless steal or titanium (and perhaps combined with a gem, such as a diamond or her birth stone), you can find a nice jewelry gift that fits within your budget. Consider shopping around at a few local jewelry stores in your area, or visiting an online-based jeweler, such as BlueNile.com (*www.bluenile.com*). As you're making your jewelry selection, remember, you're buying a gift that is a symbol of your love, not a measure of it. In other words, it's the beauty and thoughts behind the gift, not the value of the gift itself that's truly important. Also, try to coordinate your jewelry selection with pieces she already owns. If she has pearl earrings, for example, consider giving her a matching pearl bracelet or necklace.

- **Lingerie**—"Appropriateness" is the word to keep in mind if you decide to purchase lingerie for your girlfriend. There's definitely a strong sexual connotation associated with this type of gift, so be sure you and your girlfriend are ready to explore a sexual/intimate aspect of your relationship prior to presenting this type of gift. As any guy knows, Victoria Secret (*www.victoriassecret.com*) is one of the best places to shop for romantic and intimate lingerie. If you're uncomfortable visiting a Victoria Secret retail store, you can shop online or request one of their famous catalogs.

- **Personal Scrapbook or Photo Album of a Special Event**—If you have a collection of photos of you and your girlfriend, you can create an extremely sentimental and loving gift by transforming a set of loose photos into a scrapbook or photo album. Creating a scrapbook takes some creativity and can be themed around a specific event or occasion. Your girlfriend will probably appreciate the time you invest in creating this type of one-of-a-kind gift that can celebrate and showcase your relationship.

- **Teddy Bear**—A teddy bear makes for a romantic and light-hearted gift, especially if the bear is dressed in an outfit to commemorate a special occasion. The Vermont Teddy Bear Company (800-829-BEAR/ *www.vermontteddybear.com*) offers more than 100 different bears that can be shipped anywhere. You can also visit a Build-A-Bear retail store (found at many local malls) or the company's website to order a designer teddy bear (877-789-BEAR/*www.buildabear.com*). Plan on spending between $50.00 and $150.00 for this type of gift.

- **Perfume/Spa Products**—Perfume or spa products can be a great gift for your girlfriend, especially if you know what types of product(s) she likes and uses. It's best not to experiment or guess, because these products are based a lot of personal preference. If you want to buy your girlfriend perfume, check to see what she already wears and likes. Don't simply purchase a popular brand of perfume.

Tips For Buying Jewelry As A Gift

Buying any type of jewelry as a gift can be extremely romantic. However, buying this type of gift can be a bit confusing. "I know what you're thinking. Jewelry is complicated, totally foreign, and you're not sure you can trust that guy behind the jewelry store counter. In survey after survey women almost always rank jewelry as their most-wanted gift. Even better, it almost always fits. It matches everything. It's always romantic, and can last a lifetime," said John Baird, a spokesperson for BlueNile.com.

The first step to finding the perfect piece of jewelry for your girlfriend is to do your research. "Visit websites, like *BlueNile.com*, and visit several jewelry stores, to become educated on the different types, qualities, and values of jewelry. Next, go through your girlfriend's jewelry box. Think about the jewelry you've seen her wear and what she already owns," said Baird. "Determine if she prefers silver or gold. Does she wear earrings? You might want to ask her mother or her friends for advice. Finally, consider her personality. Is she more of an evening gown and fine wine type of woman, or a jeans and beer type of girl?"

When deciding about the type of jewelry to buy as a gift, Baird suggests, "Don't chase jewelry fashion trends. What's on the cover of *Vogue*, will either be gone next month, or just as likely won't fit her personality. Instead, focus on buying a classic jewelry piece, such as diamond stud earrings, pearl strands, or a diamond tennis bracelet. This will assure that the item will fit her personality and always be in fashion. A classic jewelry piece can also be worn for almost any occasion."

Protect Yourself from Sexually Transmitted Diseases

When your dating relationship with your girlfriend gets more serious and the topic of sex comes up, be prepared to protect yourself against STDs. The National Institute of Allergy and Infectious Diseases (*http:// biodefense.niaid.nih.gov/factsheets/stdinfo.htm*) report, "Sexually transmitted diseases (STDs), once called venereal diseases, are among the most common infectious diseases in the United States today. More than 20 STDs have now been identified, and they affect more than 13 million men and women in the U.S. each year."

According to WebMD.com (*www.WebMD.com*) and The Cleveland Clinic, "Sexually transmitted diseases, commonly called STDs, are diseases that are spread by having sex with someone who already has an STD. You can get a sexually transmitted disease from sexual activity that involves the mouth, anus, vagina, or penis. STDs are serious illnesses that require treatment. Some STDs, like AIDS, cannot be cured and are deadly."

You can learn more about STDs, how they're caused and about treatments for them by visiting the WebMD website or contacting a medical professional. Because it's critical that you have accurate information, don't rely on your friends or relatives to provide you with information about STDs or birth control, unless the person you're consulting is a trained medical professional.

Some of the more common STDs include:

- Chlamydia

- Genital Warts (Human Papilloma Virus)

- Gonorrhea

- Hepatitis B

- Genital Herpes

- HIV/AIDS

- Syphilis

- Trichomoniasis

Almost any doctor can administer tests for STDs. To find a testing facility in your area, you can also point your web browser to *www.ehivtest.com/locator.asp*.

There are a handful of things you can do to help protect yourself from STDs. Before participating in any type of sexual activity with your partner, it's important to have a basic understanding of STDs and how to prevent them. You can learn more by visiting the WebMD website (*www.WebMD.com*), speaking with your doctor or a medical professional, or by visiting another medical-oriented website, such as The Sexual Health Info Center (*www.sexhealth.org/std*).

WebMD reports that some of the common strategies to protect yourself from STDs include:

- Understand that not having sex or sexual relations is the *only* guaranteed way to prevent STDs.

- Always use a latex condom when you engage in sexual activities. (If using a lubricant, make sure it's water-based.) A condom is also a form a birth control. Unless you're willing to run the high risk of impregnating your girlfriend/lover, it's important that you always use some form of birth control when engaging in intercourse or other forms of risky sexual contact.

- Avoid being sexually promiscuous and having multiple partners. WebMD reports, "The more partners you have, the more likely you are to catch an STD."

- Practice monogamy. This means having sex with only one person and being faithful to that person. Your partner, however, must also have sex with only you to reduce your risk.

- Select your sex partners carefully and try to learn as much as you can about their sexual history. WebMD suggests, "Don't have sex with someone whom you suspect may have an STD."

- If you're sexually active, visit a doctor, medical clinic or medical professional on a regular basis and have yourself checked for STDs. Speak with your doctor to determine how often you should be tested.

- WebMD reports that people are less likely to use a condom if they're drunk or under the influence of drugs when they engage in sexual activities. For this reason, don't use alcohol or drugs before you have sex.

- Do research and learn the signs and symptoms of STDs. Look for them in yourself and your sex partners. The more you know about STDs, the better you can protect yourself.

Not Every Relationship Works: Quick Tips For Calling It Quits

In any relationship, as the guy, you want to be chivalrous and considerate of the woman's feelings, no matter what. That being said, if you need to break off a relationship, do it tactfully. Remember, everyone has feelings! Avoid breaking up with someone is a tasteless way, like having her discover you've been cheating or by sending her an impersonal email. While breaking up is never easy and typically involves a lot of emotional drama, it's always best to do it in-person. Try to leave off in the best way possible, whether you've been seeing the person a few days or a few years.

Of course, before breaking things off all together, if this is someone you care about, do everything possible to determine if the relationship can be salvaged. Remember, when two people have chemistry together and get along well, even if there's a strong love between the two, it often takes hard work to make a long-term relationship truly work.

8

Entertaining Yourself: Things To Do With Your Free Time

You work, perhaps you go to school, plus you have countless personal responsibilities. Virtually every minute of every day, including your weekends, seem to be taken up by a seemingly endless array of things you *have to* (as opposed to *want to*) do. Unfortunately, this is an all too common scenario. There's so much to do, with too little time to do it.

As you discovered in Chapter 1, learning basic time management skills can help you free up some of your valuable time, allowing you to take more control over your life and enjoy the activities you want to participate in.

Once you've allocated some free time for yourself, if you want to thoroughly enjoy that valuable time, pinpoint some of the ways you can best spend it. Whether you're an active person or prefer to spend what little free time you have camped out on your couch watching DVDs, how much quality personal time you allocate for yourself and how you spend that time is a personal decision.

This chapter offers a bunch of suggestions for how you can best experience your free time, get the most out of it, have fun and hopefully add balance in your life between your work, other responsibilities and your ability to enjoy what life has to offer. Later in this chapter, you'll also read about a handful of "must have" gadgets" for bachelors which can be used to improve your quality of life in many different ways.

Free Time?!?!? What's That?

So, what do you like to do when you have free time? Are you a spontaneous person or do you prefer to pre-plan your activities? As you decide how you'd like to enjoy your personal time, consider the following:

- How much free time (personal time) is available to you and when will you be able to enjoy it?
- What activities do you enjoy?
- With whom do you like spending your personal time with?
- Based on what you like to do, how much pre-planning, if any, is required?
- Is it necessary for you to actually block out personal time in your schedule? Do you prefer to set an appointment with yourself each day or week to enjoy free time, or are you able to break away from your daily responsibilities without having to actually block it out of your schedule?
- Are you someone who enjoys doing things you're comfortable with, or do you prefer to meet new people, try new things and constantly broaden your horizons by engaging in new types of activities?

Fun Things To Do With Your Free Time

Everyone is different. We all enjoy doing different things, spending time with different people and engaging in different activities, based on our own personalities, skills, budget and personal preferences. Based on your situation, consider how you enjoy spending your personal time.

If you're bored and looking to experience new things, consider one of the activities described within this section:

BBQ/Tailgate Party

An outdoor grill or barbeque can be a fun and extremely social way to enjoy quality time with friends and loved ones. Best of all, cooking on a grill/BBQ doesn't require a whole lot of cooking skill, yet it's relatively easy to prepare a wide range of delicious meals involving steak, burgers, hot dogs, chicken, fish and vegetables. Add some cold soda or beer and you've got the perfect meal.

Purchasing an outdoor grill can cost anywhere from under $100.00 to several thousand dollars, depending on the features you're looking for and the size of the unit itself. For a typical bachelor who will be cooking for himself and a few friends, the Coleman RoadTrip Outdoor Grill (Item #9941-768, price: $179.95, 800-835-3278, *www.coleman.com*) offers ease-of-use and a compact size (perfect of a tailgate party, a deck or a backyard), plus it operates using 16.4 ounce cylinders or 20 pound tanks of propane (sold separately.)

Once you have your grill and you're ready to cook, Coleman has teamed up with The Clever Brothers to offer a bunch of delicious BBQ recipes. Check out these two websites:

- *www.coleman.com/coleman/roadtrip/rtrecipes.asp*
- *www.clevercleaver.com*

Call Friends or Your Mom

Whether you have a cell phone or traditional phone at home, use it to stay in touch with friends and family. Especially if you're constantly caught up with work or school, use some of your free time to call people whom you need to catch up with. Many phone companies, such as Verizon and MCI, offer a flat-rate monthly service that includes unlimited local and long distance calls, plus a handful of calling features (like Caller ID, Call Waiting and Voice Mail). With a service like this on your home phone, you can call anyone, anytime and not have to worry about unexpected phone charges.

Another option is to purchase inexpensive pre-paid calling cards. Find a card that offers a very low per-minute rate, without any extra per-call connection fees or surcharges. These phone cards can be used from your home phone, from work or from most public telephones. For information on discounted pre-paid phone cards, using any search engine, type in the search phrase "Discount Phone Cards". You should be able to find a per-minute long distance rate of less than a nickel. Before purchasing a phone card, read the fine-print to insure you won't be billed extra per-call or activation charges.

Many cellular phone plans, from companies like Sprint PCS or T-Mobile, offer unlimited nights and weekends (with no roaming or long distance charges). This is a great way to stay in touch with people close to you, with incurring a high phone bill.

Go Camping

Pack a tent, your sleeping bag and some additional camping gear and take yourself and perhaps one or two friends on a local camping adventure. Even if you just get away for one night, camping can be a great way to relax, enjoy nature and get away from your hectic daily live. Coleman (800-835-3278/*www.*

coleman.com) offers a large selection of camping supplies, including: tents, sleeping bags, coolers, portable lights and other needed gear. Visit any sporting goods store to learn more about what equipment you'll need to safely go camping, based on where you'll be going and how long you'll be going for.

Visit the Family Camping Gear website (*www.familycampinggear.com*) for a selection of recommended packing lists to insure you don't forget important camping gear or supplies.

Go on a Date

Expand your social horizons and improve your romantic life by going on some dates. Find a woman you like, ask her out and plan a fun and romantic evening together. See Chapter 7 for details.

Hang Out with Friends

Call up one or more friends and make some plans. Whatever you were planning to do for fun on your own, consider making it a social event and sharing the experience with your buds.

Listen to Music/Attend a Concert

Whether you're in a car listening to the radio, working out with your Walkman, sunbathing while listening to your MP3 player or engaging in any other activity with music in the background, listening to your favorite tunes can help improve your mood, make it easier to relax or help motivate you while exercising.

In addition to simply listening to the radio, MP3s or CDs, if you have an evening free, consider going to a live concert. Check out the entertainment listings in your local newspaper and see what concerts are being held at local bars and clubs, plus major venues in your area. You can also call Ticketmaster (*www.ticketmaster.com*) or visit DigitalCity.com (*www.digitalcity.com*) for a listing of local events.

Participate in Your Hobby

Spend some of your free time participating in the hobby (or hobbies) you really love, whether it's playing golf, fishing, boating, doing home improvement projects, building models, playing a musical instrument, photography, painting or repairing your car. Figure out what you love to do and pursue it as a hobby. Whether your hobby involves spending quality alone time or socially interacting with others, it's important that you choose one or more hobbies that offer you countless hours of enjoyment and personal fulfillment.

Plan a Romantic Night Away With Your Girlfriend

Sure, you can go on a basic date, but if you'll be spending the night together and want to do something extra special, consider planning a one night get-away. Instead of booking a hotel/motel reservation, spend the night at a romantic bed and breakfast (B&B) in your area. There's no need to travel great distances to find a romantic setting. A change of scenery and some quality time alone with your girlfriend could do wonders for your relationship, plus it doesn't have to cost a fortune.

Play Sports/Workout

Physical activity will help keep you in-shape and healthy. For many people working out is a pleasurable activity. What can be even more fun, however, is participating in your favorite sports with friends. Get together for a quick round of golf, a one-on-one game of basketball, a hike or even a bike ride.

The great thing about working out and exercising is that you can do it almost anytime and anywhere (depending on the activity). Sure you can visit a health club and work out on the latest equipment, but you can stay home and exercise as well. After a long day sitting at your desk at work (or behind a desk at school), some type of physical activity will help improve your physical and psychological well-being.

Play Video Games

Have 10 minutes or a few hours to spare? Want to save the galaxy, pretend you're a professional athlete, rule a great civilization or beat your own high-score at a game of skill? Well, million of people each day enjoy playing their favorite video or computer games. No matter what type of challenge you're looking for, whether it's one that requires strategy, quick reflexes or both, there are literally thousands of different video games available for the popular systems.

To learn more about the hottest games, check out what's available from: Nintendo (*www.nintendo.com*), Microsoft (*www.xbox.com*) and Sony (*www.playstation.com*) and their third-party game developers. If you're into sports, you've love the realism of the sports simulation games from EA Sports (*www.easports.com*). These sports games, for example, can be played alone (against computer-controlled opponents) or against your friends.

Read

Relax your body while you send your mind on an exciting adventure by reading a novel. Learn new skills or expand your knowledge base by reading a non-fiction/how-to book. Need a recommendation, check out Amazon.com (*www.amazon.com*) or Barnes & Noble (*www.bn.com*), or visit your local bookstore.

In addition to books, consider grabbing a few magazines from the local newsstand and catch up on the latest news about whatever interests you. Some great general interest or guy-oriented magazines include: *Time, Newsweek, People, Entertainment Weekly, Details, GQ, Maxim, Sports Illustrated, Playboy* and *Penthouse.* To catch up on the latest current events or discover what's happening in your local area, pick up a newspaper.

For many people, spending a few minutes reading before bed every night offers a great way to relax, clear one's mind and prepare for a good night's sleep. If you've never become interested in reading for pleasure, because you think of boring school textbooks every time the idea of a book goes through your head, try finding something that you enjoy reading about, and give reading for pleasure another chance now that you're older and more mature.

Take a Walk

In addition to being good exercise, doing something as simple as taking a 15 or 30 minute walk around the block, to the park or to the local convenience store is a great way to enjoy some fresh air, clear your head and reduce stress. If you're walking alone, bring along your Walkman, CD player or MP3 player (Apple iPod). Otherwise, use the time to catch up with one or more friends as you walk with them or call them from your cell phone.

Visit a Club or Bar

Bored sitting at home doing the same old thing every evening? Consider getting dressed up and hanging out at a dance club, perhaps meeting women. You could also chill with your buds at the local bar. Getting drunk on a work or school night is certainly not recommended, but enjoying one or two drinks in a social atmosphere can be fun, relaxing and help improve your social life.

Visit a Museum, Gallery or Attend a Cultural Event

Everyone should have a little culture in their lives. Consider exploring a museum or gallery. If you're not into art or history, a visit to the local science museum or aquarium might be better suited to your taste. No matter where you live, chances are there are a wide range of cultural events and activities taking place, plus special exhibits and events at local museums and galleries. Check your local newspaper or DigitalCity.com to learn what's happening in your area. Cultural events are often an excellent way to meet women in a casual, non-threatening environment. If you live in or near a major city, your options will be plentiful.

Visit a Spa

One of the most relaxing and rejuvenating experiences you could have is to indulge yourself in a full-body massage and/or facial from a day spa. Don't worry, spas, massages, body wraps and other spa treatments, aren't just for girls and gay guys. In fact, there's nothing feminine about experiencing a massage, whether it's administered by a trained and licensed male or female. In America alone, there are over 5,700 spas, according to a study done by Price-Waterhouse-Coopers, and a large portion of the clientele at these spas are guys.

A good day spa will offer a menu of services designed to relax and rejuvenate your mind and body. A one-hour massage can cost anywhere from $50.00 to $300.00, depending one where you go, but the results will be felt instantly as the pent up stress your body holds literally melts away. As you get used to the pampering treatment, you might want to experience a body wrap or aromatherapy, for example, to make your spa visit even more relaxing.

If you're interested in experiencing a massage, contact any local day spa or health club. While on vacation, you'll also find spa facilities available at many hotels, resorts and aboard cruise ships. Chapter 9 offers more information about traveling "bachelor style" and vacation opportunities that involve a spa visit.

Watch a Movie or Television

Television offers the ultimate in passive entertainment that has the power to keep even the biggest couch potato entertained. Yes, if you're a television junkie, chances are you won't be able to get enough of the shows you enjoy watching.

Aside from what's on television, no matter where you live, chances are there's a video store somewhere nearby. Renting a movie or two and then spending an afternoon or evening at home can be a way to spend time with someone close to you, or pass the time if you're alone.

If you find yourself renting at least several movies per month, consider joining a service, called Netflix (*www.netflix.com*). Instead of having to trek down to the local video store to pick up your movie, and then worry about returning it on time to avoid late fees, Netflix offers a wonderful alternative.

For a flat monthly fee of under $20.00, members can visit the Netflix website and choose up to three DVDs at a time from the company's library of over 15,000 titles. The DVDs are then immediately mailed directly to your home. When you're done watching them, you simply insert the DVD back into the included pre-paid mailing sleeve and drop it in any mailbox. You can keep the movies as long as you wish, without worrying about late-fees. Netflix offers incredible convenience, a much better movie selection than most local video stores, and plenty of flexibility in terms of when you watch the movies.

For people who travel a lot, using Netflix, you can rent a few DVDs before you leave on a business trip, for example, watch them on the airplane using your laptop computer's built-in DVD player (or a portable DVD player), then return the DVDs when you return home.

Need recommendations about what movies to watch, well Netflix offers its members detailed information and reviews of each title it offers. You can also get movie reviews from the Movies.com (*www.movies.com*), Film Critic (*www. filmcritic.com*), E! Online (*www.eonline.com/Reviews/Movies/index.html*) or Yahoo Movies (*http://movies.yahoo.com*) websites.

When you want to get out of your home, Hollywood offers a constant selection of motion picture blockbusters "now playing at a theater near you." To learn about what movies are playing at your local theater and obtain reviews, check your local newspaper or go online and check the Moviefone website at *www. moviefone.com*. If you have a wireless Palm PDA, you can also access Moviefone movie listings from anywhere by first downloading a free program from the company's website.

Watch Sports

For sports fans, watching your favorite sport on television (or attending an actual sporting event) is a no-brainer. Especially if you're a subscriber to cable television or a satellite TV service, there's never a shortage of sports programming to watch. Most guys consider ESPN and FOX Sports to be their favorite TV networks. If there's a big game, whether is the Super Bowl or World Series, consider inviting a few friends over and throwing a small impromptu party as you watch the game.

If you're planning your own Super Bowl type party (or a party for any sporting event), here's a shopping list of "must have" items:

- Assortment of junk food (pretzels, popcorn, etc.)
- Chicken/buffalo wings

- Chips & dip

- Ice

- Nachos & melted cheese

- Pizza (Call your local Domino's Pizza)

- Soda and beer (if you're over 21)

To transform your party into a more elaborate event, consider preparing some full meals for your guests. Check out the Cooks Recipes website for a selection of easy Super Bowl Party recipes (*www.cooksrecipes.com/holiday-recipes/super-bowl-party-recipes.html*).

Work On Home Improvement Projects

Whether you live in a house, condo or apartment, chances are you can improve your living space with some basic home improvement or decorating projects. Doing simple things, like painting one or two walls in a room, replacing the carpeting or flooring, or updating the window treatments, you can radically change the look of your living space.

Doing basic home improvement projects isn't as difficult or expensive as you might think. For most projects, all you need is a basic tool set, some directions and the time and motivation to conceive and then complete the project. Brookstone (866-576-7337/*www.brookstone.com*), for example, offers an excellent all-inclusive, 112-piece toolset that comes in its own case. Priced at $150.00, the Comprehensive 112-Piece Tool Set (item #361725) is the type of toolkit that every bachelor pad should be equipped with, because it's ideal for small jobs or larger ones. A slightly less expensive, 89-piece toolkit is also available from Brookstone ($99.00, item #320044).

Even if you don't consider yourself a handyman, home improvement projects can be fun, rewarding and allow you to improve your quality of life at home without spending a fortune. In addition to reading books and magazine articles, places like Home Depot offer free and low-cost courses for beginners on a wide range of home improvement topics. You'll also find knowledgeable people at most hardware stores to walk you through how to complete many types of projects.

The Home Depot website (*www.homedepot.com*) also offers the free Home Improvement Project Index. Here, you'll find easy-to-follow, illustrated directions for completing hundreds of different home improvement-type projects.

Each set of directions also includes a complete list of tools and supplies you'll need to complete the project.

In addition to saving money by not having to hire professionals, completing some or all of your home improvement projects will provide hours worth of entertainment and a true sense of accomplishment as you complete each project successfully.

Worship

Everyone's life has several important components—personal, professional, financial and spiritual. For some busy people, it's the spiritual aspect of their lives that sometimes gets put on the backburner as we deal with the challenges daily life offers. No matter what your religious beliefs are, if you consider yourself to be a religious or spiritual person, it's important to make time for this aspect of your life. How you express your religious or spiritual beliefs is entirely up to you. You can attend religious services, worship at home, read religious materials (such as the Bible) or simply take a few moments each day to reflect on your beliefs.

For many people, it's their religious or spiritual beliefs that offer them an anchor as they face life's challenges. Thus, it's important not to neglect this aspect of your life if it's important to you. Being a religious or spiritual person, however, doesn't necessarily mean that you must adhere to the beliefs and practices of an organized religion. Your beliefs are your own, so how you incorporate those beliefs into your life is entirely up to you.

Hopefully, after reading this section, you'll be able to keep yourself entertained and avoid boredom. As you decide how you'll spend your free time, focus on pursuing new experiences, doing things you enjoy and spending time with people you care about. Allowing yourself to experience happiness and pleasure in this aspect of your life will make it easier to deal with situations and circumstances that may be less pleasant, such as schoolwork or your day-to-day job.

Muscles Are Hot, Flab Is Not!

For those who like to work out in order to stay healthy and fit, you can join a health/fitness club and pay a one-time sign-up fee along with monthly dues (which can range for $19.95 to $200 or more per month). You'll find gyms and health clubs like Gold's Gym, Bally Total Fitness, 24-Hours Fitness and LA Fitness located across America.

You can also invest in free weights or purchase a complete home gym system, such as the popular Bowflex from The Nautilus Group Inc. (888-563-6485/ *www.bowflex.com*).

With over one million Bowflex systems currently in use, Bowflex is one of the most popular home fitness machines in the world. You've probably seen the info-mercials for this system, which ranges in price from $700 to $2000 (with finance plans as low as $25.00 per month available).

Joey Osborne is a personal trainer and the Director of Training for The Nautilus Group Inc. He explained that a system like Bowflex allows you to do all of the exercises and experience all of the benefits of working out at a gym, however, you can do it in the comfort and privacy of your own home. "You can achieve fat loss, muscular strength or achieve any of your fitness goals using a system like Bowflex," said Osborne.

No matter what home gym system you purchase, there are several things to look for in a unit, in addition to its price. Osborne explained that the versatility of the system is very important. "I want to be able to pick a muscle group and then choose from several different ways to work out those muscles," said Osborne, who also said that someone should make sure that the equipment they purchase will be able to fit their level of fitness as they progress. The system should be able to offer adequate resistance and be able to increase as you get stronger.

The size and weight of the unit is also an important consideration. Make sure you have ample space to use the system in your home, but also pay attention to how compact the system can get when it's folded up for storage. The Bowflex units, for example, folds up and has a two-foot by two-foot footprint.

Finally, make sure the home gym system you purchase is capable of offering a total body workout solution. The Bowflex Ultimate XTLU, for example, delivers a real, whole-body workout with over 90 exercises. It comes fully loaded with a Lat Pulldown Attachment to build upper-body strength, a Low Pulley/Squat Station for your glutes and core muscles, Leg Extension/Leg Curl Attachment to build leg muscles and a built-in Adjustable Pulley System to vary how you target your muscle groups. Other types of home workout equipment only focus on one muscle group or a single part of the body.

Working out using a home system offers several advantages. For example, you can save considerable time traveling to and from the gym or health club. You can also work out around your own schedule and not have to wait-in-line for equipment to become available. It's also often cheaper to finance a home workout system, like Bowflex, than it is to join a gym and pay the ongoing membership dues.

The drawback to a home system is that you don't have access to the health club's other facilities, like a sauna, steam room or fitness classes.

Especially if you've never worked out before, once you purchase your home gym equipment, Osborne suggests that you start off by reading the manual carefully and watch the accompanying video (if applicable). It's also important to define your goals and know what you're trying to achieve. A goal might be to lose 20 pounds, improve your overall strength or to build muscle in your legs. Once you define your goals, you can develop a specific work out regiment to achieve them. "It's important to read the manual that comes with the workout equipment you use and not try to figure stuff out on your own," said Osborne.

"We've developed a six week fat-loss program, for example, which guarantees results if you follow the program. We have developed very specific programs to help people to achieve specific results, whether it's muscle growth or fat loss. For a beginner, I strongly recommend hiring a certified or licensed personal fitness trainer to visit your home and help you get started using the home gym system. This will help insure that you're using the equipment and doing the exercises correctly," added Osborne.

Bowflex has also introduced specialized sport-specific training programs for enthusiasts of golf and Pilates, for example. The trick to achieving results from any home workout system is to follow the directions, stay motivated and to stick with the program. "Becoming physically fit requires 10 percent working out, 10 percent maintaining proper nutrition and diet, and 80 percent motivation. To stay motivated, I recommend listening to music as opposed to watching TV during the workout. Watching TV or even talking with a buddy can be distracting and keep you from fully utilizing your work out time. If you don't use the system correctly, it's not going to work," explained Osborne. "If you measure your results every week and you see positive results, you're more apt to stay motivated."

Becoming healthy and physically fit requires exercise, however, proper diet is also critical. "Being in shape consists of strength training, cardiovascular training, nutrition and developing your flexibility. Those are the four elements of fitness," explained Osborne.

Sure, it's easy to say you don't have time to work out and exercise, however, the short and long-term benefits you'll receive from investing as little as 15 minutes per day into exercising and then eating right are tremendous. You'll look healthier, feel healthier, have more strength and feel better about yourself. Just like your personal relationships, professional obligations and the spiritual element in your life, fitness is an aspect of your life that shouldn't be ignored.

Top 10 "Must Have' High-Tech Gadgets For Guys

One of the benefits to being a bachelor is that you have nobody to support financially, except for yourself. Thus, if you have a decent income and learn how to properly manage your money, you should have some left over income to treat yourself to some fun "toys."

Obviously, a sports car is probably at the top of most guys' toy wish lists, whether you're young and first getting your license or you're going through a mid-life crisis. While you're single and have no family to support, you might consider indulging in the purchase of a sports car if it fits within your budget.

The following is a list of ten types of high-tech gadgets, toys and tools that could easily fit into your bachelor lifestyle. Many of these items aren't needed to get through life, but can be considered luxury items that can make your quality of life better.

#1—Broadband Internet Connection with a Wireless Router

In today's fast-paced, information-oriented world, having the power of the Internet at your fingertips is more important than ever. No matter what you use the Internet for, having a high-speed connection via DSL or Broadband (cable), you'll have virtually instant access to a broad range of information and Web content that could otherwise take hours to access using a standard dial-up Internet connection.

Using a high-speed Internet connection, you can send/receive email, download software, play online-based games, surf the Web and have access to an incredible amount of Web-based content anytime. In addition to offering countless hours worth of entertainment, the Internet can also be a valuable tool for finding a new job, performing any type of research, managing your finances or meeting new people (through chat rooms.)

Most cable television providers now offer broadband Internet connections for under $50.00 per month. Slightly slower DSL connections are available from a wide range of service providers, including most local phone companies and America Online.

Once you have a high-speed Broadband Internet connection in your home, if you'd like additional computers to also have access to the Web, there are many ways to make this happen. The easiest method, if your computers operate using Windows XP (or later), is to add a wireless router to your cable modem. This will cost under $100.00 for the router, then under $75.00 for each adapter needed to connect additional computers to the web wirelessly.

Using a wireless router to connect to your cable modem allows you to add as many computers as you want to a single Internet connection, without running additional cables or wires throughout your home. LinkSys (*www.linksys.com*), for example, offers an extremely easy-to-use wireless router as well as the required wireless adapters for additional PC-based desktop or laptop computers. Using this type of wireless connection, your laptop computer, for example, could be used anywhere in your home and have high-speed Internet access available. This type of wireless solution is also ideal if you have one or more roommates and each of whom has their own computer.

#2—Cell Phone

Cell phones have become commonplace in America. In addition to having a traditional phone line, most people now carry a handheld cellular phone, making them available to anyone, virtually anytime. If used correctly, a cell phone can be a valuable tool in business, or it can keep you in touch with those close to you, even when you're not at home or sitting near your desk at work.

Cell phones are available from dozens of manufactures and offer a wide range of features and functionality, besides simply allowing you to make and receive calls. For example, many cell phones now allow you to surf the web, take and send digital pictures, have built-in PDA functionality, allow you to play video games and/or listen to MP3 music.

Every few months, a few generation of cell phones are released that offer more power and capabilities. Nokia (*www.nokia.com*) has launched an all-in-one handheld video game, cell phone, web browser and PDA, called the N-Gage, while PalmOne offers its power-packed Treo 650, which offers wireless web browsing capabilities and a lot of other functionality in a cell phone.

As important as it is to have a cell phone that offers the features and functionality you'll want and need, choosing the right service plan is equally important, since when you sign up with a cellular service provided, you typically have to commit to a one or two-year service plan that carries a several hundred dollar penalty if you cancel your service early.

The way around making a long-term commitment with a cellular service provider is to purchase pre-paid cellular service, however, the per-minute costs of your phone calls (and related long distance and roaming charges) will be significantly higher than if you signed up for a standard plan from a company like Sprint PCS, A&T& Wireless/Cingular, T-Mobile or Nextel, for example. The best thing to do when shopping for the best cellular plan is to visit any mall and speak with representatives from each of the major service providers to compare rates, features and plans, based on your personal needs.

As you shop around for the best deals, consider things like:

- The total cost of the monthly plan.

- How many daytime minutes the plan includes.

- How many night and weekend minutes the plan includes.

- Whether or not the plan includes roaming charges, or if you'll be billed extra each time you leave your calling area.

- What geographic area the plan covers. Most companies offer local, regional and national calling plans.

- Whether or not long distance call charges are included.

- What calling features are included with the plan, such as call waiting, caller ID and voice mail.

- Whether or not you can access the Internet using your phone.

- Whether or not you can send/receive text messages and/or photos.

- How much extra you'll need to pay for insurance on the phone. Typically, for just a few dollars per month, you can insure the phone against loss, theft or damage. Thus, if something happens to your phone, you'll only need to pay a small deductible (usually around $35.00) instead of purchasing a new phone, which could cost several hundred dollars.

Once you think you've found the perfect plan, based on your needs, make sure you understand all of the fine print associated with the plan, then use your phone responsibly. For example, you could sign up for a $30.00 per month plan, but quickly go over your allocated number of minutes. Once you do this, you could be billed up to 50 cents (or more) per minute of usage, and that will increase your bill considerably. Make sure you understand how many minutes your plan offers, when you can use those minutes and whether or not roaming and/or long distance charges will apply to some or all of your calls.

Finally, based on your personal needs, determine what cell phone accessories you'll need. For example, you may want to protect your phone with a case, purchase additional batteries for the phone, or buy a car power adapter for the phone. A phone headset is also ideal if you'll be using the phone while driving or if you need your hands free while you're talking.

#3—Digital Camera

Digital cameras have changed the way people take pictures. Instead of dealing with traditional film and processing, a digital camera takes pictures, stores them on digital media, then allows you to edit, store or print your photos using your computer. You can also have your digital pictures processed by a photo lab to obtain professional quality prints.

Companies like Olympus, Nikon, Canon, Gateway and Minolta all offer powerful digital cameras. The cost can vary from a under $100.00 to several thousand dollars. The biggest thing to consider when purchasing a digital camera is its resolution, which is measured in megapixels. This will determine the quality of the photos you'll be able to take with the camera. Next, consider what type of memory media the camera uses and how many photos you'll be able to store before filling up the memory card. Finally, consider the features the camera offers, such as a zoom lens, how easy it is to connect the camera to a computer in order to transfer images, and its overall size and weight.

According to Microsoft's website (*www.microsoft.com*), when it comes to digital cameras, its "resolution determines the quality of your digital photos. Each digital image is composed of tiny dots called pixels, which are tiny light-sensitive squares. The number of pixels in an image is referred to as the image's resolution. The greater the number of pixels in an image, the higher the resolution. And the higher the resolution, the better and larger the print you can make from your Windows XP-based computer and printer."

In terms of the camera's memory, the Microsoft website explains, "The number of images you can store in a memory card is based on the capacity of memory on the card, the resolution of your camera, and the quality selection you choose for the images and how the camera compresses the images. Before you settle on a specific size of memory card, get your camera manufacturer to tell you how many pictures you can fit on a given-size card at each resolution. Most digital cameras include a starter memory card. Starter cards are usually low capacity memory cards that allow you to get started with your new camera right away, but ultimately become a source of frustration because of the limited number of images the camera is able to store. When you upgrade to a larger memory card, you can take more photos before you have to make decisions about which images to keep and which to delete."

Once you've taken your photos and you'd like to make prints (as opposed to viewing the images of your computer screen), one option is to purchase a photo printer, from a company like Epson and print out the photos you want on special photo paper (sold separately). Another option is to use a service like America Online's "You've Got Pictures" that allows you to upload your images to the service and have professional quality prints mailed to you within a few days. Depending on the size print you want, the cost can be anywhere from $ .29 to $3.99 each.

Using a digital camera, creating electronic scrapbooks or photo albums is easy using specialized software. This type of software often comes with the camera or can be purchased separately. You can also share your images by posting them on web pages or emailing them directly to friends and family.

#4—Apple iPod (or any .MP3 Player)

In the 1980s and 90s, the Sony Walkman allowed people to listen to the radio or cassettes while on the go. Later, the Discman offered superior sound quality in a portable device. These days, the next big thing in portable audio is being able to listen to your music using an MP3 player. These devices allow you to download music or convert music from your audio CDs and store them digitally in an MP3 player. These units offer superior sound quality and typically enough storage to hold dozens or even hundreds of songs.

The "Rolls Royce" of MP3 players is Apple's popular iPod (*www.ipod.com*). Available in a variety of memory configurations, including 20GB or 30GB (which determine the number of songs the unit can hold), the iPod unit is super-slim.

According to Apple, it "redefines what a digital music player should be. It's lighter than 2 CDs, can hold up to 10,000 songs, and downloads music at blazing speeds. Now you can take your entire music collection with you wherever you go. Apple's iPods are available for Mac and Windows starting at $299." The newer iPod Shuffle is a "no frills" digital audio player that starts in price at just $99.00.

As for audio quality, Apple reports that its iPods are, "designed to give you the best portable digital music experience ever. The iPod delivers the highest sound quality from input to output. iPod supports the most popular audio formats—including MP3 (up to 320 kbps), MP3 Variable Bit Rate (VBR) and WAV—giving you access to a wide range of audio file types. And, iPod is the only portable digital music player that supports the AAC format (Mac-only), which features CD-quality audio in smaller file sizes than MP3, so that even more songs fit on your iPod."

In a unit that's much smaller than a pack of cigarettes, the iPod offers a high-tech design and an incredible amount of storage for your music. Transferring your MP3 files between a Mac computer and the iPod is very simple. Connecting the iPod to a PC-based computer via FireWire or USB is a bit more complex, but definitely doable. In addition to the iPod player, Apple offers the iTunes Music Store, which allows you to legally download thousands of songs (for a small, per-song fee). The iPod also supports a service, called *Audible.com*, which for a low monthly fee, allows you to download and listen to audio books and other types of audio content using your iPod or other MP3 player.

Of course, you can take the less legal route and download music and other content from a free service, like Kazaa (*www.Kazaa.com*) or WinMX (*www.winMX.com*), but there are copyright infringement issues when you take this approach.

If you enjoy listening to music while on the go, while exercising, jogging, commuting to work, etc., an MP3 player offers the latest technology for truly enjoying your music. The days of 8-track tapes, cassettes and LPs are long over. MP3s and other formats of digital music are quickly replacing even CDs.

For those who consider themselves true audiophiles and want to experience the very best quality sound from their MP3 player, consider investing in noise-reduction headphones from a company like Shure (*www.Shure.com*). The cost of Shure's E series earphones start at about $100.00.

Shure's website reports, "All Shure earphones employ small in-ear speakers, called 'drivers.' These tiny, efficient devices deliver rich, accurate sound to give you a unique listening experience. In-ear earphones are designed to fit snugly and securely inside your ear, making them the perfect choice for sports, workouts, or other activities where headphones or ear buds might shift or fall out. By isolating you from background noise, in-ear earphones are ideal in many situations where interference from outside noise causes you to turn up the volume on your headset (mass transit, airplanes, gyms, work)."

#5—Laptop Computer

Having a laptop or notebook computer allows you to work from virtually any-where, whether it's at home, on an airplane or while sitting at Starbucks. With a laptop, you have all of the computing power and capabilities of a desktop com-puter, but with complete portability. Shopping for a laptop is very much like shopping for a desktop PC. You want to focus on the unit's technical specifica-tions. When it comes to laptop computers, however, you also want to consider the unit's weight and battery life.

Virtually every desktop computer manufacturer also offers a line of laptop computers, so it's important to shop around for the best deals. Just as you would with a desktop PC, first consider exactly what you'll be using the laptop for, where you'll be using it and what applications you'll be running. Also, think about what accessories you'll need. Next, consider some of the other features many laptops now offer, like the ability to watch DVD movies. This is particularly appealing if you travel a lot on airplanes, for example.

Finally, consider how the laptop can connect to the Internet and what types of connections you'll need. One of the latest trends is for public places like airports, hotels and coffee shops, for example, to offer Internet HotSpots. With the right type of hardware, you could connect to the Internet wirelessly from these locations. If this is appealing, make sure your laptop will have this capability.

Laptops range in price from just under $600 to over $4,000, depending on the unit's capabilities. For most users, a hardware investment of about $1,500 should get you a well-equipped, Windows-based laptop that will handle all of your computing needs. When purchasing your laptop, consider investing in the optional insurance that most dealers offer. This will allow you to get the unit repaired or replaced should it be lost, damaged or stolen. If you'll be traveling a lot and plan to make a significant investment in the purchase of a new laptop, the insurance can be a great additional investment.

When shopping around for a laptop, do your research on the web, read a few computer magazines and then visit at least two or three computer or electronics dealers, like CompUSA, Best Buy or Circuit City. It's important to have a general understanding of the buzzwords associated with a computer system. Some of the things you'll need to know and compare when evaluating each of the computer models from a technical standpoint include:

- Processor Class/Type

- Processor Speed

- Installed Memory

- Maximum Memory Expansion

- Hard Drive Capacity

- CD-RW Write, Re-Write and Read Speed

- DVD Read Speed

- Included Drives

- Sound Support

- Video Chipset

- Screen Resolution
- Display Size
- Display Type
- Ports
- Card Slots
- Network Support
- Input Devices
- Battery Life
- Installed Operating System
- Included Software
- Unit Size and Weight
- Warranty Length & Details

#6—PDA (Personal Digital Assistant)

As you've already learned from Chapter 1, a PDA can be an excellent time management and organizational tool that could quickly become an indispensable part of your life. These units, from companies like PalmOne, are easy-to-use, palm-size computers with offer a wide range of functionality and expandability. Thus, you can customize your PDA to handle many different types of applications, from working as an electronic scheduler and appointment book, to an electronic address book. By adding software and accessories, you can transform a PDA into a digital camera, wireless Internet device or even a GPS (Global Positioning System).

All PDAs available now work under one of three operating systems—Palm, Pocket PC or Linux. Each offers the ability to easily transfer files and data between any desktop and laptop computer and the PDA, plus offers a suite of built-in applications. For details about the different types of PDAs, visit any consumer electronics or office supply superstore, such as Circuit City, Staples, Office Max or Best Buy, or check out these websites:

- PalmOne—*www.palmone.com*
- Pocket PC/Windows Mobile—*www.microsoft.com/windowsmobile*
- PalmGear H.Q.—*www.palmgear.com*

If you're in the market for a PDA, you can save money, especially on older models, by visiting an online auction site such as eBay.com. The cost of new PDAs, however, start at under $100.00 and go up to about $800.00, depending on the model and its functionality. For students and young professionals, the Palm Zire line, for example, offers a full-color screen, built-in digital camera, built-in MP3 player and a nice suite of built-in software applications (including date book, address book, calculator, to-do list manager and memo pad.) The higher-end PalmOne Treo 650, for example, offers wireless communication and web surfing capabilities along with a suite of built-in applications.

#7—GPS (Global Positioning System)

It's no secret that guys hate asking for driving directions. Most guys would rather drive around aimlessly instead of asking for directions or referring to a map. Well, if you're not about to give up your manhood enough to start asking for directions, but you're sick of getting lost, consider investing in a car GPS system.

Imagine looking at a small LCD screen and seeing a detailed map of exactly where you are and where you're going, plus have a voice telling you exactly what turns to make and when you need to make them, in order to reach your destination. Auto GPS systems are coming down in price and are now available as an optional accessory for most makes and models of vehicles. You can also purchase less powerful and less expensive handheld GPS systems, which you can use in your car or while hiking, camping or bike riding for example. Many PDAs can also be converted into a handheld GPS system.

GPS systems use satellites to pinpoint exactly where you are, anywhere on the planet, then utilize current maps to help you get exactly where you're going. Even if you can't afford a GPS system in your own vehicle, when you rent a car from Hertz, for example, for just a few extra dollars per day, you can have the Never-Lost GPS system added to the car. This is extremely convenient if you'll be driving around an unfamiliar city and want some assistance navigating. NeverLost, for example, will help you find any address, popular tourist destination or any hotel, restaurant, gas station or business with ease.

According to Magellan (800-707-9971/*www.magellangps.com*), the manufacturer of several different GPS systems for vehicles, "Motor vehicle enthusiasts and casual drivers alike know that navigation can be the trickiest part of the driving adventure. GPS is an indispensable navigational instrument providing a wealth of information including speed, heading, time to destination and your precise position, allowing you to concentrate on the road and the experience without worrying about getting lost or finding your way. Whether you're rolling down the highway, racing to a business conference, driving on a delivery schedule or 4-wheeling off road, your GPS receiver will get you there and back quickly and safely."

While many car manufactures now offer GPS as an optional add-on, it won't be long before this technology becomes standard is all vehicles as the technology improves and the cost continues to come down. Right now, a handheld GPS system will cost around $300.00, while a unit that gets installed into a vehicle can cost upwards of $1,500.00. But just think, with GPS, you'll never have to ask directions again, nor will you ever have to worry about getting lost or even figure out how to read a map.

#8—TiVo

Forget VCRs! Thing DVRs (digital video records) when it comes to watching and recording your favorite shows. We've certainly come a long way since the introduction of the black and white television set. Well, if you're an avid television viewer and enjoy the convenience of taping your favorite shows on a VCR for later viewing, just wait until you check out what TiVo offers! This is probably the greatest television-related advancement since the first color TVs were introduced.

TiVo (888-921-TIVO/*www.tivo.com*) is an easy-to-use digital video recorder that works very much like a VCR, however, the shows you tape are stored digitally, on the TiVo unit's hard drive. In addition to recording up to 80 hours of your favorite programs, however, TiVo also allows you to watch television and pause or rewind what you're watching at anytime. The unit also offers complete and detailed TV listings up to two weeks in advance.

The TiVo website reports, "TiVo is a service that automatically finds and digitally records your favorite shows, every time they air, even if the schedule changes. Now you can watch what you want, whenever you want. On your schedule, at your convenience. No tapes, no timers, no worries."

The price of a TiVo Series 2 DVR unit, which connects to your television set (and can work in conjunction with digital cable, satellite dish and your VCR) starts around $200.00, plus the cost of the monthly program listing service ($12.95 per month or $299.00 for lifetime service).

TiVo radically changes how you watch television and will quickly become a device you'll wonder how you ever lived without—it's that incredible! To learn more about TiVo, check out the company's website or visit any consumer electronics retailer.

If you already own one of the original TiVo units, but want to expand the capabilities of your system without investing in an entirely new unit, check out the TiVo upgrade kits offered by WeakKnees (888-WeaKnees/ *www.weaknees.com*). In less than 15 minutes, and for under $175.00, you can give your original TiVo a major upgrade and enjoy the ability to record many more hours worth of programming. Imagine storing upwards of 300 hours of your favorite shows, without having to delete programs or transfer them to VHS or recordable DVDs.

#9—Video Game System

If you grew up playing classic video games, like Space Invaders or Pac-Man, you're in for a huge surprise when you see how far video games have evolved in just a few short years when it comes to graphics, sound and overall realism. No matter who you are, chances are you'll easily be able to find a handful of video games you'll enjoy.

Sports simulations, shoot'em ups, role playing games, action/adventures and puzzle games are just some of the types of games you'll find for the popular home gaming systems from Nintendo, Sony and Microsoft—the three leaders in the video game industry. Thanks to ever advancing technology, home video game systems are now capable of connecting to the Internet, so players can experience massively multiplayer online-based games and compete against other people from around the world while sitting comfortably in their living room or bedroom.

For under $150.00, you can equip yourself with a state-of-the-art video game system that connects directly to your television set. Each game, however, is sold separately and will cost anywhere from $19.95 to $59.95 each. At the time this book was written, the popular home video game systems included the Nintendo GameCube, Sony PlayStation 2 and the Microsoft Xbox. As for hand-held gaming, the Nintendo DS and PlayStation PSP offered some of the best possible game play available while on the go.

Every few years, however, new video game systems are released, each offering the very latest technology. Nintendo (*www.nintendo.com*), Sony (*www. playstation.com*) and Microsoft (*www.xbox.com*) have all announced plans to release new systems in 2005 or 2006.

Each of these popular gaming systems have hundreds of different games available for them. So, which system should you purchase? Your best bet is to first decide what types of games you enjoy playing, then find the system that offers the best games in that genre. For example, Nintendo specialized in action/adventure type games featuring its famous characters like Mario Bros. and Donkey Kong.

Microsoft, however, has been focusing more on offering online game play. Each system offers a wide assortment of games suitable for people of all ages.

#10—XM Radio

Imagine being able to drive from New York and Los Angeles and being able to listen to your favorite radio station for the entire trip, without static. That's what's possible with XM Satellite Radio (*www.xmradio.com*). From somewhere up in space (about 22,000 miles above the earth's surface), two satellites, known as "Rock" and "Roll" broadcast over 100 digital radio stations that can be heard using an XM compatible radio receiver. Offering music, news, comedy, sports, talk and a wide range of other programming, XM Radio is the next generation of traditional AM and FM radios.

In addition to buying a special XM compatible radio receiver for your home, computer or car, you'll also need to pay $9.95 per month for programming, but if you're an avid radio listener or spend a lot of time in your car, you'll find the programming well worth it.

XM Radio can best be described as cable television for your radio, with specialized programming from MTV, VH1, Radio Disney, USA Today, E!, Fox News, CNN, ABC, CNBC, The Weather Channel, Bloomberg, C/Net, C-Span, ESPN, Fox Sports, Sporting News, Nascar, Discovery Channel, Playboy and over 70 music radio stations, you're always apt to find programming you'll enjoy.

For under $200.00 (plus the monthly programming), you can add XM Radio to any vehicle without replacing your existing radio. There are, however, a handful of replacement car stereo systems available as well as several units that allow you to add XM Radio to your home entertainment center or existing stereo system at home. For under $70.00, you can even add XM Radio to your desktop PC.

XM Radio is a huge improvement over AM and FM radio, not just from a quality of programming standpoint, but from a quality of sound and programming selection standpoint as well. With over one million subscribers in America, XM Radio is now available wherever car audio systems are sold, as well as from consumer electronics retailers, like Best Buy, Good Guys and Circuit City.

9

See The World:
Traveling Bachelor Style

One of the most fun and exciting things you can do in life is explore the world, travel and spend your vacation experiencing new things, seeing new sights, exploring new places, plus being exposed to different cultures. Thanks to the on-line based travel-related websites, planning a fun, exotic and memorable trip doesn't have to cost a fortune. With proper planning, you can experience an amazing trip, even on a tight budget or if your time is limited.

This chapter is all about traveling and planning incredible vacations. Before choosing a destination and packing your bags, there are multiple things you need to consider, including:

- Your vacation/travel budget.

- Whom you'll be traveling with. Do you plan to travel alone, with male friends, with your girlfriend or with family?

- What type of accommodations you'll need.

- What type of ground transportation you'll need.

- When you'd like to travel. Choose specific dates, or if you have flexibility, a time frame, such as a week in mid-November or around Thanksgiving. If you have some flexibility in your travel dates, you can often find better deals. For example, it's often cheaper and easier to find available flights if you depart and/or return on a Tuesday, Wednesday or Thursday.

- The duration of your trip.

- What activities you'd like to experience while traveling. Are you looking to relax and unwind, sightsee, experience the nightlife where you'll be traveling to and/or participate in activities (like various sports)?

It's important to consider each of these factors, in advance, in order to properly plan your trip and decide on a destination. Your budget will be a major factor in determining where you can go and how long you can go for. Remember, your budget should include all of your trip-related expenses, including: airfares, ground transportation, lodging accommodations, meals, souvenirs, activities, etc.

Once you know how much you have to spend, who you'll be traveling with, when you'd like to travel (specific dates) and how long you'd like to travel for, begin exploring your options. Some of the ways you should shop around for the best travel deals include:

- Check out the Travel section of any major newspapers to learn about destinations and see ads for travel specials and package deals.

- Contact the American Automobile Association' s (AAA) Travel department (if you're a member).

- Meet with one or more travel agents that specialize in the type of travel you're planning.

- Contact the travel providers (airlines, hotels, rental car companies) directly by telephone *and* visit their respective websites in search of Internet-only rates.

Using on-line based travel services, you can save anywhere from 20 to 70 percent off normal, published rates for airfares, hotels, rental cars, cruises and all sorts of vacation packages. Furthermore, you can usually save this money without a 14-day advanced purchase and without a Saturday night stay that most airlines require.

Depending on the time of year you'd like to travel, you may find that a fun and exotic trip to Europe will be much chapter than vacationing somewhere in America.

As you decide where you'll travel, do research to determine what types of activities are offered at various destinations. One of the perks to traveling as a bachelor is that you're free to try new and exciting activities and experience things you wouldn't normally do at home, whether it's hiking, snorkeling, parasailing, skiing, horseback riding, playing golf, experiencing a day spa to relax or going clubbing. The possibilities are endless and by trying new things and wanting to visit new places, you're more apt to experience a vacation you'll remember for a lifetime.

Popular Online-Based Travel Services

Are you ready to save a fortune on virtually any type of travel, whether you're planning a weekend get-away, week-long exotic vacation or a trip home during winter break from college? Well, the savings are only a few mouse clicks away when you book your travel online.

When booking your travel with the majority of the online-based travel services, keep in mind there are some major restrictions. For example, in order to get the really low rates on airfares, you can't always pick your exact travel times or airlines. You can, however, select your travel dates.

When booking a hotel, you can pick your dates, the geographic area where you'll stay and the star-rating for the property, but you can't always choose the exact hotel or motel. Also, once your reservations are paid for online, they can not be changed for any reason whatsoever and all sales are final. No refunds will be given for any reason and travel dates and times can not be altered.

Unfortunately, you will not receive frequent flier miles for airline tickets purchased online from one of the discounted travel services. Keep in mind, each of the online-based travel sights offer different services and work a bit differently, so read all of the information on the computer screen carefully before booking your travel.

As you plan your travel online, keep in mind that many of these travel websites offer even greater savings if you book your airfare, hotel and/or rental car simultaneously. Also, look for special weekend get-away packages or other special promotions offered by these websites.

Popular Travel-Related Websites

Cheap Tickets	*www.CheapTickets.com*
Cheapfares	*www.CheapFares.com*
Expedia	*www.Expedia.com*
Hotels.com	*www.Hotels.com*
Hotwire	*www.Hotwire.com*
Last Minute Travel	*www.LastMinuteTravel.com*
Orbitz	*www.Orbitz.com*
Priceline	*www.Priceline.com*

Travelocity	*www.Travelocity.com*
Yahoo Travel	*http://travel.yahoo.com*

One of the more unique travel related websites is Priceline.com. Instead of being given a price for your airfare, hotel, cruise, vacation package and/or rental car, you can make an offer and see if it gets accepted. You've probably seen Priceline's rather bizarre TV commercials starring William Shatner (Captain Kirk from *Star Trek*). Well, this service may have unusual ads, but using this service can save you a fortune when booking any type of travel.

The catch is, while you can choose what dates you want to fly, for example, you can not choose your departure times or airlines. Likewise, when booking a hotel, you can choose the quality of the hotel (between one and four stars) and the approximate location, but you can't choose a specific hotel chain or exact location. With rental cars, you can choose your rental dates and class of car, but not the rental car company you'll be using. Priceline, however, only works with the nation's top travel providers.

If you're willing to make these concessions, the benefit is that you can name your own price for what you're looking for. After researching the best possible airfare you can find, you can typically make an offer to Priceline for between 30 and 70 percent off of that best published fare, and receive your airline tickets for that discounted price.

Once you visit Priceline.com, the whole process takes about 20 minutes and you must have a major credit card. Upon making an offer, if Priceline is able to find the airfare, hotel or rental car you're looking for at the price you offered, you must make the purchase. Travel arrangements made through Priceline are not changeable or refundable.

According to Priceline, "We work with the best in the business—the names you know and trust—to bring you savings you won't find anywhere else. Our name-brand partners are willing to give you their best prices because you agree to be flexible with the brand and the specific itinerary or product that you want to buy. It's a simple concept, but by 'shielding the brand' from you until your price is accepted, our partners can now offer you prices not available to the general public. Our brand-name partners will accept your price based on their availability at the time you 'Name Your Own Price'. Of course, this requires some flexibility on your part, but this is what allows you to save up to 40 percent on brand-name products every day. For each of our products, you tell us exactly what you're looking for and how much you want to pay, and then agree to be flexible with what we find for you. For example, if you use Priceline to purchase round-trip airline tickets you can save up to 40 percent over the lowest published fares for the dates and cities of your choice. In return, the exact airline and flight times are not disclosed to you until after your tickets are purchased."

When booking airline travel through Priceline, the chances of having your 'Name Your Own Price' offer accepted improve greatly if you accept any or all of the following options (you will be prompted for each):

- You're willing to fly from one of several airports in your area (you'll be given specific options.) For example, if you live in New York, you'll be asked to select from LaGuardia Airport, Kennedy Airport and/or Newark Airport.

- You're willing to fly into any of several airports (you'll be given specific options)

- Your departure and/or return dates are flexible (you can provide specific dates)

- You're willing to accept flights with one or two connections each way

- You're willing to fly in non-jet aircrafts (operated by a major airline)

- You're willing to fly during off-peak hours (typically red-eye flights)

Assuming you have flexibility in your travel schedule and you're willing to cope with the concessions you're forced to make when using Priceline, there are some amazing travel deals to be had, especially if you're booking your trip last minute (with no seven or 14-day advance purchase and/or no Saturday night stay).

Working Directly with Travel Providers

For the maximum amount of control over your travel plans, you can make your reservations directly with the airline, hotel, rental car company, cruise ship or resort for example. If you choose to do this, call the toll-free number of the travel provider (such as the airline) first. Next, go to the website for that same travel provider and see if any lower online only rates are offered. If you're a member of AAA or AARP any other organization that offers discounts with travel partners, be sure to mention this when making your reservation. You can often save at least 10 percent if you're a AAA member and you mention this when making your reservation with a hotel or rental car company, for example.

The following listings of major airlines, hotel chains and rental car companies can be reached via telephone or online. The toll-free numbers listed here can be reached from anywhere in America and Canada.

Major Airline Contact Information

Aer Lingus	800-223-6537
Aeromexico	800-237-6639
Aeropostal	888-912-8466
AirTran Airways	800-AIR-TRAN
Alaska Airlines	800-426-0333
All Nippon Airways	800-235-9262
Aloha Air	800-367-5250
America West Airlines	800-235-9292
American Airlines	800-433-7300
British Airways	800-247-9297
Continental Airlines	800-525-0280
Delta Air Lines	800-221-1212
El Al Israel Airlines	800-223-6700
Icelandair	800-223-5500
JetBlue Airways	800-538-2583
KLM	800-374-7747
Lufthansa	800-645-3880
Midway Airlines	800-446-4392
Midwest Express Airlines	800-452-2022
Pan Am	800-359-7262
SAS Scandinavian Airlines	800-221-2350
Song Delta Air	800-359-7664
Southeast Airlines	800-359-7325
Southwest Airlines	800-435-9792

Spirit Airline	800-772-7117
SWISS	877-359-7947
TAP Air Portugal	800-221-7370
United Airlines	800-241-6522
US Airways	800-428-4322
USAir Shuttle	800-428-4322
Virgin Atlantic	800-862-8621

Major Hotel Chains, B&Bs & Resort Contact Information

The following is a listing of popular hotel, motel and resort chains, as well as website URLs that offer directories for bed & breakfast accommodations throughout the world. Once you know where you'll be traveling, you can contact the various hotel chains directly to shop around for the best deals.

<u>Average Room Rate</u>

$ = Under $50 per night
$$ = $51 to $99 per night
$$$ = $99 to $199 per night
$$$$ = Over $200 per night

Hotel Name	*Toll-Free Phone Number*	*Website*	*Price Range*
Bed & Breakfasts Nationwide Directories		*www.theinnkeeper.com* *www.travelassist.com/reg/reg_m_us.html* *www.bnbfinder.com* *www.bedandbreakfast.com*	$$ to $$$$
Best Western	(800) 780-7234	*www.bestwestern.com*	$$ to $$$
Club Med	(888) 932-2582	*www.clubmed.com*	$$$$
DoubleTree	(800) 222-TREE	*www.doubletree.com*	$$$

Hotel Name	Toll-Free Phone Number	Website	Price Range
Four Seasons	(800) 819-5053	www.fourseasons.com	$$$$
Hilton	(800) 774-1500	www.hilton.com	$$$ to $$$$
Holiday Inn	(800) 465-4329	www.holiday-inn.com	$$
Hyatt	(888) 591 1234	www.hyatt.com	$$$
Marriott	(888) 236-2427	www.marriott.com	$$
Motel 6	(800) 4-MOTEL6	www.motel6.com	$ to $$
Omni Hotels	(800) THE-OMNI	www.omnihotels.com	$$$ to $$$$
Ramada	(800) 2-RAMADA	www.ramada.com	$$$
Ritz-Carlton	(800) 241-3333	www.ritz-carlton.com	$$$$
Sandals Resorts	(888) SANDALS	www.sandals.com	$$$ to $$$$
Sheraton	(800) 325-3535	www.sheraton.com	$$$ to $$$$
Sonesta	(800) SONESTA	www.sonesta.com	$$$$
W Hotels	(877) 946-8357	www.starwood.com/whotels	$$$$
Westin	(800) 228-3000	www.westin.com	$$$
Wyndham	(877) 999-3223	www.wyndham.com	$$$ to $$$$

Major Rental Car Company Contact Information

Thifty	800-847-4389	*www.thrifty.com*
Hertz	800-654-3131	*www.hertz.com*
National	800-CAR-RENT	*www.nationalcar.com*
Enterprise	800-RENT-A-CAR	*www.enterprise.com*
Budget	800-527-0700	*www.budget.com*
Alamo	800-462-5266	*www.goalamo.com*
Dollar	800-800-3665	*www.dollar.com*
Avis	800-230-4898	*www.avis.com*

Addition Travel-Related Resources

Airline Flight Trackers (Receive flight delay information, etc.)	*http://tracker.flightview.com/amex/flight_tracker/ft_main.asp* *www.flightarrivals.com* *http://tracker.flightview.com/htUSAToday/ff.htm* *http://airlinetracker.com*
America Automobile Association (AAA) (Travel Information, Travel Agency)	(877) TRIPTIK (Information)/ (800) 222-7448 (Reservations)/*www.aaa.com*
AmTrak Trains	(800) USA-RAIL/*www.amtrak.com*
Currency Converters	*www.xe.net/ucc* *www.oanda.com/convert/classic*
Five-Star Adventure (A travel agency specializing in active vacations, involving bicycling, walking and multi-sport getaways.)	(800) 462-2848/*www.backroads.com*
Greyhound Bus Lines	(800) 229-9424/*www.greyhound.com*

International Expeditions (A travel agency specializing in small group ECO travel and expeditions throughout the world.)	(800) 242-4686/*www.ietravel.com*
MapQuest (Driving Directions & Maps)	*www.mapquest.com*
Rail Europe (Eurail passes and European train tours)	(877) 803-RAIL/*www.raileurope.com*
The Weather Channel (Worldwide Weather Forecasts)	*www.weather.com*
Travel Insurance Providers	(866) 807-3982/*www.accessamerica.com* (888) 457-4602/*www.travelex-insurance.com* (800) 826-4919/*www.travelguard.com* (800) 243-3174/*www.travelinsured.com*
U.S. Dept. of State Travel Warnings	*www.state.gov/travel.cfm*
U.S. Passport Information (Applying For & Renewing Passports)	*http://travel.state.gov/passport_services.html*
Worldwide Embassy Directory	*www.embassyworld.com/embassy/directory.htm*

Packing For Your Trip

Once you know where you're going and when, determine what activities you'll be participating in and what the weather will be like while you're there. This will help you pack the appropriate clothing for the trip. Ideally, without over-packing, you want to bring clothing that's appropriate for the climate and the activities you'll be engaged in.

According to Tilley Endurables (800-363-8737/*www.tilley.com*), a company that specializes in easy-to-care-for and stylish clothing made specifically for frequent travelers, "When packing for a trip, pack light. That means coordination. Pick a couple of shirts that mix-n-match with a couple of pair of pants or shorts. A jacket or vest to top it off and you can go casual or dressed for dinner without packing your entire wardrobe. Ease-of-care and wrinkle-free clothing items are important musts. Tilley products, for example, can be washed in the hotel sink at night, hung to dry and be ready to go for breakfast."

No matter where you'll be traveling, don't forget to protect yourself properly from the sun. Tilley makes a collection of weather-proof hats and caps which offer excellent sun production without compromising style.

Tilley reports, "If you aren't planning to wear a hat en route, a Tilley hat, for example, can be easily squished inside your suitcase, golf bag or pocket ready to go when your adventure begins. No matter what type of hat you wear, make sure it shades your the face, ears and neck. Ideally, you want to wear a brimmed hat that offers certified protection from UV rays. Tilley hats have been rated with an Ultraviolet Protection Factor (UPF) of 50+ —the maximum rating given." Tilley hats, like the popular Airflo hat which weights four ounces, offer excellent sun protection, are rain repellent, stylish, offer a hydrofoil anti-sweat band and they even float.

As for the rest of your wardrobe, while on vacation you want to be comfortable, stylish and protected from the elements. The experts at Tilley recommend wearing loose, closely woven clothing made of lightweight material to stay cool while providing your body with shade from burning rays. For those times when bare skin is an absolute necessity, provide shade by applying sunscreen with a SPF 15 or higher. For your eyes, make sure your shades offer the sun protection of UV filters."

A sun burn (as opposed to a sun tan) is not sexy, plus it can be painful and damaging to your skin. If you want to go for six hours on the beach on the first day of your holiday, you're definitely going to hurt. Enjoy yourself by timing sun exposure. The sun can do the most damage between 10:00 a.m. and 2:00 p.m., when it's directly overhead.

Depending on where you're traveling, pickpockets and theft might be a concern. For this reason, you should wear pants, shorts, jackets or vests that offer sealable pockets for your wallet and valuables. Velcro or zippered pockets that are hidden from view offer the most security.

The following are some additional packing tips:

- Never pack and check (at the airport) any items that you absolutely must have when you get off the plane, such as prescription medications. If you're planning to pack fancy cloths that can't get wrinkled, use a garment bag or a suitcase with a special compartment designed for suits.

- Instead of folding casual clothing, try rolling them and then placing the articles in your luggage. This takes up less space and works best with jeans and casual pants, socks, non-dress shirts, sweaters, sweatshirts, and other casual clothing items.

- Place shampoos, cologne bottles, toothpaste, and anything else that could leak in sealable plastic bags.

- While packing your luggage, make a list of each bag's contents and leave the list at home. If your bag gets lost or stolen, having a list of missing items will help you get reimbursed by the airline or insurance company.

- Once your bags are packed and you're ready to leave your home, keep your bags with you at all times until they are safely checked with the airline at a designated baggage check-in location, such as the airline's ticket counter. Never leave your bags unattended at the airport, and never accept any packages or items from strangers at the airport.

- All of your travel documents (airline tickets, etc.), should be kept in a pocket or in a carry-on bag while you're traveling.

To help you decide what to bring and insure you don't forget to pack something important, visit the following websites which offer packing lists appropriate to different types of trips:

- Packing Lists—*www.travelsmith.com/ts/packlist.jsp*
- Packing Advice—*www.packitup.com*

Choosing The Right Luggage

Luggage comes in a wide range of styles and sizes. When packing for your trip, you'll save a lot of hassle by choosing luggage designed for the type of travel you'll be doing. For example, an "overnight bag" is typically designed to hold one change of clothes and some toiletries. A garment bag will hold one or two suites without wrinkling them, while a duffle-type bag will allow you to pack a lot of casual clothes in a relatively compact space.

In addition to making your stuff easy to carry around when traveling, you want your belongings to stay protected and organized. For convenience, luggage with built-in wheels is a must for any bag that's larger than your basic overnight bag. You also want the luggage to be made of a durable material, such as Ballistic nylon.

Buying luggage is an investment and one that should last you for many years. Thus, you want to choose luggage that's well-made, durable, stylish and that's designed for the type of traveling you'll be doing. There are dozens of popular luggage manufacturers. If you can't afford to buy luggage that's appropriate for the type of trip you'll be taking, borrow some from friends or relatives.

Tumi Luggage, Inc. (800-322-TUMI/*www.tumi.com*) manufactures a line of top-quality, high-end luggage in a wide range of styles. Unlike many other luggage manufacturers, Tumi's products are covered by a lifetime guarantee against defects in materials and workmanship. All of the company's products are made in the U.S.A., using ultra-strong Tru-Ballistic nylon or napa leather. In addition to providing superior workmanship, each bag is expertly designed with multiple (and often expandable) compartments and storage pockets.

According to Tumi, if you don't yet own luggage that's suitable for airplane travel, the first step is to determine how you'll be using your luggage. The actual pieces of luggage a business traveler might purchase are very different from the luggage a family going on vacation would use. A family that takes just one trip per year doesn't need to spend as much on their luggage as an individual or family that travels often.

Luggage that will be checked at the airport, as opposed to being carried on an airplane, needs to be extremely durable. Some luggage is specifically designed to keep clothing, such as suits, wrinkle free, while other luggage pieces are designed to hold a lot of casual clothing.

Ballistic nylon is pretty indestructible, and when you realize what your bags go through once you check them at the airport, you'll appreciate the strength of this material. The outer covering of bags tend to go through a lot of wear and tear. Some less expensive luggage materials simply can't hold up to repeat abuse, which means it'll have to be fixed or replaced much sooner. No matter what style or brand of luggage you purchase, choosing luggage manufactured with durable fabric is critical.

Likewise, if you're buying luggage with wheels, it's important to evaluate the quality of those wheels. Do they spin smoothly? Do they wobble? Tumi, for example, uses the same wheels used on in-line skates, so they have a minimum of friction. This is important when you're dragging 30 to 60 pounds of luggage behind you through the airport, which often requires walking over one-half-mile along crowded airport concourses.

Don't forget to examine the handle system on the luggage. Look for handles that are strong, comfortable and durable. Tumi's luggage, for example, offers a steel core that is surrounded by three layers of padding and high quality leather. The handles are then secured to the bag using solid steel rings and screws.

Overall, luggage needs to be strong and lightweight. All of the stitching should be tight, with no loose threads visible. Another thing to look for when choosing luggage is to examine how well it's laid out. Are the compartments where you'd want to put them? Do the compartments provide added efficiency? Also, is all of the space in the bag useable for packing? Can any of the pockets be accessed from the outside? You should be able to open the bag and say to yourself, 'Wow, this bag was laid out well and will be able to hold all of the belongings I plan on traveling with.'

These days, the materials and fabrics used to manufacture soft-body luggage is as durable, if not more durable, than hard body luggage. In addition, thanks to expandable compartments, most soft-body luggage is much lighter weight and can often hold more than same-size hard body luggage or suitcases. Ballistic nylon, used to manufacture many soft-body pieces of luggage, is water-resistant, usually puncture proof, and much easier to carry and store.

When shopping for luggage, visit a specialty luggage store or a major department store that carries a lot of luggage styles, from different manufacturers. Since many pieces of luggage look alike, and most bags come in standard solid colors, like black, it's a good idea to make your bag look a bit different when you check it at the airport. To make your bags stand out, so that the wrong person doesn't accidentally pick it up off the baggage claim conveyor belt, tie a bright colored ribbon around the handle. Also, make sure you have at least one well-attached luggage tag on each bag. It should clearly list your full name, address and phone number. (Some people choose to use a work address and phone number for security reasons.)

In addition to having this information on a luggage tag on the outside of the bag, it's also an excellent idea to include this information inside the bag, so if your bag gets lost, and the luggage tag falls off, the person who finds it can still contact you.

If your luggage gets damaged or lost by the airline, it's critical that claims be made in-person, before leaving the airport. Should a problem arise, visit your airline's lost baggage counter located near the baggage claim area in the airport.

Along with Tumi, dozens of different manufacturers offer luggage in a wide range of colors and styles, and at a variety of price points. Keep in mind, quality varies greatly between manufacturers, and while two bags from different manufacturers might look similar, their overall quality level and price might be very different, which is why examining each bag before you purchase it is important.

Other popular luggage manufacturers include: Altantic, American Tourister, Andiamo, Biggs & Riley, Dakota Metro, Hartmann, Kipling, Samsonite and TravelPro.

Who Says You Can't Take It With You?

Whether you're being a tourist and exploring a new city, hiking through a jungle, or spending your days sunning at the beach, while on vacation, you'll want to travel light, but at the same time, carry some items with you wherever you go. Instead of overstuffing your pockets, consider carrying a comfortable, durable and weather-resistant (waterproof) shoulder bag with multiple pockets.

Tilley Endurables offers a rugged, masculine and stylish looking Shoulder Bag made from Cordure nylon (item #TA367, price: $175), while Tumi offers a selection of shoulder bags made from Tru-Ballistic nylon that are ideal for people on the go. These shoulder bags also make excellent airplane carry-ons. Once you've picked the shoulder bag that offers the functionality and look you need, here's a list of items you might want to carry in it while traveling:

- Book or magazine
- Camera with film (if applicable) and extra batteries
- Cell phone
- Hat
- Handheld Video Game System
- Pen and paper
- Small first aid kit (including headache medication)
- Small flashlight
- Sunglasses/Prescription Glasses
- Sunscreen
- Travel guide/maps
- Walkman or iPod

Dealing with Airport Security

Since the September 11th terrorist attacks, how people travel through airports has changed forever. The security precautions being taken at major airports and tourist destinations change regularly. Thus, even if you're a frequent traveler, be sure to show up at the airport at least 90 minutes prior to any domestic flight and at least two hours before an international flight.

Be sure to leave extra time to park your car at the airport (if applicable), and be prepared to wait in long lines at the airline's ticket counter and then again to go through security. Always keep your printed boarding passes, airline tickets and related paperwork easily accessibly to show to airline and security personnel. You'll also need to show your photo ID (driver's license, passport or military ID) multiple times as you check in for a flight.

When you travel, you and everything you're carrying with you (or checking within your luggage) is subject to be searched. To make this process as stress-free as possible, don't carry with you anything that has been banned by the airlines. Follow the directions of airline and security personnel to make the airport check-in and airplane boarding process easier.

Visit The Transportation Security Administration's website (*www.tsa.gov*) for additional information about airport security and what you can and can't take with you on the airplane and within your checked baggage. Click on the 'Travelers & Consumers' icon at the top of the main webpage.

Before You Go, Create A Detailed Travel Itinerary

Especially if you're not an experienced traveler, create a detailed travel itinerary for yourself. This will help to insure you're in the right place at the right time, and have the appropriate travel documentation (reservation numbers, paper-based tickets and confirmation letters, etc.) with you. The following is a template for creating a personalized travel itinerary.

Travel Itinerary

Name of Traveler(s): _____

Departure Date: _____

Airline Information

Airline: _____

Airline's Phone Number: _____

Reservation and/or Record Locator Number: _____

Departure Flight Number(s): _____

Departure Time: _____

Departure City: _____

Destination City: _____

Arrival Time: _____

Seat Assignment: _____

Connection Flight Information: _____

Frequent Flier Number for Airline: _____

Method of Payment: _____

Number of Bags to be Checked: _____

Number of Carry-Ons: _____

Accommodations

Hotel Name: _____

Reservation/Confirmation Number: _____

Address: _____

Phone Number: _____

Fax Number: _____

Check-In Date: _____

Departure (Check-Out) Date: _____

Room Accommodations Requested: _____

Room Rate ($): _____

Method of Payment: _____

Rental Car Information

Name of Rental Car Company: _____

Confirmation/Reservation Number: _____

Rental Car Company's Phone Number: _____

Pick Up Date/Time: _____

Pick Up Location: _____

Return Location: _____

Return Date/Time: _____

Daily/Weekly Rate ($): _____

Method of Payment: _____

Train Information

Train Number: _____

Train Service Phone Number (Amtrack: 800-USA-RAIL): _____

Confirmation Number: _____

Departure City/Station: _____

Departure Time: _____

Destination City: _____

Arrival Time: _____

Seat Number: _____

Method of Payment: _____

When actually traveling, it's easier to stay within your budget if you keep track of expenses. This can be done using a small pad and paper, or a personal digital assistant (PDA). For each expense, keep track of the following information:

Date: _____

Vendor: _____

Expense Description: _____

Method of Payment: _____

Attendees (if applicable): _____

Notes: _____

With all of your travel plans pre-arranged and organized before you leave, the chances of you better enjoying your trip and avoiding common travel-related mishaps is much better.

Awesome Vacation Destinations for Bachelors

The following are just a few vacation destination options suitable for bachelors traveling alone, with friends or with their girlfriend. Where you ultimately go is a personal decision, based upon what you like to do, what you'd like to see, your budget and what type of weather you'd like to experience.

To visit any of these exciting vacation destinations, you can contact a travel agent or an airline and inquire about special package deals, or book your airfare, accommodations, ground transportation and activities on your own by contacting the providers directly or by using an online-based travel website.

Just a few exciting vacation destinations for bachelors include:

- Cancun/Mexico

- Caribbean

- Hawaii

- Iceland

- Lake Tahoe/Aspen, CO

- Las Vegas, NV/Atlantic City, NJ

- London

- Los Angeles, CA

- Miami (South Beach)

- New York City

- Paris

- Phoenix

Take A High Seas Vacation Aboard A Cruise Ship

Cruise ships offer an incredible and exciting vacation opportunity. Leaving from major U.S. ports, such as Miami, Florida, you can book a three, five or seven night (or longer) cruise to a variety of locations. Whether you want to see the Caribbean, Europe, Hawaii, Alaska or virtually anywhere else in the world that's accessible from the ocean, a cruise aboard a well-known cruise line offers plenty of shipboard activities, incredible meals, comfortable cabin accommodations and a convenient way to visit multiple ports of call.

Excellent package deals (that include airfare, shipboard cabin accommodations and meals, for example) are available from all of the cruise ship companies and many of the online-based travel websites.

Keep in mind, each cruise line typically offers a fleet of ships. Each ship often caters to a different type of audience, so speak with the reservations consultant or a travel agent to help you choose a cruise that's most suited to your desires. For example, there are cruises targeted to singles and others that cater to people looking for adventure as opposed to relaxation.

Before booking a cruise, contact the various cruise lines and request brochures and/or promotional videos to learn more about what's offered. Taking a cruise is a very different type of vacation experience than flying to your destination and staying at a hotel. To get the most out of a cruise experience, pre-planning what you do at each port of call is important.

Experience A Royal Caribbean Cruise

The secret to experiencing the ultimate cruise vacation is to choose a cruise line and ship that specializes in vacation opportunities that cater to your specific wants and needs.

Royal Caribbean International (800-398-9819/*www.royalcaribbean.com*) offers luxury accommodations and exotic activities aboard each of its ships. Whether your destination is the Caribbean, Alaska, Bermuda, Europe, Hawaii, Mexico or The Panama Canal, Royal Caribbean offers a wide range of vacation options at many different price points.

Along with choosing a destination, you'll want to speak with your travel agent or a cruise ship reservations specialist to determine which ship is best for you. For example, some cruises cater to singles and young adults, while others are more oriented to newlyweds (honeymooners), families or senior citizens.

In addition to the usual activities you'd expect aboard a cruise ship, for bachelors, the Royal Caribbean ships each offer nightly entertainment (featuring Broadway-quality talent), plus multiple swimming pools, a casino, bars, dance clubs, a rock climbing wall, an ice skating rink, multiple dining rooms, a sports bar, shopping, a full spa and health club, plus dozens of other shipboard activities. In short, what you'll find aboard any Royal Caribbean ship is a floating city, that's dedicated to your enjoyment.

At each port of call, there are also dozens of optional land excursions you can participate in (for an additional fee) to make your trip truly memorable. One of the great things about a cruise ship is that you unpack once in your cabin and that's home for the duration of your voyage. There's even a cabin attendant on-hand to cater to all your needs.

During your voyage, you'll visit multiple ports of call and be able to spend the day exploring different places. All-you-can-eat gourmet meals and many ship-board activities are all included in the price of the cruise (drinks cost extra), plus each day, you'll be given a multi-page itinerary of every activity and event taking place on the ship. So, you can spend every minute of every day and night participating in various activities, or you can kick back and relax on the deck, perfect your suntan and do nothing. How you spend your time is entirely up to you.

When planning your budget, calculate the price per person for the voyage (Royal Caribbean prices its cabins on a per-person basis, based on double occupancy), then plan on spending at least several hundred dollars per person on extras, depending on what activities you want to participate in and how much shopping you plan to do. You're also expected to tip your cabin attendant, waiter and several other crew members you encounter on the ship, so that adds up to at least $100.00 per cabin.

Unlike a typical hotel room, space within the passenger cabins aboard cruise ships is limited, yet all offer bunk beds or various bed configurations (such as a single queen-size bed or two twin-size beds) to accommodate the passenger's needs. Space for storing luggage is also limited, typically to a small closet as well as under the bed, so it's important to pack conservatively. While much of your time will be spent wearing a bathing suit or casual attire, there are formal (black-tie optional) dining nights aboard many cruise ships.

When traveling, be sure you bring your passport and a major credit card. When traveling aboard a Royal Caribbean ship, a 'SeaPass' identification/charge card account will be set up for you, so you can charge all of your onboard purchases directly to a major credit card. At the time you book your cruise (or up to 10-days prior to your departure date), you can pre-book your land excursions after selecting them from a detailed catalog available from Royal Caribbean. Some of the land excursions fill up quickly, so advance reservations are recommended. You can, however, book your land excursions once you actually board the ship (usually up until the last minute) for each port of call.

Be sure to pack plenty of sunscreen, film for your camera, batteries and other essentials, including multiple bathing suits and comfortable walking shoes. All of this can be purchased on the ship (or on land when the ship docks), but you'll often pay a premium. You should also pre-purchase international pre-paid calling cards (that allow you to call from your overseas destinations to the U.S.) if you'll want to call home from any of the ports of call. Ship-to-shore calls can be made while aboard any Royal Caribbean ship, for example, for $7.95 per minute (or $.50 per minute to surf the Internet).

The experience you have aboard a cruise ship is entirely up to you, yet for most people, taking a cruise becomes an experience they'll remember for a lifetime.

Contacting The Popular Cruise Lines

Carnival Cruise Lines	(888) CARNIVAL	*www.carnivalcruiselines.com*
Celebrity Cruise Lines	(800) 722-5941	*www.celebrity.com*
Disney Cruise Lines	(800) 951-3532	*http://disneycruise.disney.go.com*
Holland America Cruise Lines	(877) 724-5425	*www.hollandamerica.com*
Norwegian Cruise Lines	(800) 327-7030	*www.ncl.com*
Princess Cruise Lines	(800) PRINCESS	*www.princess.com*
Radisson Seven Seas	(866) 592-5224	*www.rssc.com*
Royal Caribbean Cruise Lines	(800) 398-9819	*www.royalcaribbean.com*
Windstar Cruises	(800) 258-SAIL	*www.windstarcruises.com*

All-Inclusive Vacations Take The Stress Out of Travel

If you're looking to vacation someplace that's tropical, plus you want to leave the hassles of vacation planning behind, consider experiencing an all-inclusive vacation from Club Med (800-WEB-CLUB/*www.clubmed.com*) for example. Located in more than a dozen exotic destinations around the world, Club Med offers a complete vacation for a flat fee. Much like a cruise ship experience, all of your meals, activities and travel expenses are all pre-paid, so once you arrive at your destination, all you need to do is have fun.

Each of Club Med's properties offer a different selection of activities and overall vacation experience, so it's important to contact Club Med or your travel agent to determine which location offers the most of what you're looking for, based upon who your traveling with and what activities you'd like to experience. Club Med offers a very social environment, so whether you're traveling alone, with guy friends or someone you're romantically involved with, you'll have a chance to socialize with other guests during meals and during organized activities you choose to participate in.

Spas Aren't Just For Chicks

For many guys, a vacation is the perfect time to relax, unwind and rejuvenate their mind and body. If this is the type of vacation you're hoping to experience, consider staying at a resort with a full service spa. Phoenix and nearby Scottsdale, Arizona are quickly becoming premier spa destinations in America. With over a dozens world-class spas located in this area, it's the ideal place to relax and pamper yourself, plus play golf on some of the best courses in the country.

While women have enjoyed the spa experience for decades, only recently have guys begun enjoying and benefiting from what spas have to offer. These days, many of the best spas, including virtually all of them in the Arizona area, now cater to men, offering specialized treatments, massages and therapies that cater to what a guy needs.

If you thought that a massage, body wrap or even a facial were treatments only for women, you're wrong. Not only can the various spa treatments be enjoyed by men, but guys can really benefit from the treatments if they're looking to relax or recuperate after an intense workout or after participating in sports.

In addition to offering world class spas, many resorts in the Phoenix and Scottsdale area, for example, also offer many activities for guys, plus top-notch restaurants. These resorts are perfect for getting away with friends or for romantic get-aways.

Some of the most popular four and five-star rated resorts in the Phoenix area that offer full-service day spas, swimming pools, golf and a wide range of other activities (horseback riding, hiking, tennis and fine-dining opportunities) include:

- Pointe Hilton Squaw Peak Resort (800-876-4683/*www.pointehilton.com*)

- Pointe Hilton Tapatio Cliffs Resort (800-876-4683/*www. pointehilton.com*) featuring The Tocaloma Spa & Salon

- The Arizona Biltmore Resort & Spa (800-950-0086/*www. arionabiltmore.com*)—a resort visited by every American President since Herbert Hoover and some of Hollywood's biggest celebrities since 1929.

- The Boulders Resort (800-553-1717/*www.wyndhamluxury.com*) featuring The Golden Door Spa

- The Four Seasons Resort (480-515-5700)

- The Hyatt Regency Scottsdale (800-55-HYATT/*www.hyatt.com*)

- The Royal Palms (602-840-3610/*www.royalpalmsresortandspa.com*) featuring The Alvadora Spa

Even if you don't have the time or money to visit a world class spa in the Phoenix area, you can most likely find an upscale day spa in any U.S. city or area where you'll be traveling. Whether you enjoy a one hour massage, a more exotic body treatment (such as a mud wrap) or experience a full-day of treatments, a visit to a spa will help you relieve tension, relax and allow help the stresses of everyday life to literally melt away.

10

Getting Yourself Out of Trouble & Cleaning Up Your Act

Sometimes, things don't go as planned or as you'd like'em to. In other words, shit happens! While it's impossible to plan for every possible emergency, you should determine, in advance, how you'll handle problems when they arise. This chapter focuses on a handful of common emergencies and offers basic advice on how to deal with them. Of course, these are only basic guidelines. If you get caught up in a bad situation, seek help immediately.

Hopefully, you'll never need any of the information offered in this chapter. However, there's a good chance that you or someone close to you will need to know what's offered here sometime in your life, so be prepared!

As a general rule, if you experience any type of emergency that requires police, fire or medical assistance, dial: 9-1-1 from any telephone.

Life Isn't Always Fair: What To Do If...

There are certain bad things in life that virtually everyone of us will be forced to experience at some point. It's often not a matter of if, but when. Proper planning, in advance, can help you get through many of these negative experiences with the fewest possible long-term negative implications.

One way to protect yourself, for example, is to obtain the best possible heath, auto and homeowner's (renter's) insurance you can afford. Having insurance will help protect you financially when negative things happen in your life. It's an excellent idea to sit down with one or two independent insurance brokers at least once every few years to make sure you have adequate insurance protection based on your lifestyle, finances and needs.

In addition, it's important to keep all of your important personal information and legal documents in one place, preferably in a fire-proof lockbox, safe or bank safe deposit box. Documents (either originals or copies), such as your birth certificate, passport, car registration, a copy of your driver's license, insurance binders, bank account information, credit card information, a detailed list of your wallet's contents (including credit card numbers), etc., should all be kept in a safe place that's easily accessible. Make sure at least one trusted friend or relative knows where you keep this information.

Also, keep a list of important phone numbers in your wallet, within your PDA and with your important papers. These important phone numbers should include your:

- Accountant
- Auto Mechanic/Car Dealership
- Banks & Financial Institutions
- Chiropractor (if applicable)
- Contact Information for Close Relatives
- Credit Card Companies
- Dentist
- Doctor
- Eye Doctor
- Hospital/Emergency Room/24-Hours Walk-In Medical Center
- Insurance Broker(s)/Insurance Providers (Health Insurance, Auto Insurance, Life Insurance, Homeowner's/Renter's Insurance, Long-Term Disability Insurance, etc.)
- Lawyer
- Local Police, Fire Department and Ambulance
- Pharmacy (and all prescription information)
- Psychologist/Psychiatrist (if applicable)
- Veterinarian (if you have pets)

When disaster does strike, chances are you'll have a lot on your mind and won't be thinking clearly. By having all of your important documents and information in one place, you'll be better prepared to contact people you need to get in touch with immediately and deal with whatever emergency arises. It's also an excellent strategy to think carefully about how you'll handle various types of situations, to help you better prepare to deal with them.

The following are some common emergencies ordinary people, like you, sometimes have to deal with, as well as strategies for handling these situations in the best way possible. Under each category, you'll see what you can do to prepare for this type of emergency, and then learn what to do if the situation actually happens.

…You Get Arrested

Preparation: The obvious answer about how to avoid getting arrested is simply not to do anything illegal—or at least don't get caught. No matter what, it's always a good idea to carry in your wallet the name, address and phone number of your personal or family attorney (or someone you know who is a lawyer). This way, you know exactly whom to call if you get arrested, for whatever reason. On this same card or sheet of paper, list emergency contact information for one or two relatives.

Dealing with the Situation: If you do get arrested, be polite and friendly with the police officers, but do not answer their questions until after you have spoken with your lawyer. Simply provide the arresting officer with the name of your attorney. Do not try to talk your way out of the situation, negotiate with the officer or run from the situation. If you can not reach your own lawyer (or you don't have one), once you've been arrested, you are entitled to consult with an attorney that's provided for you.

Once a police officer arrests you, you will be read your Miranda Rights. At the conclusion of this, the officer will say something like, "Knowing your rights in this matter, are you willing to talk to me now?" Respond "No." Request to speak with a lawyer immediately. Do not discuss the situation with the police officer(s) without your lawyer present. If you are being arrested, the situation is serious and should be dealt with accordingly. Contrary to popular belief, aside from speaking with a lawyer, you are not entitled to make a telephone call once you've been arrested.

…Your Car Gets Towed

Preparation: To prevent this from happening, do not park illegally or on private property. Follow the parking signs and/or local parking regulations. Also, make sure you pay all parking violations in a timely manner. Having excessive out-standing parking tickets could result in your car getting towed.

Dealing with the Situation: If your car was towed from a privately owned park-ing lot, the name and contact information for the towing company should be posted on a nearby sign. You can also contact the local police or the owner of the lot where you were towed from. Determine who towed your vehicle and where it was towed to. If you were towed from a private lot, you will most likely have to pay towing charges in addition to storage fees and perhaps a processing fee to retrieve your vehicle. If your car was towed by the police, you will be responsible to pay whatever fines are applicable to retrieve your car.

Once your car gets towed, it's important to retrieve it as quickly as possible. Most towing companies charge a hefty storage fee for each 12 or 24 hour period they keep your vehicle. Be prepared to pay in cash (or with a money order), but insist on obtaining a receipt for your payment. In some instances, credit cards may be accepted, but personal or company checks are almost never accepted by towing companies.

In addition to payment, to retrieve your car, you'll almost always need to show a photo ID, a copy of your car's registration and perhaps proof of insurance. As soon as you retrieve your car, inspect it for any damage and make sure all of your personal property was left intact. Report any problems immediately to the towing company and the police.

...You Get Into A Car Accident

Preparation: There were an estimated 6,356,000 car accidents in the U.S. in 2000. There were about 3.2 million injuries and 41,821 people were killed in auto accidents in 2000. To avoid becoming a statistic, keep your car properly maintained, never drink and drive, avoid driving if you're exhausted, and at all times, pay attention when you're behind the wheel. Always keep a notepad, pen, first aid kit and flashlight in your vehicle.

Dealing with the Situation: If anyone has been injured in the car accident, call 9-1-1 and request medical assistance immediately. Be prepared to give your exact location and know the closest cross street or main road to where you are.

Assuming nobody is injured, consider contacting the police and having an officer complete an accident report while everyone is still on the scene. If you're involved in a minor accident, exchange information with the other driver. Also, be sure to get the names, phone numbers and addresses of any other passengers and witnesses in the area, even if there's no apparent damage to either vehicle. The following websites offers free basic advice for people involved in a car accident:

- FreeAdvice.com—*http://accident-law.freeadvice.com/auto*
- State Farm Insurance—*www.statefarm.com/claims/autoacc.htm*
- Maine Bar Association—*www.mainbar.org/documents/Accidents.pdf*

When exchanging information with the other driver and gathering information about the accident, you'll want to obtain the following:

- The driver's name, address, phone number and driver's license number
- The make, model, color and year of the vehicle(s) involved in the accident
- The license plate number of each vehicle involved in the accident
- The driver's auto insurance provider and policy number
- If you have a camera, take pictures of the vehicles and the accident scene
- Obtain contact information from all witnesses to the accident
- Immediately write down all of the details relating to the accident, including the location (exact address), time, date, and the circumstances that caused the accident. You don't want to forget anything.
- If there's a police officer on the scene, get his/her name, badge number and contact information. Also, ask if there's a number associated with the accident report. No matter what, be sure to file an accident report with the police after the accident.
- Even if you were at fault, never admit fault after the accident until after you've spoken with your insurance company and your lawyer.
- Contact your auto insurance company at your earliest convenience. (The sooner, the better.)
- Never leave the scene of an accident without exchanging information with the other drivers and/or pedestrians involved.
- Consider contacting your lawyer after the accident, especially if there was damage to your vehicle or if you were injured.

…You Lock Your Keys In The Car (or Lose Your Keys) or It Breaks Down

Preparation: It's an excellent strategy to keep an extra copy of your important keys (home and car keys, for example) at home, at work and/or with a friend.

Dealing with the Situation: If you lock your keys in your vehicle, call AAA (800-AAA-HELP) or any emergency road side service provider you're a member of. You can also call the local police department or any local locksmith. If your vehicle is equipped with OnStar (*www.onstar.com*), for example, call the toll-free number provided by OnStar or your car dealer. If you have a child or pet locked in the vehicle (with no windows open, call the police immediately and explain the situation. Do not, however, leave the child unattended. Ask to borrow a cell phone, if necessary.

If your car breaks down, light one or two emergency flares, turn on your vehicle's hazard lights, contact an emergency road side service provider (such as AAA) and/or call the police. If the car is stuck along a major road, try moving the vehicle to the side of the road, but do not wait for help inside the vehicle. Move yourself to someplace safe while you wait for help to arrive. To show your car is broken down, you may want to raise the hood of your vehicle in addition to turning on the hazard lights. Also, depending on the situation, it's often a good idea to wait for professional help to arrive as opposed to seeking the help of a passerby. If someone volunteers their services, simply ask them to call the police on your behalf if you haven't already done so.

…You Get Fired From Your Job

Preparation: There are many reasons why people lose their job. This can't always be prevented. Of course, while on the job, you should follow your company's procedures and rules and not do anything illegal. It's also an excellent idea to have enough money in saving to support you for at least two to three months, assuming you lose your job and can't get a new one right away. Don't count on unemployment benefits to cover all of your ongoing expenses.

Dealing with the Situation: Getting fired from a job can be an emotional experience, plus one that causes a tremendous amount of stress in your life. If you get fired, downsized or dismissed from your job, for whatever reason, first determine what severance pay and/or unemployment benefits you're entitled to and when they kick in. Next, apply for those benefits and start figuring out your personal financial situation.

Immediately start updating your resume and begin looking for new job opportunities. Depending on the type of job you're looking to fill and the strength of the overall economy, you may find yourself unemployed for a few weeks, several months or even up to a year. If money is tight, consider contacting and working with a temporary employment agency to bring in an income while you're looking for full-time work. It may also become necessary to take on some other type of job, just to pay the bills, while you're looking for the perfect employment situation.

No matter why you've lost your job, it's important to begin taking steps to rectify the situation immediately. Sure, you may feel angry or depressed, but it's important to put aside these emotions and take positive steps toward finding and landing a new job quickly. To help cover any long gaps in your employment history, consider signing up for one or more night classes. This way, you can tell future potential employers that you chose to expand your education, which is the reason for a two, three or six month gap from when you initially lost your job.

No matter how you feel about the employer that's let you go, always act professionally. Do not attempt to steal any of the company's equipment or records as you leave for the final time. Also, do not threaten any superiors or coworkers. If possible, try to obtain a written letter of recommendation from a superior prior to leaving. For strategies for finding and landing a new job, see Chapter 3.

...You Get Into A Fight with Your Girlfriend

Preparation: Be kind, respectful and considerate. Don't cheat! Assume that as the guy, you're never right and your opinion means nothing. That being said (in jest, of course), it's important to develop an open and honest relationship with your significant other. Being able to discuss your thoughts and feelings, and allowing your girlfriend to do the same, will help keep the relationship healthy. Try to discuss your disagreements instead of allowing them to fester until the situation blows up into an all-out argument.

Dealing with the Situation: When people are angry at each other, they tend to say hurtful things, which causes the disagreement to escalate. Instead of allowing this to happen, try to have a mature and honest conversation with your girlfriend when a disagreement arises. If the situation is very serious, seek out help from a third party, such as a professional counselor, and participate in couples counseling. You may be able to reach an amicable solution simply by sitting down once with someone who can facilitate better communication between you and your girlfriend. Remember, the key to any successful relationship is compromise, listening to the other person and respecting their thoughts, opinions and feelings.

If you're in the wrong and you know it, be man enough to admit your fault(s) and apologize. Adding flowers, jewelry or expensive chocolates to your apology often works well, but don't try to buy off your girlfriend's affection. The apology gift should include a heartfelt apology.

Need flowers in a pinch? You can drop into any local florist, or call 1-(800) FLOWERS (*www.1800flowers.com*) to have flowers, a plant or a gift delivered to your girlfriend. Same day and next day delivery is often available. To have an adorable, custom-created teddy bear delivered, contact The Vermont Teddy Bear Company (800-829-BEAR/*www.vermontteddybear.com*). Be sure to check out the company's 15-inch "I'm Sorry" or "I Love You" bears.

...You're Running Out of Money

Preparation: Set aside money from your weekly paycheck and deposit it into a savings account. Ideally, you want to have enough money in savings to support yourself for up to three months and/or cover emergency expenses. If you're not earning enough money to cover all of your expenses, it's important to immediately take control of your spending and establish a budget for yourself. Don't rely on credit cards to continue living beyond your financial means. Chapter 4 deals with managing your money.

Dealing with the Situation: Virtually everyone goes through times when money is tight. The first thing to do is carefully evaluate your spending habits and eliminate all excessive or unnecessary spending. If you have large balances on high interest credit cards, try to transfer those balances to cards with lower interest rates and pay off the outstanding balances as quickly as possible.

Many people have trouble getting their finances under control. If you're one of these people, sit down with a financial advisor or accountant and get help organizing your finances, analyzing your spending and creating a budget. You're always better off borrowing money from friends or relatives (as long as you plan on paying it back promptly) then relying on high interest credit cards, which will increase your financial debt and cause more problems in the long-run.

It's important to live within your means. This requires you to understand how much money you earn, how much you need to cover your living expenses and how to properly manage all aspects of your finances. No matter how bad the situation is, chances are it can be fixed over time as long as you don't ignore the situation. Once you identify the causes of your financial woes, work with a professional to develop a plan to fix the situation and always learn from your mistakes.

The initial investment you spend hiring a financial advisor or accountant to help you fix your financial situation and get the most out of the money you have available will most likely save you hundreds, if not thousands of dollars in the future.

...You Get Robbed or Mugged

Preparation: If you're in an unsafe area, avoid walking alone at night or putting yourself in situations where you could become an easy target for criminals.

Dealing with the Situation: Getting robbed is a scary experience. Obviously, you want to protect yourself and your own safety. The best way to do this is to give the robber what they want (your wallet, etc.). As you interact with the robber, try to remember as much as you can about them, such as their looks, what they're wearing, how they sounded, etc. Be sure to contact the police as soon as possible after the incident. If your wallet is stolen, you'll also want to contact the various credit card companies (and the financial institutions that provided your debit cards) and report the theft. Request a replacement replacement driver's license from The Department of Motor Vehicles, and contact your home owner's insurance company to file a claim if items of significant value were stolen. One of your first steps after being robbed should be to contact the local police and file a report.

...You Lose Your Wallet

Preparation: Aside from being careful, there's not too much you can do to avoid losing your wallet or getting it stolen. It's never a good idea to carry around too much cash. Plus, you want to keep a list of your wallet's contents, including all of your credit cards (account numbers and customer service phone numbers), in a safe place. Avoid carrying your Social Security card or anything with your Social Security Number within your wallet.

Dealing with the Situation: If you lose your wallet, immediately determine what credit card(s) and/or debit card(s) you were carrying and contact those financial institutions immediately. Most credit card companies can send you replacement credit cards within a few days. If you were carrying any blank checks in your wallet, call you bank and instruct them to cancel those checks. Finally, call the Department of Motor Vehicles and obtain a replacement driver's license (if the original was in your wallet). As for other important documents, such as insurance cards and membership cards, etc., call the appropriate organizations to obtain replacements at quickly as possible.

It's important to protect yourself financially if you lose your wallet, however, you also want to protect your identity. For several months after you lose your wallet, pay careful attention to your credit card statements and request copies of your credit reports to make sure you don't become a victim of identity theft. If you lose your wallet and your keys simultaneously, it's a good idea to have the locks changed at your home to insure you don't get any unexpected visitors. Also, be sure to file a report with the local police department, if you believe your wallet was stolen.

...You Have A Medical Emergency

Preparation: Keep taking care of yourself, eating right and exercising.

Dealing with the Situation: If you experience a medical emergency, go directly to a hospital or dial 9-1-1. If the situation isn't life threatening, call your doctor or visit a walk-in medical center. If you have medical/health insurance, make sure you bring your membership card when you seek our medical treatment. Chances are, your health insurance provider offers a toll-free member services number you can call for a doctor referral or to discuss your coverage.

...You Get Caught In A Natural Disaster or Terrorist Attack

Preparation: No matter where you live, it's always good to be prepared for a natural disaster or unexpected terrorist attack. The best way to do this is to have a collection of non-perishable food, water and supplies on-hand and ready to use. Also, stock up on batteries, flashlights, and have a portable (battery or solar powered) TV and/or radio available to you.

Dealing with the Situation: If disaster strikes, listen carefully to news reports on the radio or television and follow the advice and direction or police, fire or military personnel. You should also read documents prepared by The Federal Emergency Management Agency and The U.S. Department of Homeland Security about how to prepare for unexpected emergencies.

The following are informative resources for learning how to prepare yourself and for gathering the supplies you may need in case of an emergency. From these websites, you'll also find detailed lists of useful items and supplies, in addition to the non-perishable food and water you should have on-hand at home and/or in your car (and stored in a waterproof container):

- Code Red Survival Kits—(888) 267-1872/*www.coderedkits.com*

- Emergency Packs & Survival Kits—*www.firstaidsurvivalkits.com*

- Federal Emergency Management Agency (FEMA)—*www.fema.gov/rrr/emprep.shtm*

- Leatherman Pocket Tools—(800) 847-8665/*www.leatherman.com*

- Quake Care, Inc.—*www.quakekare.com*

- U.S. Dept. of Homeland Security—*www.ready.gov/make_a_kit.html*

Breaking Your Bad Habits

For a wide range of reasons, people become addicted to substances like tobacco, alcohol and various types of drugs. Even a minor addiction can have a major impact on your health, finances and overall well-being.

Breaking an addiction can be difficult. While there are plenty of resources to help you do this alone, it's always easier to surround yourself with people who will support your efforts, including trained professionals.

This section will help you find the resources and help you need to break unwanted addictions and deal with other common problems that many people face, like depression and stress.

Stop Smoking: Breaking Your Nicotine Addiction

Out of the millions of people around the world who smoke, research shows that a huge percentage of those people would like to quit. Breaking a nicotine addiction can be extremely difficult, but it's not impossible! There are many programs you can participate in, therapies that you can utilize and both prescription and non-prescription drugs that can help. The first step, however, is to make the decision for yourself that you truly want to quit. Next, choose a quitting method, based on your research (and advice from medical professionals) that will work best for you.

Whether you decide to quit cold turkey, get hypnotized, use the patch or chew nicotine replacement gum, it's important to learn all about the quitting method you choose, including what the various potential side effects are.

Extensive research has shown that when you're ready to quit, following these five steps will make the process easier:

Step 1—Get ready. Start by setting a date to quit, get rid of your ashtrays and other smoking paraphernalia, determine why past quitting attempts have failed and stay away from other smokers (while they're smoking.)

Step 2—Get support. Seek out the help of friends, family and coworkers. Also, obtain assistance from a health care provider (such as a doctor, nurse, pharmacist, psychologist, or smoking counselor.)

Step 3—Learn new skills and behaviors. Whenever you would have smoked a cigarette in the past, adopt a new, more positive behavior. Also, develop methods for dealing with the stress associated with breaking a nicotine habit.

Step 4—Get medication and use it correctly. There are a handful of medications you can use to help you quit. With the help of your doctor, pick one that's best for you, then carefully follow the directions for using it.

Step 5—Be prepared for a relapse. You might not be successful at breaking your addiction right away. Be prepared to face challenges and setbacks, but stick to your plan.

Step 6—Take full advantage of the free resources available to you. In addition to the resources listed here, consider joining some type of support group (one that meets in person or online) so you can share your experiences with others and benefit from that added support. The more time and effort you invest in your quitting efforts, the greater your chances of success will be.

Nicotine Replacement Therapy

WebMD (*www.WebMD.com*) offers an extensive amount of information for people looking to quit smoking. One popular method is to use over-the-counter drugs, in the form of nicotine gum, patches, nasal spray or an inhaler. WebMD reports that each form of nicotine replacement is a little different. For more detailed information about these treatments, point your web browser to: *http://my.webmd.com/content/healthwise/124/30767*. You'll discover the pros and cons of using the various nicotine replacement treatments.

According to WebMD, "Nicotine gum is a nicotine-containing compound (nicotine polacrilex) that has a texture similar to chewing gum. It contains 2 mg or 4 mg of nicotine per piece. Nicotine gum is designed to release nicotine slowly into the mouth when chewed and then placed between the cheek and gum. Nicotine gum (Nicorette) is available without a prescription.

"A nicotine patch looks like an oversized adhesive bandage. The outer part of the patch sticks to your skin, while the inner portion presses against and slowly releases nicotine into your skin. Nicotine patches are available with and without a prescription."

Nicotine patches are available as:

- Nicoderm CQ (24-hour patch, 7 mg, 14 mg, or 21 mg of nicotine per patch).

- Nicotrol (16-hour patch, 15 mg of nicotine per patch).

- Habitrol (24-hour patch, 7 mg, 14 mg, or 21 mg of nicotine per patch; requires a prescription in the United States and some other countries).

WebMD also reports that, "Nicotine nasal spray is used like any nasal spray, by squirting mist into each nostril. Nicotine nasal spray must be used carefully because the nicotine it delivers can be harmful if used too often. Nicotine nasal spray (Nicotrol NS) is available without a prescription. Nicotrol NS contains 0.5 mg of nicotine per spray. The total dose is 1 mg when sprayed in both nostrils.

"A nicotine inhaler looks very much like a cigarette. It holds a cartridge containing nicotine, and it delivers a puff of nicotine vapor (in a measured dose) into your mouth and throat area, where the nicotine is absorbed. A nicotine inhaler (Nicotrol Inhaler) is available by prescription only. It contains 10 mg of nicotine per cartridge."

Using a drug isn't necessarily the best or easiest way to quit smoking, nor is it suitable for everyone. Finding the best way to quit for you is a personal decision.

It should be made, however, with the help of a medical professional. The following are some additional resources and organization you can contact to help you on your quest to quit smoking:

QuitNet—*www.quitnet.com*

This service has a simple mission—to help people worldwide quit using tobacco. According to QuitNet, "In the U.S., 70 percent of all adult smokers say they want to quit smoking and half will try each year. Operational since 1995, Quit-Net today is host to the world's largest community of smokers and ex-smokers helping each other quit."

U.S. Public Health Service—*www.surgeongeneral.gov/tobacco/ consquits.htm*

According to this free service, there are many reasons to consider breaking your smoking addiction, such as: You will live longer and live better; quitting will lower your chance of having a heart attack, stroke, or cancer; if you are pregnant, quitting smoking will improve your chances of having a healthy baby; the people you live with, especially your children, will be healthier; and you will have extra money to spend on things other than cigarettes.

To help in your quitting efforts, The U.S. Food and Drug Administration (FDA) has approved five medications to help you quit smoking:

- Bupropion SR—Available by prescription.
- Nicotine gum—Available over-the-counter.
- Nicotine inhaler—Available by prescription.
- Nicotine nasal spray—Available by prescription.
- Nicotine patch—Available by prescription and over-the-counter.

Research shows that any of these medications will more or less double your chances of quitting and quitting for good. Before using any type of drug to help you break your nicotine habit, it's important to speak with your health care provider and obtain advice. Also, carefully read all of the information on and within the packaging for the product or medication(s) you use.

Office of the Surgeon General—*www.surgeongeneral.gov/tobacco*

Statistics from the Centers for Disease Control and Prevention show that smoking related diseases claim more than 400,000 lives annually and cost the United States tens of billions of dollars in medical expenses and lost productivity. To help people quit, the Surgeon General's website offers a vast amount of free information and resources.

<u>Additional Resources</u>

American Heart Association
7272 Greenville Avenue
Dallas, TX 75231
(800) AHA-USA1 (242-8721)

American Cancer Society
1599 Clifton Road, NE
Atlanta, GA 30329
(404) 320-3333
www.cancer.org

American Lung Association
1740 Broadway, 14th Floor
New York, NY 10019
(212) 315-8700
www.lungusa.org

National Cancer Institute
Bethesda, MD 20892
(800) 4-CANCER (422-6237)

Office of Smoking and Health
Centers for Disease Control and Prevention
800-CDC-1311
www.cdc.gov/tobacco

Quit Drinking: Dealing with Alcoholism

People drink alcohol for many reasons. For most people, however, drinking small amounts of alcohol in social situations is commonplace and safe (if done responsibly). There are, however, people who tend to drink too much, too often. Some of these people become alcoholics, which means they become dependant on alcohol.

Drug Rehabs (866-762-3712/*www.drug-rehabs.com*) is a free online-based service dedicated to the treatment of drug addictions. The organization provides information and treatment resources for individuals suffering all types of addictions, including alcohol. Its website reports that alcoholism, also known as 'alcohol dependence,' is a disease that includes four symptoms:

1.   Craving: A strong need, or compulsion, to drink.

2.   Loss of control: The inability to limit one's drinking on any given occasion.

3.   Physical dependence: Withdrawal symptoms, such as nausea, sweating, shakiness, and anxiety, occur when alcohol use is stopped after a period of heavy drinking.

4.   Tolerance: The need to drink greater amounts of alcohol in order to "get high."

"Alcoholics are in the grip of a powerful craving, or uncontrollable need, for alcohol that overrides their ability to stop drinking. This need can be as strong as the need for food or water. Although some people are able to recover from alcoholism without help, the majority of alcoholics need assistance. With treatment and support, many individuals are able to stop drinking and rebuild their lives," reports The Drug Rehabs website. "Alcohol abuse differs from alcoholism in that it does not include an extremely strong craving for alcohol, loss of control over drinking, or physical dependence."

If you're having trouble controlling your alcohol consumption, The Drug Rehabs website recommends that you determine if you have any of the following symptoms or engage in any of these negative behaviors that might require treatment:

•   Failure to fulfill major work, school, or home responsibilities

•   You drink in situations that are physically dangerous, such as while driving a car or operating machinery

•   You've recently experienced recurring alcohol-related legal problems, such as being arrested for driving under the influence of alcohol or for physically hurting someone while drunk

- You've continued drinking, despite having ongoing relationship problems that are caused or worsened by the drinking

To determine if you have an alcohol abuse problem, also ask yourself these four questions.

1. Have you ever felt you should cut down on your drinking?

2. Have people annoyed you by criticizing your drinking?

3. Have you ever felt bad or guilty about your drinking?

4. Have you ever had a drink first thing in the morning (as an "eye opener") to steady your nerves or get rid of a hangover?

According to the Drug Rehabs website, "One 'yes' answer suggests a possible alcohol problem. If you answered 'yes' to more than one question, it is highly likely that a problem exists. In either case, it is important that you see your doctor or other health care provider right away to discuss your answers to these questions. He or she can help you determine whether you have a drinking problem and, if so, recommend the best course of action.

Even if you answered 'no' to all of the above questions, if you encounter drinking-related problems that impact your job, relationships, health, or the law, you should seek professional help. The effects of alcohol abuse can be extremely serious—even fatal—both to you and to others."

Alcoholics Anonymous—*www.aa.org*

One of the best-known worldwide organizations that's dedicated to helping people deal with their alcohol consumption and addiction problems is Alcoholics Anonymous, which, according to the organization, is a fellowship of men and women who share their experience, strength and hope with each other that they may solve their common problem and help others to recover from alcoholism.

"The only requirement for membership is a desire to stop drinking. There are no dues or fees for AA membership; we are self-supporting through our own contributions. AA is not allied with any sect, denomination, politics, organization or institution; does not wish to engage in any controversy, neither endorses nor opposes any causes. Our primary purpose is to stay sober and help other alcoholics to achieve sobriety," reports the organization.

Local chapters of Alcoholics Anonymous can be found across America and throughout the world. To seek out help or more information, look for "Alcoholics Anonymous" in any telephone directory. In most urban areas, a Central A.A.

office, staffed mainly by volunteers, will be happy to answer your questions and/ or put you in touch with those who can. You can write to: A.A. World Services, Inc., P.O. Box 459, New York, NY 10163 or call (212) 870-3400. A directory of all AA chapters worldwide can be found on the organization's website.

Break A Drug Addiction

You've seen the public services announcements on television—you already know drugs are bad…very bad. Sure, you may think it's fun and enjoyable to "experiment" with various illegal substances, however, for a variety of reasons this is dangerous and possibly deadly.

Once you start experimenting with drugs, it becomes all too easy to become addicted. Your life can and will quickly spin out of control. While it's never a good idea to use any type of recreational drugs, especially illegal ones, if you do find yourself in over your head, it's vitally important that you seek help immediately. Do not try to deal with the addiction yourself. Get in contact with any medical professional, such as your doctor. You can also contact any hospital for assistance. How you break your addiction will depend on what you're addicted to. Remember, even casual drug use can put you at risk.

For more information or to seek out help, contact:

- The National Alcohol & Drug Abuse Hotline—(800) 252-6465
- The Cocaine Helpline—(800) 262-2463.
- Narcotics Anonymous—*www.na.org*
- National Institute on Drug Abuse—*www.nida.nih.gov*

Dealing with Depression, Stress & Suicide

Sure, everybody feels sad or blue now and then. But, if you're sad most of the time, and it's causing you problems that impact one or more aspects of your life, the underlying problem could be depression.

Sometimes people get seriously depressed when experiencing something like a divorce, major financial problems, someone you love dying, a messed up home life, or after breaking up with girlfriend. In some instances, depression just happens.

If you're experiencing long-term depression, stress or anxiety for any reason, the good news is that you can get treatment and feel better soon. Clinical depression is a serious illness that can affect anybody. It can affect your thoughts, feelings, behavior, and overall health.

Most people with depression can be helped with treatment. The majority of depressed people, however, never get the help they need. When depression isn't treated, it can get worse, last longer, and prevent you from getting the most out of this important time in your life. Over 60 percent of all people who die by suicide suffer from major depression. If one includes alcoholics who are depressed, this figure rises to over 75 percent.

There are a number of ways to determine if you're truly depressed or if the stress and anxiety you're often experiencing needs to be treated. It's important to understand, there are two kinds of depressive illness: *major depression* and *manic-depression* or *bipolar disorder* (when feeling down and depressed alternates with being speeded-up and sometimes reckless.)

You should definitely get evaluated by a professional if you've had five or more of the following symptoms for more than two weeks, or if any of these symptoms cause such a big change that you can't keep up your usual routine:

Symptoms of Depression

- You feel sad or cry a lot and it doesn't go away.

- You feel guilty for no reason; you feel like you're no good; you've lost your confidence.

- Life seems meaningless or like nothing good is ever going to happen again. You have a negative attitude a lot of the time, or it seems like you have no feelings.

- You don't feel like doing a lot of the things you used to like—like music, sports, being with friends, going out—and you want to be left alone most of the time.

- It's hard to make up your mind. You forget lots of things, and it's hard to concentrate.

- You get irritated often. Little things make you lose your temper; you overreact.

- Your sleep pattern changes; you start sleeping a lot more or you have trouble falling asleep at night. Or you wake up really early most mornings and can't get back to sleep.

- Your eating pattern changes; you've lost your appetite or you eat a lot more.

- You feel restless and tired most of the time.

- You think about death, or feel like you're dying, or have thoughts about committing suicide.

Symptoms of Manic-Depression

- You're rebellious or irritable and can't get along at home or school, or with your friends.

- You feel high as a kite…like you're "on top of the world."

- You get unreal ideas about the great things you can do…things that you really can't do.

- Thoughts go racing through your head, you jump from one subject to another, and you talk a lot.

- You're a non-stop party, constantly running around.

- You do too many wild or risky things: with driving, with spending money, with sex, etc.

- You're so "up" that you don't need much sleep.

Having depression or experiencing extreme stress or anxiety doesn't mean that you're a weak person or a failure. Most people with depression can be helped with psychotherapy, medicine, or both together. Short-term psychotherapy typically means talking about feelings with a trained professional who can help you change the relationships, thoughts, or behaviors that contribute to depression. Medications have been developed that effectively treats depression that is severe or disabling. Antidepressant medications are not "uppers" and are not addictive. Treatment can help most depressed people start to feel better in just a few weeks.

Even if you don't have health insurance, there are many organizations and clinics that offer free treatment to those who can't afford it. So, if you're feeling overwhelmed by severe stress, anxiety or depression, seek out help. More than 29,000 people in the United States die by suicide every year. It is this country's 11th leading cause of death, and is often characterized as a response to a single event or set of circumstances. No matter why you may be feeling suicidal, there is help available to you!

Suicide Prevention Hotlines & Resources

The National Hopeline Network
(800) SUICIDE/(800) 784-2433
(This free service provides access to trained telephone counselors, 24 hours a day, 7 days a week.)

American Foundation for Suicide Prevention
(888) 333-AFSP/(212) 363-3500
www.afsp.org

Suicide Awareness Voices of Education
Emergency number: (800) 784-2433
www.save.org

Girls & Boys Town National Hotline
(800) 448-3000
www.girlsandboystown.org
(For teenagers, this free service provides access to trained telephone counselors, 24 hours a day, 7 days a week.)

The Trevor HelpLine
(800) 850-8078

Other Types of Free Resources

- AIDS Hotline—(800) 342-AIDS

- American Red Cross—*www.redcross.org* (Consult your local telephone book for the American Red Cross chapter in your area.)

- Domestic Abuse Hotline—(800) 799-SAFE

- Gay & Lesbian National Hotline—(888) 843-4564

- Grief Recovery Helpline—(800) 445-4808

- Mothers Against Drunk Driving—(800) 633-6233

- National Life Center Hotline/Pregnancy Hotline—(800) 848-5683

- National Runaway Switchboard—(800) 621-4000/*www.nrscrisisline.org*

- Parents, Families & Friends of Lesbians & Gays (PFLAG)—(202) 467-8180/ *www.pflag.org*

- Poison Control Center—(800) 222-1222/*www.calpoison.org*

- Therapist Referral Service—(800) THERAPIST/*www.1-800-therapist.com*

- Victims of Crime Resource Center—(800) 627-6872

Final Thought...

It's important to remember that everyone experiences hardships or problems at various points in their lives, so you're not alone in whatever you happen to be dealing with. If you ever feel that a situation s getting out of hand, seek out the help or guidance you need to regain and then maintain control over your life. It's okay to ask for hekp when you need it!

Being a bachelor can be fun, but with life comes responsibilities and pressure that you'll need to deal with effectively.

11

This Bachelor Thing Isn't Forever...

◆

What's Next?

Many guys love the bachelor life and it's something they'll look back on fondly for the rest of their lives. However, there comes a time in almost everyone's life when they want to settle down, get married and perhaps start a family. When this happens, a guy experiences major transitions in all aspects of his life.

After you've experienced the single's dating scene, hopefully you'll find the woman of your dreams and eventually want to get married. When and if you get married and to whom are some of the biggest, yet exciting decisions you'll ever have to make. After all, when you get hitched, it's supposed to be with the person you'd like to spend the rest of your life with—your best friend, lover and partner, all wrapped up into one person.

Are You Ready For Marriage?

In America, you need to be 21-years-old to drink alcohol, 18-years-old to vote, and somewhere between 16 and 18-years-old to obtain your driver's license. These are all important milestones is someone's life, however, none compare to the significance of committing yourself to someone else by getting married. With a parent's permission, you can get married in America at a young age (depending on the state), yet deciding to get hitched is one of the most important decisions you'll make in your lifetime.

The decision to get married is never something you should rush into. This should be a decision you make based on several important criteria, the most important of which is the love you have for the other person. You must also decide if you are emotionally mature and responsible enough to be married. This level of maturity and responsibility doesn't automatically come to people at a certain age, so it's a realization you'll need to reach on your own, whether you're 18, 28 or 48.

Some people are totally ready to marry their high school sweetheart when they graduate at age 18, then go on to lead happy, healthy and prosperous lives together. Others, however, aren't emotionally ready to make the necessary commitment to another person until much later in life. These days, people get married for the first time in their late-teens, twenties, thirties and even their forties. There are no rules to follow when it comes to deciding whether or not you're ready to tie the knot and commit your life to someone else.

Once you think you've met the person you'd like to marry, search within yourself to determine if you're truly ready to give up bachelorhood, commit yourself to that one other individual romantically, take on the financial responsibilities of being a married couple, and devote the rest of your life to loving and caring for this other person. Furthermore, look to the future. Determine, without a doubt, that this is the person you'd potentially like to raise a family with; care for in sickness and in health; vacation with; come home to each and every night; share your meals with and be intimate with.

The person you ultimately marry should be your best friend; confidant; someone you trust implicitly; someone you can communicate openly with about anything; someone you're physically attracted to; and someone you truly love, respect and cherish. Most importantly, your girlfriend should feel exactly the same way about you! You two should have a love for each other that's strong today, but that will only grow stronger in the months and years to come, no matter what challenges the two of you face in the future (and there will be many challenges).

In today's world, simply loving someone unfortunately isn't enough of a reason to get married. It's perhaps the most important reason, but you two must also have the maturity, sense of responsibility and overall stability in your lives to understand that developing a happy and healthy married relationship will often take hard work, require compromises and demand that you both maintain an undying support for each other—no matter what.

Prior to popping the question and getting engaged, make sure you've thought through all of the ramifications of getting married and that in your heart you are 100 percent prepared for the added responsibilities taking this major step in your life entails. This is a decision you absolutely must be totally sure about *before* proceeding.

You probably already know that the divorce rate in America is ridiculously high. Don't enter into a marriage with the mindset that if this doesn't work out, you'll simply get a divorce and/or annulment, then move on with your life. This isn't the movies, and breaking apart a marriage is never easy, either emotionally or financially. Instead, enter into this relationship with the commitment and expectation that your marriage will last for the rest of your lives and will be a true partnership in every sense of the word.

Obviously, the decision to get married isn't one that should be made lightly. Even if you've found the absolute perfect mate, there will probably be some lingering doubts in your mind due to the enormity of the commitment you're about to make. It's always a good idea to seek out the advice and guidance of people you love and trust, such as relatives, friends, or even a psychiatrist, relationship counselor or a religious leader (your priest, rabbi, etc.). Ultimately, however, the decision about whom you'll marry and when you'll get married should be entirely up to you (and your girlfriend).

Everyone dreams of finding their soul mate early in life and then living out a storybook romance. While this is something you should certainly strive for, you must also consider reality. Even if you're head-over-heels in love with your girlfriend, prior to popping the question and getting engaged, make sure you'll be compatible in every aspect of your life, or at the very least, you will both be willing to make serious compromises to insure your well-being and stability as a married couple.

As you decide whether or not you've already met your perfect partner, think about how she'll fit into each area of your life—now and in the future—and how you'll fit into her already established life. Consider what changes you and she will be forced to make in your lives, what compromises will be required, and how you'll both adapt to the changes required. After all, once you're engaged and ultimately married, every aspect of your lives will be impacted.

Also, consider your own long-term personal, professional and financial goals. Realistically, how will getting married impact your ability to achieve these goals in the future? What additional challenges will you face? How will your timeline for achieving your goals be altered upon getting married?

After considering how married life will impact your ability to achieve your goals, take a look at every major area of your life and determine the impact of getting engaged and ultimately married with have.

Area of Your Life	Things To Consider
Career	• Does the career path you are following mesh with your girlfriend's career path? What about in the future? Consider salary, work schedule, potential promotions, etc. • Will one of you have to relocate in the future? How will a potential relocation impact the other person's career? • Will one or both of you continue working once you're married? • When you're ready to have kids, will your wife be able to take the necessary time off? What about your work schedule? • Does your girlfriend understand your need to work long hours in order to earn a specific promotion or achieve a career goal? Do you understand her career objectives?
Family Situation	• Do you get along with your girlfriend's parents and relatives? Does she get along with your family members? • How might these relationships impact your marriage, in terms of having to deal with in-laws, for example? • Does your girlfriend want to remain living close to her parents? Do you want to live close to your parents? Will this impact the geographic area you'll be able to live in the future? • How involved will you and your wife need to be as your respective parents retire and/or need to be cared for in their old age? • What are your desires in terms of expanding your own family? Do you want kids? How many? When? Are your desires compatible with your girlfriend's desires in terms of expanding your family?

Area of Your Life	Things To Consider
Friends	• Do you get along with your girlfriend's circle of friends? Does she get along with your friends?
	• Will your respective circles of friends be able to mix in the future? For example, if you host a dinner party, will you both be able to invite your respective friends and know everyone will get along?
Future Goals	• Do you and your girlfriend have compatible long-term personal, professional and financial goals and aspirations?
	• What compromises might you and she have to make? Are you willing to live with these compromises?
Living Habits and Current Living Situation	• How compatible will you and your girlfriend be when you start living together as a couple?
	• Are you willing to make compromises in terms of your personal habits and routine. For example, will you routinely put the toilet seat down when you're done, use a glass instead of drinking directly out of the milk carton, and be willing to share the remote control when you're watching television together?
	• If your girlfriend will be moving in with you (or vice versa), are you willing to re-arrange your belongings and/or totally redecorate? Will you discard some of your stuff to make room for her?

Area of Your Life	Things To Consider
Personal "Baggage"	Everyone has personal baggage or obstacles they've overcome, challenges they've faced and personal insecurities and phobias. For example, someone's personal baggage might include: a bad relationship with their parents; bad experiences in previous relationships or marriages; a former addiction to drugs, smoking or alcohol; having survived some type of physical or sexual abuse; dealing with an eating disorder; living with a sexually transmitted disease; living with a long-term physical or mental illness, etc. Whatever personal baggage you are bringing into the relationship, is your girlfriend willing to accept it and help you overcome and/or deal with it? What about the personal baggage she's bringing into the relationship? Have you and your girlfriend discussed the baggage you're each bringing into the relationship?
Personality, Morals and Values	Everyone has their own personality, morals and values. Chances are, if you're considering popping the question, you already know that you and your girlfriend are compatible. Consider the more serious issues, however, and determine if your differences could potentially grow and ultimately cause problems in your future relationship.
Political Association	It's been said that when you're trying to get along with someone, never discuss politics or religion. Well, since you're contemplating marriage, it's important that you and your girlfriend discuss these issues and bring any disagreements out into the open. While your political beliefs probably won't have a tremendous impact on your relationship, it's important to determine to what extent you agree or disagree on political issues.

Area of Your Life	Things To Consider
Religious Beliefs	• Depending on how religious or spiritual someone is, those beliefs can have a tremendous impact on their lives and relationships. Do you and your girlfriend have the same religious or spiritual beliefs or follow the same religious practices?
	• If you come from different religions, what will you practice as a couple in your home?
	• What religion will you teach to your children?
	• Do the religious beliefs you follow impact your lifestyle? If so, how might this impact your married life?
	• Are either of you considering changing religions? If so, what's involved in that? Are you prepared to deal with the ramifications of what your families and friends might think about these actions?
	• How will your respective families react to you marrying outside of your religion (if applicable)?
	• Will you have a religious wedding ceremony? If so, who will officiate? Where will the ceremony be held?

When it comes to true love, things are seldom as straight forward or as black-and-white as you'd wish them to be. Instead, there are millions of shades of grey. Thus, while you'll want to consider the questions posed in this chapter in order to make well-thought-out decisions that relate to the rest of your life and your relationship, you should also follow your heart.

Getting Engaged: Proposing To Your Girlfriend

Every year in America alone, approximately 2.4 million weddings are performed. But, before the ceremony actually happens, either the potential groom or the bride must pop the big question and propose marriage. One of the scariest, yet most romantic and memorable moments in most people's lives is when they propose marriage (or get proposed to). Yet, upwards of 80 percent of engaged couples admit that the actual proposal was less romantic than they had envisioned it would be. Once you've found the person you'd like to propose to, it's important to figure out the very best way to pop the question in the most personalized, romantic and memorable way possible.

When the time is right and you've found the woman of your dreams, to help you plan and execute the perfect marriage proposal, the book *Will You Marry Me? Popping The Question with Romance and Style* (New Page Books) offers the following five tips.

Five Tips For Planning The Perfect Marriage Proposal

Tip #1—Once you've devised the perfect way to pop the question, put yourself in your girlfriend's shoes and consider exactly what she wants, expects and would consider romantic. Ask yourself what *she* would consider to be the perfect, most romantic and memorable marriage proposal possible. Will your idea live up to her expectations?

Tip #2—Set your timeframe to propose. Will you propose on a specific date, in conjunction with a holiday or birthday, for example? Once you have a proposal date in mind, you also now have a deadline to meet in terms of making all of the necessary arrangements leading up to your proposal.

Tip #3—Aside from you and your girlfriend, consider who will be present when you propose. Will you pop the question when you and your girlfriend are alone, or do you want friends, family and/or others to witness this exciting event? Make sure someone will have a camera on-hand to photograph or videotape your proposal.

Tip #4—Focus on the specifics regarding how you'll pop the question. Consider what you plan to say and how you'll say it. Don't memorize a speech word-for-word, but develop a list of ideas, sentiments and/or emotions you'd like to convey to your girlfriend as you ask for her hand in marriage.

Tip #5—Pay attention to detail as you plan your proposal. Once you know how and when you'll propose, and what type of scenario you'll create, proper planning is required to make sure every aspect of your scenario is well thought-out, coordinated and rehearsed. When the time comes to actually pop the question, you're going to be nervous. Being properly prepared will help insure nothing goes wrong.

After getting engaged, your life will experience a whirlwind of changes. You'll almost overnight go from a single guy to someone who is in a serious and committed relationship with the person you'll eventually be married to. One of the first things you'll want to do after getting engaged is announce it to the world—your family, friends, co-workers, etc. Once you start telling a few people, you'll be surprised how quickly news travels. Expect people to start coming up to you and/or calling with their congratulations, even if you didn't tell those people directly. Oh, and you can expect to receive engagement gifts as well.

It's best for the people who are close to you to hear about your engagement directly from you and your fiancé. Thus, you should both make a list of the people in your lives who are most important to you, then make a point to call or speak with those people directly to tell them your exciting news. Depending on your personal situation, your parents and your soon-to-be in-laws, as well as your siblings and other close relatives, should be at the top of your lists, as should your closest friends.

If you're following "tradition" (and this term is being used lightly here), between the time you get engaged and the actual wedding, there will be a considerable amount of celebrating. You and your fiancé (or your parents or soon-to-be in-laws) might decide to host an engagement party. This is a social gathering that can be formal or as casual as a backyard barbeque. An engagement party is typically attended by the soon-to-be bride and groom, along with family, friends, coworkers and anyone else you'd like to invite.

As you get closer to the wedding date, the soon-to-be groom may be invited by his best man to a bachelor party, while the bride gets whisked away by her bridesmaids for a bachelorette party. These tend to be "guys only" or "girls only" events.

What happens during these events is entirely up to those involved. Just keep in mind, however, you will have to answer to your girlfriend the following morning, so you'd best be somewhat behaved as you say goodbye to your bachelorhood.

Almost immediately after you get engaged, you and your girlfriend will need to start the process of planning your wedding. Depending on the type of wedding you envision and the number of guests you plan to invite, this can become a tremendously time consuming endeavor that will require you both to make literally hundreds of decisions. At the very least, you'll want to get your hands on at least one or two books about wedding planning in order to help you take an organized approach to this process and keep costs under control. (An average wedding in America costs over $20,000.) You might, however, consider hiring a professional wedding planner to work with you to create your ultimate dream wedding.

As the wedding planning begins, everyone will have ideas about the date, location, theme, what food should be served, the music to be played, what the wedding party should wear, etc. Even if your parents or your in-laws are paying for the wedding and handling many of the details, it's extremely important that you and your fiancé remain the final decision makers. After all, this is your wedding and it's important that you're actually able to experience the wedding you both envision.

One of the first decisions you'll need to make will involve the date for the wedding. Start off by choosing a month and year. This will give you a timeframe in which you can plan the ceremony and celebration.

At the same time you're putting the wedding plans together, you'll also need to plan your honeymoon. About 99 percent of newly married couples go on a honeymoon and wind up spending on average about $4,000 for the trip. The average length of a honeymoon is nine days. Of course, this can vary based on your budget and interests.

Your honeymoon will be your first trip together as a married couple, so you want the trip to be extremely romantic and memorable. Spend some time deciding what type of honeymoon you'd both enjoy, then consult with a few travel agents that specialize in honeymoons to fine tune your ideas and narrow down the vast possibilities. You can also visit the *HoneymoonLocation.com* or *VacationIdea.com* websites for ideas and trip planning advice. If you're on a budget, take full advantage of the online-based travel sites to save money. For example, *Hotwire.com* offers a special 'Deals & Destinations' section on its website that offers romantic get-away and honeymoon ideas that are discounted.

Honeymoon destination possibilities are limitless. Use this opportunity to visit someplace exotic that you've always dreamed about. If you're planning to travel during a peak honeymoon season, such as June or July, it's best to make your travel reservations as far in advance as possible.

Some popular honeymoon destinations or ideas include:

- Taking a trip to someplace tropical, such as Hawaii or the Caribbean, and staying at a beachfront resort.

- Going on a European sightseeing adventure—London, Paris, Amsterdam, Italy, etc.

- Taking a cruise.

- Going to a romantic destination that's sentimental to you both.

- Traveling somewhere to enjoy some type of activity together, such as skiing, mountain climbing, camping, etc.

After the marriage and the honeymoon, it's time to settle into your new life as a happily married guy. From this point on, many of the decision you make regarding your career, finances, spending, how you spend your free time and where you go on vacation, for example, will be a join effort, between you and your wife. To develop the best relationship possible, you'll want to develop an open, honest and loving relationship with your wife that's based upon trust. Your life should now be dedicated to her happiness and well-being (and vice versa).

The early days of married life will once again require a tremendous level of adjustment on your part. You'll probably have to get used to living together, sleeping together, spending your free time together and making the logistics of your life together work. This will definitely require some compromise on both your parts, so be prepared to make concessions, adapt to new ways of doing things and being willing to listen to someone else's ideas and opinions.

It won't be long before you'll be looking back on your days as a bachelor, hopefully fondly, as you take on the responsibilities of a married man. Perhaps fatherhood is on the horizon and you and your wife decide to create a family. While much of what you've learned about life in general will be useful as you get older, always be willing to learn new things, adapt to life's constant changes and engage yourself in the pursuit of happiness for yourself and your loved ones. Embrace the new responsibilities you'll have as a married man and take them seriously.

Your bachelorhood may gone once you get married, but your new life as a married man will only be starting, so enjoy!

About The Author

Jason R. Rich (*www.JasonRich.com*) is the bestselling author of more than 29 books and is a frequent contributor to numerous major daily newspapers and national magazines. He's also worked as the senior editor of *American Idol The Magazine,* the official magazine of America's most popular television show.

Some of his other recently published books, which are now available from bookstores nationwide or from *Amazon.com* or *BN.com*, include:

- *American Idol Season 3—All Access* (Prima/Random House)
- *American Idol Season 4—The Official Fan Book* (Prima/Random House)
- *The Everything Family Guide to The Walt Disney World Resort, Universal Studios & Greater Orlando*, 1ˢᵗ, 2ⁿᵈ, 3ʳᵈ and 4ᵗʰ Editions (Adams Media)
- *The Everything Family Guide To Las Vegas,* 1ˢᵗ and 2ⁿᵈ Editions (Adams Media)
- *The Everything Family Guide To The Caribbean* (Adams Media)
- *The Unofficial Guide to Starting A Business Online,* 1ˢᵗ and 2ⁿᵈ Editions (Wiley Publishing)
- *Will You Marry Me? Popping The Question with Romance & Style* (New Page Books)
- *Make Your Paycheck Last* (The Career Press)

As a freelance marketing and public relations consultant, as well as a spokesperson, Jason Rich works with numerous companies in a wide range of industries. He's currently single and lives just outside of Boston.

978-0-595-35593-8
0-595-35593-5